THE CAMBRIDGE COMPAN
LITERATURE AND THE ENVI]

CW00742792

The Cambridge Companion to Literature and the Environment is ... authoritative guide to the exciting new interdisciplinary field of environmental literary criticism. The collection traces the development of ecocriticism from its origins in European pastoral literature and offers fifteen rigorous but accessible essays on the present state of environmental literary scholarship. Contributions from leading experts in the field probe a range of issues, including the place of the human within nature, ecofeminism and gender, engagements with European philosophy and the biological sciences, critical animal studies, postcolonialism, posthumanism, and climate change. A chronology of key publications and bibliography provide ample resources for further reading, making *The Cambridge Companion to Literature and the Environment* an essential guide for students, teachers, and scholars working in this rapidly developing area of study.

LOUISE WESTLING has been teaching in the English Department at the University of Oregon since 1977. She served as a visiting professor at the University of Tübingen and a Fulbright Professor at the University of Heidelberg, and as a president and founding member of the Association for the Study of Literature and Environment. She is the author of *The Green Breast of the New World: Landscape, Gender, and American Fiction* (1996) and of the forthcoming *The Logos of the Living World: Merleau-Ponty, Animals, and Language*.

THE CAMBRIDGE
COMPANION TO
LITERATURE AND THE ENVIRONMENT

THE CAMBRIDGE
COMPANION TO
LITERATURE AND
THE ENVIRONMENT

Edited by

LOUISE WESTLING
University of Oregon

CAMBRIDGE
UNIVERSITY PRESS

CAMBRIDGE
UNIVERSITY PRESS

University Printing House, Cambridge CB2 8BS, United Kingdom

Cambridge University Press is part of the University of Cambridge.

It furthers the University's mission by disseminating knowledge in the pursuit of
education, learning and research at the highest international levels of excellence.

www.cambridge.org
Information on this title: www.cambridge.org/9781107628960

© Cambridge University Press 2014

First published 2014

A catalogue record for this publication is available from the British Library

Library of Congress Cataloguing in Publication data
The Cambridge Companion to Literature and the Environment / [edited by]
Louise Westling, University of Oregon.
pages cm. – (Cambridge Companions to Literature)
Includes bibliographical references and index.
ISBN 978-1-107-02992-7 (hardback) – ISBN 978-1-107-62896-0 (paperback)
1. Ecocriticism.   2. Nature in literature.   3. Ecology in literature.   4. Environmental
literature – History and criticism.   I. Westling, Louise Hutchings, editor of compilation.
PN98.E36C36   2014
809'.9336–dc23   2013029366

ISBN 978-1-107-02992-7 Hardback
ISBN 978-1-107-62896-0 Paperback

CONTENTS

CONTENTS

CONTRIBUTORS

JONI ADAMSON is Associate Professor of English and Environmental Studies at Arizona State University, where she is Senior Scholar at the Global Institute of Sustainability and Program Faculty in Human and Social Dimensions of Science and Technology. She is the author of *American Indian Literature, Environmental Justice, and Ecocriticism* (2001); coeditor with Mei Mei Evans and Rachel Stein of *The Environmental Justice Reader: Politics, Poetics, and Pedagogy* (2002); and coeditor with Kimberly Ruffin of *American Studies, Ecocriticism and Citizenship: Thinking and Acting in the Local and Global Commons* (2013). With coeditors William Gleason and David Pellow, she is at work on *Keywords for Environmental Studies*.

TIMOTHY CLARK is Professor of English at Durham University and a specialist in modern literary theory, continental philosophy, and Romanticism. He has published many articles in literary and philosophical journals. His books include *Derrida, Heidegger, Blanchot: Sources of Derrida's Notion and Practice of Literature* (1992); *Martin Heidegger* (2001); *The Poetics of Singularity: The Counter-Culturalist Turn in Heidegger, Derrida, Blanchot, and the Later Gadamer* (2005); and *The Cambridge Introduction to Literature and the Environment* (2011).

JANET FISKIO is Assistant Professor of Environmental Studies at Oberlin College, where she specializes in ecocriticism, agrarianism and food justice, and climate change. She has published "Unsettling Ecocriticism: Rethinking Agrarianism, Place, and Citizenship" in *American Literature* (2012); "Ecotopia and Apocalypse: Narratives in Global Climate Change Discourse" in *Race, Gender, and Class* (2012); and "A World of Difference: The Lure of Plants in Gary Paul Nabhan" in *Environmental Philosophy* (2008). At present she is working on a book called *Poetics of Climate Change: Witness, Mourning, Hospitality*.

TERRY GIFFORD is Visiting Scholar at Bathspa University and Profesor Honorifico at the Universidad de Alicante. A founding member of the Association for the Study of Literature and Environment in the United Kingdom and Ireland (ASLE-UK, now ASLE-UKI) and a widely published author of ecocriticism and mountaineering essays, he has written many books, including *Green Voices: Understanding Contemporary Nature Poetry* (1995), *Pastoral* (1999), and *Reconnecting with John Muir: Essays in Post-Pastoral Practice* (2010). He is the editor of *The Cambridge Companion to Ted Hughes* (2011).

AXEL GOODBODY is Professor of Germanic Literature at the University of Bath. One of the founders of the European Association for the Study of Literature, Culture and Environment (EASLCE), he was its first president (2004–2006). He is editor of *ECOZON@: European Journal of Literature, Culture and Environment* and the Rodopi book series Nature, Culture and Literature. Recent publications include *Nature, Technology and Cultural Change in 20th-Century German Literature* (2007); *Wasser – Kultur – Ökologie* (2008); and a coedited volume, *Ecocritical Theory: New European Approaches* (2011).

SHARI HUHNDORF is Professor of Native American Studies and Comparative Ethnic Studies and Coordinator of Native American Studies at the University of California, Berkeley. She has written many articles on Native American literature and is author of two books, *Going Native: Indians in the American Cultural Imagination* (2001) and *Mapping the Americas: The Transnational Politics of Contemporary Native Culture* (2009). She coedited *Indigenous Women and Feminism: Politics, Activism, Culture* (2010) and *Sovereignty, Indigeneity, and the Law* (2011). Currently she is working on a book tentatively entitled *Indigeneity and the Politics of Space: Gender, Geography, Culture*.

ALEX HUNT is Associate Professor of English at West Texas A&M University. He has published many articles on the American Southwest and ecology, edited *The Geographical Imagination of Annie Proulx: Rethinking Regionalism* (2010), and is coeditor of *Postcolonial Green: Environmental Politics and World Narratives* (2010).

SARAH E. MCFARLAND is Associate Professor and Department Head of English at Northwestern Louisiana State University. Author of many articles in critical animal studies, she also coedited *Animals and Agency, an Interdisciplinary Exploration* (2009).

LEO MELLOR is Roma Gill Fellow in English at Murray Edwards College, Cambridge University. He has written articles and book chapters on modernism, war journalism, and the relationship between locale and literature, and he is the author of *Reading the Ruins: Modernism, Bomb Sites, and British Culture* (2011).

KATE RIGBY is Professor of Environmental Humanities in the School of English, Communications and Performance Studies at Monash University, Australia. She is a Senior Editor of the journal *Philosophy Activism Nature*, coeditor of *Ecocritical Theory: New European Approaches* (2011), and author of *Topographies of the*

Sacred: The Poetics of Place in European Romanticism (2004), among other books. She was the inaugural president of ASLE-Australia–New Zealand.

BONNIE ROOS is Associate Professor of English at West Texas A&M University, with research interests in transatlantic modernism and postcolonialism. In addition to publishing a number of book chapters and journal articles, she is coeditor of *Postcolonial Green: Environmental Politics and World Narratives* (2010).

STEPHEN RUST is an Adjunct Instructor and Assistant Director of Cinema Studies in English at the University of Oregon, where he teaches cinema studies. He has published a number of articles, including one on *Avatar* and ecorealism, and he is coeditor of *Ecocinema Theory and Practice* (2013).

CATRIONA SANDILANDS is Professor and Canada Research Chair in Sustainability and Culture at York University, Canada. Author of many articles and book chapters, she has written *The Good-Natured Feminist: Ecofeminism and the Quest for Democracy* (1999) and coedited *This Elusive Land: Women and the Canadian Environment* (2004) and *Queer Ecologies: Sex, Nature, Politics, and Desire* (2010).

ALFRED K. SIEWERS is Associate Professor of English and Affiliate Faculty member of the Environmental Studies Program at Bucknell University. Author of articles and book chapters on symbolic landscapes in medieval literature, he has written *Strange Beauty: Ecocritical Approaches to Early Medieval Landscape* (2009) and coedited *Tolkien's Modern Middle Ages* (2009).

KAREN THORNBER is Harris K. Weston Associate Professor of the Humanities at Harvard University, where she participates in the Department of Comparative Literature, the Harvard University Center for the Environment, and the Reischauer Institute of Japanese Studies. In addition to articles and book chapters, she is author of *Empire of Texts in Motion: Chinese, Korean, and Taiwanese Transculturations of Japanese Literature* (2009) and *Ecoambiguity: Environmental Crises and East Asian Literatures* (2012).

LOUISE WESTLING is Professor Emerita of English and Environmental Studies at the University of Oregon. She was a founding member of ASLE and was its president in 1998. Author of many recent articles on ecophenomenology and literature, she has written *The Green Breast of the New World: Landscape, Gender, and American Literature* (1996) and *The Logos of the Living World: Merleau-Ponty, Animals, and Language* (2013).

WENDY WHEELER is Emeritus Professor of English Literature and Cultural Inquiry at London Metropolitan University and Adjunct Professor in Art, Environment and Cultural Studies at RMIT University in Melbourne, Australia. She has written essays on biological systems theory and biosemiotics, and her books include *A New Modernity? Change in Science, Literature and Politics* (1999) and *The Whole Creature: Complexity, Biosemiotics and the Evolution of Culture* (2006). Recently she coedited a special issue in the New Formations series on *Earthographies: Ecocriticism and Culture* (2008) and a special issue of *Green Letters* on *Ecophenomenology and Practices of the Sacred* (2010). She is currently completing a new book on biosemiotics, matter, mind, and creative process.

ACKNOWLEDGMENTS

I would like to thank Ray Ryan, Senior Editor for English and American Literature at Cambridge University Press, for his encouragement and support throughout the various stages and vicissitudes of this *Companion* project. Louis Gulino, Editorial Assistant, was courteous and efficient in his guidance through many practical details of manuscript preparation, and Production Manager Marielle Poss found an excellent production team at Newgen Knowledge Works, headed by Bhavani who was extremely helpful in answering my queries and adapting to some last-minute changes. I'm very grateful to Robert Swanson for the indexing of the book, a task that would have driven me around the bend. The contributors to the volume deserve my deep gratitude for agreeing to write chapters whose subjects were somewhat arbitrarily offered to them. All of these authors were invited to participate because of the quality of their work in environmental literary criticism, but I could not have anticipated the exciting ways they surpassed my expectations. I want to thank them all for their professionalism and willingness to accept editorial requests. Karen Ford, Head of the Department of English at the University of Oregon, was a generous supporter of this project, and I also want to thank Ryleigh Nucelli for her work in proofreading the final drafts of chapters and helping to make formatting consistent among them.

LOUISE WESTLING

Introduction

For as long as humans have been recording images of the world around them, they have been wondering about its meaning and their own status. Paleolithic caves in the Dordogne are filled with luminous paintings and carvings of aurochs, horses, mammoths, ibex, salmon, snakes, and flowering and seeding plants. Only occasionally does a small human figure appear, often with the head of a stag or in crude stick form. Tribal cultures around the world have long oral traditions in which humans belong to the whole community of living creatures and share responsibility for ethical behavior within it. But radical changes to those ancient traditions came with domestication of plants and animals and with the settled hierarchical civilizations that began to separate themselves from the rest of the natural world. Four thousand years ago Sumerian King Gilgamesh gazed over the wall of his city and saw a corpse floating in the river, lamenting, "I too shall become like that, just so shall I be."[1] His answer to the fear of mortality was to attack nature by destroying the sacred cedar forest of the gods, with tragic consequences in his epic story. That disastrous impulse born of the will to master nature was only the beginning, as landscapes on every continent were forcibly turned to human purposes by advancing technologies and burgeoning populations, which have now brought us to what many fear is the brink of global ecological collapse. In *The Country and the City*, Raymond Williams surveys the often escapist English literary responses to these changes from the landscape enclosures of the Early Modern period into the industrial era of the nineteenth century.[2] As early as Charles Dickens' *Hard Times* (1854), and then more recently with John Steinbeck's *Grapes of Wrath* (1939), and with Rachel Carson's *Silent Spring* (1962), writers have warned us about the environmental damage caused by industrial societies. In the past several decades, however, increasing dismay about environmental problems has produced new kinds of literature and a wide international focus of scholarly attention. Literature and environment studies first became formalized in American universities in the 1990s and began to spread all over the globe.[3]

Now ecocritical books, journals, and articles proliferate, scholars flock to formal conferences on environmental humanities, and students eagerly fill courses devoted to environmental literature, history, and philosophy.

The Cambridge Companion to Literature and the Environment is a guide to major areas and crucial themes in this rapidly developing interdisciplinary field of environmental literary studies. It is designed to complement Timothy Clark's Cambridge Introduction to Literature and Environment (2011), by offering examples of scholarship by a range of experts, who have done most to define the field, from several countries. Although self-conscious environmentalist attention to literature is only two decades old, rich traditions in all major cultures have focused on the human place in the natural world. Examples include not only Mesopotamian and biblical texts, but also the Ramayana, Euripides' Bacchae, Ovid's Metamorphoses, the Mayan Popol Vuh, the ancient Chinese poetry of Li Po, the work of Japanese poets Chomei and Basho, and, of course, the European pastoral. Ecocriticism reevaluates those traditions in light of present environmental concerns, examines a wide range of recent literary works that engage environmentalist perspectives or imagine ecological catastrophe, questions the very categories of the human and of nature, probes theoretical positions that can offer rigorous grounding for ecological thought, and necessarily turns toward the life sciences to restore literary culture to the fabric of biological being from which it has emerged and within which it will always be enveloped. Its scope includes poststructural critiques of nostalgia and theoretical naiveté in nature writing, Marxist and feminist exposure of political bad faith in the pastoral tradition and deep ecology, examination of literary engagement with biological sciences, links between environmental philosophy and ecocritical theory, critical animal studies and literary animals, postcolonial and globalist perspectives on literature from around the world, "posthumanism," attention to new media that has grown out of literature, and rhetorical studies of public and governmental discourse about the environment. Studies in literature and the environment are expanding so rapidly, both geographically and intellectually, that this book cannot include many important topics and global traditions such as premodern literatures, science fiction, literary attention to plants and agriculture, and literatures from Asia, Africa, and precolonial America.[4] Nevertheless, the chapters that follow indicate the complex texture of possible approaches to virtually every literary tradition.

Writing about the natural environment has a long protohistory in Britain and Ireland, as both Alfred Siewers' chapter on "Green Otherworlds of Early Medieval Literature" and Terry Gifford's "Pastoral, Anti-Pastoral, Post-Pastoral" demonstrate. But aside from Celtic traditions, and long history of pastoral, writing about the natural world in the past was often negative. Grim winter scenes of crags, wolf-haunted valleys, tangled forests, and stormy heaths appear from *Beowulf* and *Sir Gawain and the Green Knight* to Shakespeare's *King Lear*. John Donne wrote of the world's disfigured proportions, with "warts and pock-holes in the face/ Of th'earth,"[5] and the Pilgrim colonists arriving on the coast of Massachusetts in 1620 saw only a howling wilderness or haunt of Satan.[6]

The late seventeenth century, however, brought dramatic changes in taste. The beginnings of modern science and industrial technology, together with aesthetic influences from India and China, led to delight in vast perspectives, dramatic storms, huge mountains, and raging torrents as well as more ordinary rural scenes. The concept of the Sublime was resurrected from the treatise of Longinus, an otherwise unknown Greek rhetorician of the first or third century AD, and popularized by the Earl of Shaftesbury and Edmund Burke in the eighteenth century, while Kant theorized the Sublime in German philosophy around the same time. As Marjorie Nicolson pointed out, this movement amounted to the invention of a new way of thinking about the natural world, one deeply entangled in theological, philosophical, and scientific debates.[7] For Kant, the Sublime was a response to the vast powers of the natural world that elevates the imagination to a rational understanding of infinity, which dwarfs nature. He wrote that such sights as towering, craggy mountains; erupting volcanoes; violent hurricanes; lofty waterfalls; and turbulent oceans "exhibit our faculty of resistance of trifling moment in comparison with their might. But *provided our own position is secure*, their aspect is all the more attractive for its fearfulness. ... Therefore nature is here called sublime merely because it raises the imagination to a presentation of those cases in which the mind can make itself sensible of the appropriate sublimity of its own being, *even above nature* (emphasis added)."[8] Raymond Williams anatomized the class privilege involved in such attitudes by noting that "the wild regions of mountain and forest were for the most part objects of conspicuous aesthetic consumption."[9] Only those with adequate security could afford to wander at leisure and aestheticize such regions. Thus we can understand why colonial control of vast new lands and industrial production offering domestic comfort and wealth for literary Europeans might make aesthetic appreciation of dramatic natural scenes a possibility. They were no longer so threatening. The aesthetics of Romanticism were made possible by relative privilege and environmental domestication at home, and by conquest abroad. This was true as well for the American landscape painters of the Hudson River School and for James Fenimore Cooper's fictional forests of the same period. The actual forests of early New England had long been mowed down, as environmental historian William Cronon explains, and the national mythology about wilderness erased the violent appropriation of the continent by European settlers.[10]

Romantic attention to the natural world must thus be understood as double-edged, part of a reaction against the environmental blight of industrialism, at the same time that it was primarily the work of a privileged elite, associated with imperial conquest. Jonathan Bate's inaugural British study in environmental criticism, *Romantic Ecology: Wordsworth and the Environmental Tradition*, seeks to rehabilitate Wordsworth's poetry of nature as an awakening of genuine ecological interest.[11] And as Bate demonstrates in a later book, poems such as Byron's "Darkness" and Keats's "To Autumn" respond to genuine environmental events. In this case they respond to the consequences of the Indonesian Tambora volcano eruption in 1815, which filled earth's atmosphere with dust that caused lowered temperatures and failed harvests all over Europe for three years. Keats's ode celebrates the return of normal harvest bounty in 1819.[12] But Timothy Clark remarks that while reaffirming the importance of the natural world for literary criticism, Bate risks "over-idealising premodern and capitalist ways of life."[13] Dickens was far ahead of our own ecocritical interest in environmental justice, with novels such as *Hard Times* and *Bleak House* depicting grim industrial cities and the miasmic squalor of London slums. His heroes and heroines, however, typically escape into the safety of comfortable bourgeois establishments surrounded by green spaces. Across the Atlantic, Emerson's foundational essay "Nature" begins by claiming "an original relation to the universe" through the natural world for American writers, but goes on to feminize Nature and describe her meekly receiving the dominion of man. "Nature" ends with a heroic call for the kingdom of man over nature.[14] Thoreau's essay "Walking" similarly aims to speak a word for Nature and claims that "in wildness is the preservation of the world," yet celebrates the westward migration of European settlers into this "wildness" as the nation's destiny.[15] Scottish immigrant John Muir followed the American pattern of moving westward to California for such adventure. But he chopped down primeval redwood forests before turning to worship the sublime landscapes of the Sierras and to fight to save Yosemite and other "wilderness" landscapes – while evicting the indigenous inhabitants who had lived there for thousands of years. One of the clearest ironies of this historical moment is Emerson's trip across the continent on the new transcontinental railroad that ensured the domestication of the "wilderness," where he met Muir in the redwood forest and had a giant Sequoia tree named after him by his admiring follower.

Everything changed for Western culture's sense of the human place in the natural world when Darwin published *On the Origin of Species*. Its effect was widely evident in nineteenth-century English literature, as Gillian Beer has demonstrated in *Darwin's Plots: Evolutionary Narrative in Darwin, George Eliot, and Nineteenth-Century Fiction.* Evolutionary notions about the struggle for life began to enter the novels of George Eliot and shape Thomas Hardy's depiction of life in the countryside, no longer a site of pastoral ease or *otium.* Similarly, American literary naturalism applied evolutionary assumptions about heredity and environmental struggle to grim settings, from Jack London's Alaska to Theodore Dreiser's grimy Chicago and Frank Norris's California landscapes of bloody struggle between farmers and railroad monopolies. Enormous vistas of human development from primeval origins during millennia of geological upheaval and climate change have haunted European and American literary constructions ever since, ranging from Virginia Woolf's repeated motif of mastodons and rhododendrons in Picadilly hovering behind the modern world to Faulkner's Mississippi swamps and Seamus Heaney's Irish bogs. Twentieth-century sciences of relativity theory, quantum physics, paleoanthropology, evolutionary biology, and studies in ecological dynamism have challenged literary explorations of human experience in most major cultures by now.

Ecocriticism grows out of this context, in some ways reviving pastoral and romantic attitudes toward the natural world, but informed by modern science and responding to alarm about the fragility of biological environments increasingly devastated by human technologies. Mid-twentieth-century works such as Aldo Leopold's *Sand County Almanac* urged an ethics of nature and wildlife preservation, and Rachel Carson's *Silent Spring* dramatized the devastating ecological effects of pesticides, creating a national uproar that helped to launch the American environmental movement and spread its influence around the world.[16] Leo Marx's *The Machine in the Garden* (1964) and Raymond Williams's *The Country and the City* (1973) launched critical reevaluations of pastoral traditions in light of environmental change and its relation to industrialism, political power, and colonization.[17] During the explosion of environmental interest in the 1970s, Joseph Meeker introduced explicit environmentalist criticism in *The Comedy of Survival: Studies in Literary Ecology,* followed by William Rueckert's essay "Literature and Ecology: An Experiment in Ecocriticism."[18] By 1990, Glen Love was calling for an ecological criticism in the United States, and around the same time in the United Kingdom, Jonathan Bate published *Romantic Ecology: Wordsworth and the Environmental Tradition.*[19] Love's challenge stimulated a group of young American scholars to organize the Association for the Study of Literature and Environment in 1992, with its first international conference held in Colorado in 1995. Lawrence Buell published his pioneering work, *The Environmental Imagination: Thoreau, Nature*

Writing, and the Formation of American Culture, that same year.[20] Greg Garrard organized the first ecocritical conference in the United Kingdom in 1997 at Swansea, followed a year later by the inaugural ASLE UK meeting in Bath.[21] Interest in environmental criticism spread quickly, and international affiliate organizations began to spring up in many Asian countries and in Europe, as well as in the Commonwealth.[22] New challenges from globally spreading pollution, wildlife extinction, climate change, and increasing environmental injustice for vulnerable communities in the global south have stimulated poets and fiction writers to increase their attention to environmental dangers. Novels such as P. D. James's *The Children of Men*, Amitav Ghosh's *The Hungry Tide*, Frank Schätzing's *The Swarm* (original German *Das Schwarm*), Octavia Butler's *Parable of the Sower*, Don Dilillo's *White Noise*, Margaret Atwood's *Oryx and Crake*, and Cormac McCarthy's *The Road* all testify to this trend.

As chroniclers of ecocriticism's development have noted, we have moved quite rapidly beyond efforts in the 1990s to define ecocriticism and develop a canon of texts that are consciously environmental in their orientation. While challenges to pastoral nostalgia, self-indulgent nature writing, class and gender privilege among environmental activists, the myth of "*wilderness*," and unproblematic appeals to "nature" have been voiced by some ecocritics from the beginning of the movement,[23] increasingly complex and theoretically sophisticated analyses of environmental literature have come to dominate the field by its third decade.[24] Environmental criticism has moved beyond earlier preoccupations with subjective experience of wild or rural places to increasing considerations of urban environments, collective social situations such as those of oppressed minorities forced to live in polluted surroundings, postcolonial social and political realities, and global threats from pollution and climate change. Environmental justice criticism has become especially influential since the publication of Joni Adamson's 2001 book *American Indian Literature, Environmental Justice, and Ecocriticism* and *The Environmental Justice Reader: Politics, Poetics, and Pedagogy*, which she co-edited with Mei Mei Evans and Rachel Stein. This emphasis has become global, as seen in Rob Nixon's *Slow Violence and the Environmentalism of the Poor*.[25] Increasing attention to the wider community of life in which human cultures are immersed leads some ecocritics to explore literary engagements with evolutionary biology and animal studies. Graham Huggan and Helen Tiffin's *Postcolonial Ecocriticism: Literature, Animals, Environment* explores the overlap between postcolonial concerns and the global problem of our relationships with other creatures, while Philip Armstrong's *What Animals Mean in the Fiction of Modernity* considers human-animal relationships in the context of colonialism, decolonization, globalization, and scientific animal studies in fiction from *Robinson Crusoe* and *Moby Dick* to Yann Martel's *Life of Pi*. Global risk from climate change is another area of expansion, as in Ursula Heise's *Sense of Place and Sense of Planet: The Environmental Imagination of the Global*.[26] Theoretical approaches to "the crisis of the natural" and posthumanism engage a number of ecocritics, and renewed attention to European philosophy provides further conceptual sophistication. As Timothy Clark explains, because of the intersection of so many exciting subjects for critical attention, the potential for ecocriticism is to be "work engaged provocatively both with literary analysis and with issues that are simultaneously but obscurely matters of science, morality, politics and aesthetics."[27] It is part of a profound, many-faceted cultural effort to reconsider the human place in the world.

The chapters in this volume are organized into four main categories: "Foundations," Theories," "Interdisciplinary Engagements," and "Major Directions."

Foundations offers three studies of traditions that are precursors to contemporary environmental approaches to literature. Terry Gifford's opening chapter on "Pastoral, Anti-Pastoral, and Post-Pastoral" surveys this central European genre focused on rural settings, which was established by Theocritus more than two thousand years ago. Its complex presence continues everywhere European cultures have spread their influence. In Shakespeare we see comic as well as much darker questionings of the habit of escape from corrupt urban spaces into charmed or terrible countrysides, from *Midsummer Night's Dream* and *As You Like It* to *King Lear* and *The Tempest*. Gifford describes how American colonization gave rise to new pastoral concepts associated with wilderness, discusses ecocritical controversies about whether or not the tradition has outlived its usefulness, and offers the "post-pastoral" as a concept that reaches beyond the limitations of pastoral conventions while continuing to explore their valid dimensions.

In "The Green Otherworlds of Early Medieval Literature," Alfred Siewers adapts Northrup Frye's concept of "green world comedy" to read key early Celtic texts that evoke a natural yet magical realm beyond that of everyday human experience. From the twelfth-century Welsh *Mabinogi* to Old Irish tales, the heroic *Táin Bó Cúailnge*, and *Sir Gawain and the Green Knight*, a sense of the "other side" of nature, which humans cannot fully know or control, informs the depiction of landscapes, forests, and countryside. Siewers ties these traditions to more recent theories about the agency of the nonhuman world such as Gilles Deleuze and Félix Guattari's ideas about early art, biosemiotics, and Merleau-Ponty's philosophy of embodiment.

Shari Huhndorf examines Native American literary resistance to landscape appropriation in her essay, "'Mapping by Words': The Politics of Land in Native American Literature." Using a case study of D'Arcy McNickle's novel *Wind From an Enemy Sky*, Huhndorf demonstrates how contemporary texts such as *Wind* provide counterhistories to dominant narratives that erase Native people, and they lend moral weight to Native claims by depicting the obscured violence of colonization. These texts deploy traditional indigenous senses of space to dispute ecologically destructive colonial privatization and manipulation of the land.

Theories includes four essays about theoretical perspectives on the natural world in modern philosophy, gender studies, and literary treatment of wilderness. In "Romantic Roots and Impulses from Twentieth-Century European Thinkers," Axel Goodbody examines approaches from Heidegger's and Merleau-Ponty's phenomenology to Adorno's Marxism, Deleuze's and Westphal's theories of spaciality, Uexküll's *Umwelt* theory, and Derrida's and Agamben's posthumanism. Coherent theoretical frameworks for environmental criticism can be developed from such positions that question Western traditions of human exceptionism and help to revise our sense of the human place in the biological community. In a complementary way, Timothy Clark's "Nature, Post Nature" offers a sustained critique of environmental debates about this concept in the second decade of the twenty-first century. Demonstrating how problematic conventional notions of a nature/culture divide have proven, he reviews historical contrasts between Hobbes's and social Darwinists' concept of a nature defined by violent struggle on the one hand, and Rousseau's definition of an innocent pre-cultural condition as the natural state of man on the other. Clark sees a new kind of romantic humanism arising in the ecocriticism of Jonathan Bate and Lawrence Buell, but cautions that far more skeptical and provisional cultural diagnoses are now required in this era of the Anthropocene, when the environments in which our hominid ancestors evolved are forever gone.

Catriona Sandilands uses Shani Mootoo's novel *Cereus Blooms at Night* to identify interhuman and multispecies encounters at the heart of almost surreal gendered, colonial, and sexual violence. This essay shows how Mootoo breaks down comfortable boundaries assumed to separate humans from other species, even invertebrates and plants. It disrupts similar gender distinctions among people as it explores interrelationships between pleasure and pain that produce radically reoriented understandings of human and ecological community.

In "The Lure of Wilderness," Leo Mellor recalls biblical and Old English texts describing wild places as terrifyingly *other*, as typical of many European traditions until the Romantic Sublime transformed them to settings where fear combines with wonder to allow reassessments of self and world. He surveys complex ways poets and novelists have continued to explore wildness from Romantic poetry and American wilderness preservation appeals to descriptions of verdant bombsites during World War II, as well as writing haunted by environmental dangers today. Scope narrows in the new British nature writing of naturalist Richard Mabey and Robert Macfarlane, who locate wildness in overlooked cracks of city life and hidden corners of apparently domesticated and menaced landscapes, suggesting possible resilience.

Interdisciplinary Engagements includes three chapters on the new interdisciplinary field of biosemiotics, Thoreau's natural science in relation to ethnobotany, and critical animal studies. Wendy Wheeler's essay on "Biosemiotics and the Book of Nature" describes a revolution in the sciences of evolution and ecology growing out of the new interdisciplinary movement of biosemiotics. Realizing that mechanistic descriptions of organisms and natural processes are insufficient, a group of scientists and linguists in Europe and semioticians in North America propose instead that biological information must be understood as biosemiosis – the action of signs, and communication and interpretation in *all* living things from the single cell to complex multicellular organisms. This means that what we understand by "mind" and "knowledge" must necessarily shake off its purely anthropocentric connotations, and that human culture evolved and remains within this matrix. Thus humanistic disciplines – and literary studies – are linked with science in exploring what Jesper Hoffmeyer calls "signs of meaning in the universe," and metaphor is not merely a figure of speech but the literary expression of the play of similarity and difference that defines all biological and ecological meaning.

In "Sauntering Across the Border" Janet Fiskio connects Thoreau's natural history practices of playful sauntering with Gary Paul Nabhan's trespassing of material boundaries between Mexico and the United States, as well as disciplinary borders of literature, botany, and food politics. Nabhan extends Thoreau's work by theorizing border-crossing as essential to environmental justice and by making community integral to this practice. Fiskio shows how Nabhan contributes to ecocritical practice and environmental activism through rhetorical forms, which mediate between the Western science of conservation biology and the indigenous science of the Comcáac Indians of the Sonoran Desert, in a mixture of indigenous languages, Spanish, English, and Latin.

Sarah McFarland uses critical animal studies to question the human/animal aspects of the self/other binary and the arising consequences to subjectivity and species definitions in "Animal Studies, Literary Animals, and Yann Martel's *Life of Pi*." Through layers of ambiguity in the relationship between the boy Pi and the tiger Richard Parker as they struggle to survive on a lifeboat in the middle of the Pacific Ocean, Martel dramatizes how we can imagine worlds where the challenges to concepts such as "humanity" and "animality" are multifaceted, diverse, and various. Ultimately, McFarland argues, humans must develop an ethics of respect for the subjective integrities of other animals.

The concluding category is "Major Directions" and includes chapters on environmental justice, climate change, Asian literatures, and eco-media. In "Environmental Justice, Cosmopolitics, and Climate Change" Joni Adamson suggests that traditional folktales, proverbs, trickster stories, and animal tales might be considered as "seeing instruments" to advance environmental understanding and justice. She describes how Anishinabe writer Louise Erdrich, novelist Richard Powers, and poets and folklorists from countries such as Columbia and Peru are reexamining indigenous stories about human relationship to animals with "situated connectivities" to specific geographies for what they might reveal about linked biophysical and social processes in response to climate change.

Reading Amitav Ghosh's *The Calcutta Chromosome: a Novel of Fevers, Delirium and Discovery* (1995), Bonnie Roos and Alex Hunt's chapter on "Systems and Secrecy" reveals a postcolonial critique that uses the metaphor of malaria to raise the specters of unspoken voices and recover their role in this history. Ghosh revives the undocumented and uncorroborated stories of those erased by imperial histories, and whose "silent" voices can be used to resist oppression and gesture toward environmental justice.

Karen Thornber emphasizes the disjuncture in East Asian cultures, where traditional reverence for nature, widely expressed in literature, has failed to prevent vast environmental degradation. Her essay, "Environmental Crises and East Asian Literatures: Uncertain Presents and Futures," examines several recent poems and stories from China, Japan, and Korea that address the problems of damaged ecosystems with a kind of *ecoambiguity* about the complex, contradictory interactions between people and the nonhuman world. Such writing illuminates deeper uncertainties about such projects as the Three Gorges Dam and earthquakes that have devastated Japan and its nuclear industry, breaking the silence about terrible environmental contingencies that threaten our future.

In her chapter, "Confronting Catastrophe: Ecocriticism in a Warming World," Kate Rigby examines the formation of modern notions of natural disaster. She surveys ecological disaster texts from Heinrich von Kleist's short story, "The Earthquake in Chile" of 1806, Voltaire's response to the Lisbon earthquake of 1755 in *Candide,* and Mary Shelley's prophetic novel *The Last Man* about a pandemic in 2100, which almost wipes out human life on the planet. She appeals to Kim Stanley Robinson's suggestion in his climate-change trilogy, that confronting catastrophe might open a path to ecosocial transformation and a vision of transpecies justice.

"Ecocinema and the Wildlife Film" brings the volume's collection to its close, exhibiting some of the increasing ecocritical interest in film and media studies. In a brief history of the wildlife film genre, Steve Rust describes many of the myths, complex motivations, and questionable corporate alliances that have accompanied the evolution of films claiming to capture the "real lives" of wild animals. He exposes the sentimentalities and anthropomorphic constructions that too often underlie popular wildlife films, from Walt Disney's "True Life Adventures" and *National Geographic Specials*, to Jacques Cousteau's undersea adventures, to the French film *Microcosmos* about the busy lives of tiny creatures in a meadow, and finally to documentaries about the horrors of industrial food production, dolphin-hunting and Timothy Treadwell's gruesome end in Werner Herzog's *Grizzly Man*. But he suggests that in spite of its flaws, this genre expresses a deep need to connect with our fellow creatures and shed the anthropomorphism that lies at the heart of the planet's tragedy of species extinction.

Together, these essays indicate the wide range of sources, themes, theoretical approaches, and new directions in the rapidly developing interdisciplinary field of literature and the environment. A bibliography of "Further Reading" that follows the essays offers possibilities for further explorations. Already the problems of extreme weather events, pollution, drought and attendant food shortages, increasing changes in global climate, and the plight of the animal communities on every continent make it clear that environmental concerns require the kinds of profound reevaluations of our place in the world that this volume represents.

NOTES

1 Sumerian Version A in A. R. George (trans.), *The Epic of Gilgamesh* (London: Penguin Books, 2003), p. 151.

2 Raymond Williams, *The Country and the City* (New York: Oxford University Press, 1973).

3 See Cheryll Glotfelty and Harold Fromm (eds.), "Introduction" to *The Ecocriticism Reader: Landmarks in Literary Ecology* (Athens: University of Georgia Press, 1996), pp. xv–xxxvii; Greg Garrard, *Ecocriticism* (London and New York: Routledge, 2004); and Ursula Heise, "The Hitchhiker's Guide to Ecocriticism," *PMLA* 121 (2006), 503–516.

4 See, for example, Elizabeth DeLoughrey, Renée K. Gosson, and George B. Handley (eds.), *Caribbean Literature and the Environment: Between Nature and Culture* (Charlottesville: University of Virginia Press, 2005); Nirmal Selvamony, Nirmaldasan, and Rayson K. Alex (eds.), *Essays in Ecocriticism* (Chennai and New Delhi: OSLE-India and Sarup & Sons, 2007); Shuyuan Lu (ed.), *Nearing the Primeval Forest: Ecodiscourses of Forty Humanities Scholars*

(Shanghai: Shanghai Literary and Artistic Publishing House, 2008); Andrew Biro (ed.), *Critical Ecologies: The Frankfurt School and Contemporary Environmental Crises* (Toronto: University of Toronto Press, 2011).

5 "The First Anniversary. An Anatomie of the World," in Gary A. Stringer (ed.), *The Variorum Edition of the Poetry of John Donne*, vol. 6 (Bloomington: Indiana University Press, 1995), lines 300–301, pp. 13–14.

6 More favorable Edenic descriptions were sent home to England from the early southern colonies, but these were gendered as maternal or virginal female spaces and soon developed into accounts of rapine caused by destructive landscape practices. See Annette Kolodny, *The Lay of the Land: Metaphor as Experience and History in American Life and Letters* (Chapel Hill: University of North Carolina Press, 1975).

7 Marjorie Hope Nicolson, *Mountain Gloom and Mountain Glory: The Development of the Aesthetics of the Infinite* (Seattle and London: The University of Washington Press, 1997; orig. pub. Cornell University Press, 1959).

8 Immanuel Kant, "Of the Sublime," in Ernest Behler (ed.), *Philosophical Writings* (New York: Continuum, 1986), pp. 218–219.

9 *The Country and the City*, p. 128.

10 William Cronon, *Changes in the Land: Indians, Colonists, and the Ecology of New England* (New York: Hill and Wang, 1983); and "The Trouble with Wilderness, or, Getting Back to the Wrong Nature," in William Cronon (ed.), *Uncommon Ground: Rethinking the Human Place in Nature* (New York: Norton, 1996), pp. 69–90.

11 Jonathan Bate, *Romantic Ecology: Wordsworth and the Environmental Tradition* (London: Routledge, 1991).

12 Jonathan Bate, *The Song of the Earth* (Cambridge, MA: Harvard University Press, 2000), pp. 94–110.

13 Timothy Clark, *The Cambridge Introduction to Literature and the Environment* (Cambridge, MA: Cambridge University Press, 2011), p. 19.

14 Ralph Waldo Emerson, *Nature*, A Facsimile of the First Edition with an Introduction by Jaroslav Pelikan (Boston: Beacon Press, 1985), p. 95.

15 Henry David Thoreau, "Walking," in Robert Sattelmeyer (ed.), *The Natural History Essays* (Salt Lake City: Peregrine Smith Books, 1980), pp. 105–106, 112.

16 Aldo Leopold, *Sand County Almanac* (New York: Oxford, 1949); and Rachel Carson, *Silent Spring* (Boston: Houghton Mifflin, 1962).

17 Leo Marx, *The Machine in the Garden: Technology and the Pastoral Ideal in America* (New York: Oxford, 1964); Raymond Williams, *The Country and the City* (New York: Oxford, 1973).

18 Joseph Meeker, *The Comedy of Survival: Studies in Literary Ecology* (New York: Scribner, 1974); and William Rueckert, "Literature and Ecology: An Experiment in Ecocriticism," *The Iowa Review* 9 (1978), 71–86.

19 Glen A. Love, "Revaluing Nature: Toward an Ecological Criticism," *Western American Literature* 25 (1990), 201–215; and Bate, *Romantic Ecology*.

20 Lawrence Buell, *The Environmental Imagination: Thoreau, Nature Writing, and the Formation of American Culture* (Cambridge, MA: Harvard University Press, 1995).

21 Several years ago this organization changed its name to include Ireland, hence ASLE-UKI.

22 See http://www.asle.org/. ASLE affiliates now include ASLE Japan; ASLE Korea; ASLE UKI; ASLE India; OSLE India; the Association for the Study of Literature, Environment, and Culture, Australia-New Zealand (ASLEC-ANZ); the European Association for the Study of Literature, Culture, and Environment (EASLCE); ASLE Taiwan; and the Association for the Study of Literature, Environment, and Culture in Canada. Planning is underway for affiliated organizations in China as well.

23 See, for example, David Mazel's "American Environmentalism as Domestic Orientalism," Athens: University of Georgia Press, 2000; and Dana Phillips's "Is Nature Necessary?" in Glotfelty and Fromm, New York: Oxford University Press, 2003, pp. 137–146 and 204–222; and Kate Soper's "The Idea of Nature" and Richard Kerridge's "Ecothrillers: Environmental Cliffhangers," in Lawrence Coupe (ed.), *The Green Studies Reader: From Romanticism to Ecocriticism* (London: Routledge, 2000), pp. 123–126 and 242–249.

24 See Lawrence Buell, "Ecocriticism: Some Emerging Trends," *Qui Parle: Critical Humanities and Social Sciences* 19 (2011), 87–115; Ursula Heise, "A Hitchhiker's Guide to Ecocriticism," *PMLA* 121 (2006), 503–516; and Timothy Clark, "Introduction" in *The Cambridge Introduction to Literature and the Environment*, pp. 1–11.

25 Joni Adamson, *American Indian Literature, Environmental Justice, and Ecocriticism: The Middle Place* (Tuscon: University of Arizona Press, 2001); Joni Adamson, Mei Mei Evans, and Rachel Stein (eds.), *The Environmental Justice Reader: Politics, Poetics, and Pedagogy* (Tuscon: University of Arizona Press, 2002); and Rob Nixon, *Slow Violence and the Environmentalism of the Poor* (Cambridge, MA: Harvard University Press, 2011).

26 Ursula Heise, *Sense of Place and Sense of Planet: The Environmental Imagination of the Global* (New York: Oxford, 2008).

27 Clark, *The Cambridge Introduction to Literature and the Environment*, p. 8.

PART I

Foundations

I

TERRY GIFFORD

Pastoral, Anti-Pastoral, and Post-Pastoral

The story of the reception and transformations of pastoral in the relatively brief history of ecocriticism is a roller-coaster ride that in some ways echoes the critical history of pastoral before ecocriticism, when the countryside was not "environment" and nature was not "ecology." Ecocriticism's debates about the pastoral arise out of earlier scholarly traditions, which tend to vary between U.S. and UK scholars, sometimes to the point of outright contradiction, particularly in relation to the current usefulness of the pastoral as a concept. In part this is attributable to the desire for a distinctively American pastoral against the English and yet earlier European traditions of its origins. So an American concept of pastoral has come to challenge the notion of pastoral as a genre. Indeed, the narrative of the reception of classical pastoral would need to account for its shift from a genre, to a mode, and to a contemporary concept. What this all comes down to in the present day is the question of whether, as the British ecocritic Greg Garrard in the "Pastoral" chapter of his book *Ecocriticism* (2011) suggests, pastoral is "wedded to outmoded models of harmony and balance,"[1] or whether, as American ecocritic Lawrence Buell asserts, "pastoralism is a species of cultural equipment that western thought has for more than two millennia been unable to do without"[2] such that the current ecological crisis, in the words of the Americanist Leo Marx, "is bound to bring forth new versions of pastoral."[3] Indeed, these three usages of "pastoral" represent ecocriticism's confusion about the term that is rooted in its historical shifts in meaning. Garrard appears to be thinking of a genre with a canon of now "outmoded models" for current notions of ecology that reject "harmony and balance." Buell's "pastoralism" seems to refer to a mode of writing that engages with human relationships with land in a recognizable "species of cultural equipment." If Marx can foresee completely "new versions of pastoral" the genre must have transformed into a concept, as I argue has become the case with, for example, the ecocritical usage of terms such as "post-pastoral," "urban pastoral," or "gay pastoral."

Pastoral as a genre is really confined to two foundational texts that established the essential features of pastoral conventions and to which later writers refer back, either consciously or implicitly. In the third century BCE the Greek scholar Theocritus (316–260 BCE) wrote about the shepherds' song competitions of his youth in Sicily for his patron, the general who colonized Egypt and resided in the court at Alexandria. Thus the *Idylls* of Theocritus, the first pastoral text, gave us the word "idyllic" and established a sense of idealization, nostalgia, and escapism in a poetry of the countryside written for a court audience – all qualities that have come to be associated with definitions of the pastoral. It also created the defining pastoral momentum of retreat and return in the sense that the heightened language in which the herdsmen of Theocritus speak delivers to an urban readership insights into what Paul Alpers characterizes as common "plights and pleasures"[4] with an awareness of their limitations. There is a knowing artifice in the pastoral discourse, which is accepted because these shepherds are also representatives of everyman to readers who recognize the conventions of the genre. Thus there is a mixture that is often in tension, between realism of close encounters with nature, a simplified life, real transferable learning about inner nature from dealing with and observing outer nature, and the acceptance of a degree of artifice in this construction and its discourse. These are both real and representative shepherds who speak this poetry. So, imaginatively revisiting his youth, Theocritus returns to the Alexandrian court knowledge of human dilemmas played out in intimate contact with the rather harsh Sicilian landscape.

Retreat and return is the essential pastoral momentum – one of the defining features of this form of "cultural equipment" and the focus of the earliest ecocritical writing, which in the United States discussed journeys of retreat into wilderness (Barry Lopez's *Arctic Dreams*) or the wild (Henry David Thoreau's *Walden*). In the first British ecocriticism, on the other hand, the journeys were less important than the returns delivered from close contact with nature in the novels of Thomas Hardy, for example, or in contemporary nature poetry. Readers will notice that "return" is being used here in two ways: literal and metaphorical. This is one of the ways in which pastoral is useful to environmental criticism. Theocritus retreated in his memory to the environment of his childhood in rural Sicily and his poetry is returned to the court readership, but it also, hopefully, offers returns in the form of insights into human qualities – ideals of behavior even – that might be useful to the urban readers of the *Idylls*. Thus pastoral literature should deliver more than a narrative of a journey into the natural world. The link between pastoralists as shepherds and pastoral concerns for well-being, as in the term "pastor," is not accidental. Pastoral concern might be for human life or the life of the environment of retreat, or both.

Two centuries after the Greek *Idylls* of Theocritus, the Roman poet Virgil (70–19 BCE) added to our cultural discourse the notion of Arcadia as a literary construct of the location of pastoral retreat. Although based upon a real region of Greece, this literary Arcadia is a space in which the pastoral pretense can be acted out in its allegorical drama of interactions and dialogues between shepherds or their equivalents. In the *Eclogues* (42–37 BCE) Virgil evokes a Golden Age of the past that is set against the instability and alienation of the present. Later readers would rediscover Arcadia in Eden, the Forest of Arden, Marvell's gardens, John Muir's Yosemite, and the Georgian poets' English countryside during the First World War. The recognition of Arcadia invokes the knowing paradoxes of classical pastoral – nature and place as a literary construct, the poetic rhetoric of herdsmen, retreat in order to return, the apparent idealization that might reveal truths, fictions that examine realism, the guise of simplicity that is a vehicle for complexity. The delights of the human being embedded in nature are thus celebrated while their limitations are simultaneously examined. Much of this subtlety can be obscured by the later development of a succession of pastoral modes that varied in quality within each period and can easily be dismissed or parodied. But significantly for latter-day environmental literary criticism, a postmodern usage of pastoral is possible precisely because of the instabilities, tensions, and paradoxes embedded from the beginning in the simultaneous realism and artifice of the discourses of Arcadia – real place and cultural construct.

The diversity of pastoral modes that appeared in English literature following the European Renaissance's rediscovery of classical pastoral did not necessarily conform to all the conventions of their classical inspirations. Indeed, the term pastoral came to refer to any literature that described the countryside in contrast to the court or the city. Theme rather than form came to define the pastoral mode. Much contemporary ecocritical practice adopts this position, although, sadly, long continuities are not a feature of that practice. How often is discussion of a fiction of climate change compared to notions of the seasons in the work of Edmund Spenser? Edmund Spenser modeled his twelve eclogues of *The Shepheardes Calender* (1579) on Virgil's work, but they were longer, monthly, and incorporated more realism of the English seasons that derived from Chaucer. Their allegorical dexterity excited a Renaissance neoclassical interest in pastoral that led to Andrew Marvell's complex garden poems, which could ask metaphysical questions about what a human "green thought" might be, for example – still a question that preoccupies ecocritics from Timothy Morton[5] to Catriona Sandilands,[6] although regrettably they do not consider Marvell's take on it.

Part of this literary movement included pastoral dramas and Shakespeare was not to be left out. His wit in placing courtiers in a bucolic realism traced a journey of retreat to a return with insights gained, reconciliations (including marriages) now possible, between people, if not between the country and the city. The range of these transformations is remarkable if one thinks of the different qualities of experience of nature in Arden in *As You Like It*, in Bohemia in *A Winter's Tale*, on the blasted heath of *King Lear*, or on the island of *The Tempest*, a play that takes seriously the self-deceptions possible in working the pastoral magic at the play's devastating conclusion. As period ecocritics now turn their specialist attention to Early Modern and Renaissance pastoral literature, the rich and influential work of Shakespeare is gaining sustained study.[7] What have been regarded in the past as symbolic or allegorical references to nature in the plays are now being understood as actually also referencing real environmental concerns for forest resources, urban pollution, or issues about food sources and ethics. Indeed, Ken Hiltner has recently written a study of the period that is titled *What Else is Pastoral?* (2011) in which he cleverly argues that Renaissance texts, by gesturing away from the countryside to focus apparently upon the urban or the architectural, implicitly invoke that which is absent, thereby performing a pastoral function, such texts thus having "an environmental component."[8]

The explosion of interest in pastoral in the eighteenth century, partly driven by an Augustan valuing of supposed order and stability in Roman literature, resulted in a mixing of pastoral with georgic poetry, influenced by Virgil's *Georgics* (36–29 BCE), which gave emphasis to the practices of a human relationship with nature through the detail of husbandry. The georgic could hint at hubris in that relationship (learning from nature was necessary) just as much as it endorsed dominion over nature (the biblical command to bring forth goodness from the earth). Alexander Pope's *Windsor-Forest* (1713) exemplifies the shifts between its idealized, opening evoking Eden in England, to the work of the herbalist who "attends the duties ... to follow nature, and regard his end," to the final self-recognition of his pastoral discourse in this poem as having "sung the sylvan strains."[9] It has to be said that the potential of the georgic for contemporary environmental literary criticism (which I shall hint at from time to time in this chapter) has been largely neglected thus far, although neo-agrarian writers such as Wendell Berry are clearly working in this literary tradition that is closely aligned with – some might say is a subset of – the pastoral.

Less self-reflexive is the Romantic pastoral, which resisted the burgeoning industrial revolution (represented for Wordsworth by the railway line penetrating the Lake District at Kendal) by offering images of a rural commonwealth of pastoralists. The work of Wordsworth, often easily dismissed as idealizing nature, demonstrates the need for careful reading of pastoral, which for him in *Home at Grasmere*, for example, included both anti-pastoral disappointment at drunkenness and pastoral neighborly support in his little commonwealth. It is in this pastoral work that Wordsworth made the discovery that is still being explored by current ecocritics that the human mind is "exquisitely fitted" to external nature, enabling the possibility of an imaginative sustainability in that relationship, or indeed, the erasure of a need for a separate category of nature.

When, for the Victorians, the crisis of the diminished countryside was overlaid by a crisis of religious faith, the pastoral failed to offer much escape. Tennyson in *In Memorium* (1850) was forced to recognize that rapacious industrialism and competitive commerce might actually have been endorsed by a "creed" of nature all along. He needed to feed a hunger that was "red in tooth and claw."[10] For the Georgian poets who followed, the attempt to seek escape in the English countryside from the horrors of the First World War was doomed to be read by later critics as pastoral idealization at its most desperate.

Yet the honest enquiries of Edward Thomas and the self-challenging recognitions of natural energy of D. H. Lawrence, who both contributed poems to the Georgian anthologies that appeared between 1912 and 1922, indicate the exceptions to Georgian escapism. Nevertheless, John Barrell and John Bull, the editors of *The Penguin Book of English Pastoral Verse*, declared that the pastoral was dead in English poetry after the Georgians because the country could no longer be distinguished from the urban in the twentieth century.[11] The first nail in the coffin of pastoral in British literary criticism had been F. R. Leavis's attack on the Georgians in his 1932 book *New Bearings in English Poetry*,[12] but it was hammered home by Raymond Williams in his influential book *The Country and the City* (1973).[13] Williams was a Marxist in the English faculty of Cambridge University required to teach the English country house literature of the seventeenth and eighteenth centuries. His pre-ecocritical book was a critique of the cultural and agri-cultural falsifications of the English pastoral tradition of that period, which sought out alternatives such as John Clare and Thomas Hardy, but also the radical literature of the city such as that of Dickens. Williams' student, Roger Sales, later summed up this critique of pastoral by suggesting, in a book significantly subtitled *Pastoral and Politics* (1983), that Williams' cri-tique of pastoral could be represented by the five Rs: "refuge, reflection, rescue, requiem, and reconstruction."[14] "Refuge" refers to the element of pastoral escape and "reflection" to the backward-looking tendency for pas-toral to seek settled values in the past that require a "rescue" in a nostalgic "requiem" that is also a politically conservative "reconstruction" of history. The deception of pastoral's tendency to idealization of nature, its historical unreliability in its representation of landscape, and its view of the English countryside in a cultural class function in the analysis of Williams' influential book, predisposed English ecocritics to assume that pastoral sought to rescue a simple ecological harmony and balance. This Greg Garrard could easily dismiss as an "outmoded model."

But Williams also identified a strain of anti-pastoral literature that offered a corrective to such deceptions, often directly addressing the perpetrators. So the Wiltshire farm laborer Stephen Duck responds to Pope's image of the "joyful reaper" and James Thomson's idealization of "happy labor" in *The Seasons* (1727) with *The Thresher's Labour* (1736) in which Augustan poetic conventions are used to counter such notions: "In briny Streams our Sweat descends apace, / Drops from our Locks, or trickles down our Face."[15] But Duck's sole representation of male agricultural workers was, in turn, countered by Mary Collier's *The Woman's Labour: An Epistle to Mr Stephen Duck* (1739). Quoting Duck, Collier pointed out that it was women who raked and turned the hay. The milkmaid poet Ann Yearsley leaves no doubt about the nature of actually harvesting Pope's lofty lines about "Ceres' gifts" that "nodding tempt the joyful reaper's hand": "No vallies blow, no waving grain uprears / Its tender stalk to cheer my coming hour."[16]

Obviously the anti-pastoral here makes its correctives through the actual detail of the georgic mode. But, in fact, the anti-pastoral was embedded within the most complex pastorals from the *Idylls* onwards (which might caution easy rejections of outmoded representations of harmony that betray a lack of familiarity with the founding texts). There is a wonderful moment in the herdsmen's dialogue when Theocritus reminds his readers of the nature of a Sicilian ecology, literally grounding his idyll in unidealized fact: "You shouldn't go barefoot on the hillside, Battus. / Wherever you tread, the ground's one thorny ambush."[17] One might argue that learning how to walk the ground, in its localized and, indeed, its globalised conditions, remains as much a function of the tensions between contemporary pastoral and anti-pastoral as it was in the third century BCE. But some anti-pastoral poetry attacks the very idealizing role inherent in poetry about the English countryside. George Crabbe, in *The Village* (1783), for example, asks of the laboring poor (Pope's "joyful reapers"), "Can poets sooth you, when you pine for bread, / By winding myrtles round your ruin'd shed?"[18] That Mediterranean import into Augustan neo-classical poetry, the myrtle tree, persists from its classical roots at the very moment, Crabbe points out, when rural poverty is being exacerbated by the enclosures that are the inspiration for Oliver Goldsmith's paradoxical nostalgically idealizing anti-pastoral *The Deserted Village* (1770). It is John Clare who points the poetic political finger most knowingly and most poignantly in his poem "The Mores":

Inclosure came and trampled on the grave
Of labourers rights and left the poor a slave
And memorys pride ere want to wealth did bow
Is both the shadow and the substance now.[19]

Against this English rural reality, the colonies offered a rich source of pastoral escape, but with it came the recurring tensions of dominion and what might be called "pastoral responsibility" or stewardship. Of course, the background to the *Idylls*, written in Alexandria about Sicily, had been Greek colonial expansion into the locations of both the countryside and the court, of the retreat and the return. In *The Tempest* Shakespeare had raised awkward questions for his audience about the nature of pastoral responsibility on his enchanted isle, concluding with Prospero drowning his books of manipulative magic and asking the audience to forgive his hubris. It was James Thomson in *The Seasons* (1727–1744) who took pastoral poetry directly into the georgic challenges of the newfound lands of the exotic Americas and the East, although postcolonial ecocriticism, as yet, rarely turns its attention to this colonial legacy. For Thomson, as for the later novelist W. H. Hudson whose *Green Mansions* (1904) provides the narrative of the film *Avatar*, the untamed fertility of nature in the tropics was almost frightening in its untamable relentlessness. Here "the rugged savage" lived out his days as
A waste of time! till Industry approached,

> And roused him from his miserable sloth;
> His faculties unfolded; pointed out
> Where lavish Nature the directing hand
> Of Art demanded.[20]

The georgic "art" of directing both the slave and nature seems to be at work here where dominion dominates pastoral care.

In texts such as Thomson's the masking and displacing of environmental pillage and political conquest by nostalgic valuations of the very spaces and biosystems that are being destroyed, these literary tropes nevertheless express a yearning for ecological wholeness. Of course, this is the period of popular island narratives following the success of Defoe's *Robinson Crusoe* (1719), and in an essay titled "Problems Concerning Islands" Greg Garrard develops a postcolonial critique of five modern texts about five islands that chart the ecological effects of centuries of "the directing hand / Of Art" in a book edited by Campbell and Somerville subtitled *Ecocritical Responses to the Caribbean* (2007). Huggan and Tiffin's *Postcolonial Ecocriticism: Literature, Animals, Environment* (2010), dealing almost entirely with contemporary literature, indicates the direction that postcolonial ecocritical studies have taken in relation to works in the pastoral tradition concerned with other human and nonhuman communities.[21]

Meanwhile, America was developing its own strain of pastoral, which the Americanist Leo Marx, in his seminal and influential book *The Machine in the Garden* (1964), began by claiming *The Tempest* as Shakespeare's "American fable" of colonialism. Marx saw an American pastoral as originating in the georgics and advertisements of Beverley (1705), Crèvecoeur (1782), and Jefferson (1785), to be extended by the prose of Hawthorne, Melville, Twain, Thoreau, and Fitzgerald. The poetry of Frost and Whitman completed a distinctively American kind of pastoral, which Marx characterized as a concept that came to deal with the tensions of "technology and the pastoral ideal." At the heart of this Americanist tradition was Thoreau, whose *Walden* (1854) engaged with the possibility of a backwoods, pioneering, idealistic, retreat, while accepting the presence of the railway at the far end of Walden Pond that made retreat possible for a nation inhabiting, uneasily, a wilderness (that was actually already inhabited). Marx, in effect, claimed the individualism of the American colonizing process of its varied landscapes as a pastoral based upon a rural (one might suggest bucolic) Jeffersonian idealism that overrode idealization. Marx regarded the transcendentalists as uniquely American in their form of retreat into and beyond nature, to return again to the material world somewhat changed. For Emerson, who explicitly sought a New World, non-European philosophy, the return from transcendental experience, via intimate reconnection with nature, might be "the chant" – the artwork that conveys the insights gained. The moral obligation of the chant upon return from intense contact with nature produces the pastoral song that gives us Annie Dillard's *Pilgrim at Tinker Creek* (1974), Barry Lopez's *Arctic Dreams* (1986), and Rick Bass's *Year of the Yaak* (1996), for example. Individual epiphanies of retreat into the wilderness, wherever it is to be found, and return to deliver "the chant," are the core of American nature writing following the model of *Walden*. One can see why the earliest American ecocritics wanted to address these as texts of environmental literary inquiry.

Marx's success in his argument for an American pastoral has been as remarkable as it has been enduring. His book has never been out of print and it is the American pre-ecocriticism equivalent of Williams' *The Country and the City*. (It is a little-known fact that the two became friends when Marx was in Nottingham on a Fulbright and Marx invited Williams to lecture at MIT in 1973.)[22] What is more remarkable is the fact that his offering a means of distinguishing between what he called "sentimental pastoral" from "complex pastoral"[23] has not only been less than enduring, but that it has been a critical tool completely ignored by American critics since 1964, including latter-day ecocritics, until the Early Modern scholar Todd Borlik revived it in his 2011 book *Ecocriticism and Early Modern Literature: Green Pastures*. For Marx sentimental pastoral referred to the popular "illusion of peace and harmony in the green pasture" associated with "the simple, affirmative attitude we adopt toward pleasing rural scenery."[24] The similarity of terms here with Greg Garrard's notion of pastoral is striking, although sadly Garrard also ignores Marx's recognition of a more sophisticated complex pastoral. It is also notable that Marx does not identify an anti-pastoral line in American pastoral literature as Williams does for English literature. If the machine is already in the garden – technology is already threatening the very nature to which it gives access for celebration – the anti-pastoral is, in a sense, built-in to the American pastoral. Rather than Williams' identification of a separate counter-pastoral in English literature, Marx argues that in complex American pastoral "the pastoral design, as always, circumscribes the pastoral ideal" with a "counterforce" that undermines the idyll, as in *The Tempest* and in *Walden*. Furthermore, Marx has a sense of the limitations of the American pastoral fable:

> The outcome of *Walden*, *Moby-Dick*, and *Huckleberry Finn* is repeated in the typical modern version of the fable; in the end the American hero is either dead or totally alienated from society, alone and powerless, like the evicted shepherd of Virgil's eclogue. And if, at the same time, he pays tribute to the image of a green landscape, it is likely to be ironic and bitter. The resolutions of our pastoral fables are unsatisfactory because the old symbol of reconciliation is obsolete.[25]

Nevertheless, in a later essay on the American pastoral, Marx considered that this conclusion to *The Machine in the Garden* was too negative, expressing "an underestimation of the universality and adaptability of pastoralism" (1986: 54). Writing now as a proto-ecocritic, Marx saw that "as a result of the heightened ecological awareness of recent years, the archetypal nineteenth century image of the machine invading the landscape has been invested with a new, more literal meaning and credibility."[26] Lawrence Buell argued "American pastoral has simultaneously been counterinstitutional and institutionally sponsored."[27] *Walden*, for example, having been written from a counterinstitutional impulse was to become the most taught text in the American educational system. Echoing Marx and Buell, Borlik ends his 2011 book with the words, "The pastoral's 'staying power,' its adaptability, is precisely what we need."[28] And it was twenty years earlier that Marx, in his essay "Does Pastoral Have a Future?" (1992), had written that our modern environmental concerns were certain to produce "new versions of pastoral."[29]

In this he was gesturing toward William Empson's *Some Versions of Pastoral* (1935), which was revolutionary in turning the mode into a concept that could include "proletarian pastoral," for example, and also a consideration of *Alice through the Looking-Glass* as a version of pastoral. The point is that if pastoral can be regarded as a cultural function rather than a genre of canonical texts, or a mode of discourse about nature, it is possible to conceptualize a post-pastoral literature that includes Marx's complex pastoral, but also bypasses the British critical dead end for pastoral by identifying a version of continuity that is itself aware of the dangers of idealized escapism while seeking some form of accommodation between humans and nature. As a result of the critiques of Leavis and Williams, pastoral has become a pejorative term in English literary criticism, best characterized by the negative implication of its verb form "to pastoralize." Anyone aware that much contemporary British literature engaged with nature, the countryside, and the rural environment in a manner that escaped the closed-circuit of idealized pastoral and its anti-pastoral corrective, however, could see that the pastoral tradition was not dead, but vigorous in its transformation of the tradition in V. S. Naipaul's novel *The Enigma of Arrival* (1988),[30] for example, or in Seamus Heaney's collection *North* (1975).[31] Poet Ted Hughes was writing perhaps the most radical, varied, and complex new versions of pastoral. In 1994 I published an essay titled "Gods of Mud: Ted Hughes and the Post-Pastoral" in which I first identified what were to become the six questions that I observed to be raised for the reader by post-pastoral texts, to be elaborated in relation to poetry in the final chapter of *Green Voices* (2nd ed. 2011) and more generally expanded upon in the "Post-Pastoral" chapter of *Pastoral* (1999).[32]

The post-pastoral is unlike terms such as "postmodernism," "postcolonial," or "posthuman." "Post-" here does not mean "after," but "reaching beyond" the limitations of pastoral while being recognizably in the pastoral tradition. It is not temporal but conceptual and therefore can refer to a work in any time period. This is often misunderstood by ecocritics taking up the notion for new applications in their own work, resulting in some reduction of post-pastoral's more nuanced critical potential. It is not "intended to show how the reading and writing of rural retreat must now be tempered with an awareness of ecological threat."[33] Obviously only contemporary work can be post-pastoral in this way. Nor does it only "describe works in which the retreat serves to prompt the reader to the urgent need for responsibility and action on behalf of the environment," although this may be the case when applied to some contemporary Irish poetry.[34] The post-pastoral is really best used to describe works that successfully suggest a collapse of the human/nature divide while being aware of the problematics involved. It is more about connection than the disconnections essential to the pastoral. In illustration of the six questions typically raised for readers to some degree by post-pastoral texts each question below is followed by an example from a single poem by the English post-pastoral ecopoet Ted Hughes.

1. Can awe in the face of natural phenomena, such as landscapes, lead to humility in our species?

In his early poem "Crow Hill"[35] Hughes describes a landscape through the dynamics of processes at work in it on a macro and a micro scale. Lost in all this, "between the weather and the rock / Farmers make a little heat." Climate, geology, bird, and animal survival are such strong forces that human achievement is diminished to "a little heat."

2. What are the implications of recognizing that we are part of that creative-destructive process?

In "Crow Hill" between "humbled hills" and the vitality of the orange fox, the wind disturbs the dreams of farmers in their sleep, caught, too, in the cycles of destruction and creation in this place.

3. If the processes of our inner nature echo those in outer nature in the ebbs and flows of growth and decay, how can we learn to understand the inner by being closer to the outer?

Human dreams of sustainable vitality here, will suffer their setbacks as naturally as the impulse to make a life here represented by the bright fox and its vulnerabilities.

4. If nature is culture, is culture nature?

Nature is made culture by the discourse of this poem. But is the impulse to write the poem also nature thinking through us? If the mind, and its imagination, is our material nature, isn't the culture it produces also nature?

5. How, then, can our distinctively human consciousness, which gives us a conscience, be used as a tool to heal our troubled relationship with our natural home?

Readers will be prompted into considering to what extent this poem, and its implicit exploration of our relationship with the land here, might give us insights that are positive for our way of being in nature, or not.

6. How should we address the ecofeminist insight that the exploitation of our planet emerges from the same mind-set as our exploitation of each other, the less powerful?

There is no evident exploitation in this poem until urban readers, say, reflect upon their cultural treatment of small farmers and those farmers' treatment of the cows and pigs in the poem. Is there a cultural connection between the two in our economic and animal welfare practices? If the poem took the reader down some of these lines of thinking we might say that it is a post-pastoral poem that has extended the tradition of a pastoral landscape poem.

The post-pastoral does not so much transcend the problematics of the pastoral but explore them, seeking not a stable, complacent form of harmony in the human relationship with nature – our species' relationship with its home planet in its macro and its micro ecologies – but seeking a dynamic, self-adjusting accommodation to "discordant harmonies." To the extent that the positions taken in post-pastoral texts are provisional and open to revision, even at their most provocative and strategically didactic, they might be characterized as postmodern. But the deferral of judgments of the postmodern is not an option for ecocritics in that judgments are being acted upon daily in relation to the environment by our current "best guesses" for courses of action. At its best post-pastoral literature enacts this dynamic relationship and explores its problematics.

There is a danger that the six questions raised by post-pastoral might be used as a kind of checklist for approved texts, but it is important to realize that a single writer, or indeed a single text, might shift between all three modes of pastoral, anti-pastoral and post-pastoral. John Muir, for example, could idealize Yosemite's "temples," speak of butterflies as wonderful "mechanical inventions," and improvise a post-pastoral insight of connectedness: "When we try to pick out anything by itself, we find it hitched to everything else in the universe."[36] Indeed, might all three modes be present in Andrew Marvell's famous poem "The Garden"? Could a reader reasonably conclude that the poem's opening stanza is an anti-pastoral reminder of men's "incessant Labours"? But is the fifth stanza a classic pastoral of the absence of labor as "The Luscious Clusters of the Vine / Upon my Mouth do crush their Wine"? And isn't the conceptual challenge of the following stanza – "Annihilating all that's made / To a green thought in a green Shade" – actually a post-pastoral notion? Here is the imagination ("The Mind") creating a connection with, not just the material reality of each creature ("each kind"), but its very "otherness" in the sense of "far other Worlds" as a single vision of unified "green Thought."

Muir's and Marvell's post-pastoral conceptions each question and extend the possibilities for human reintegration with a natural universe from which much literature has assumed us to be separated. Such questions are, of course, crucial in recent apocalyptic novels of survival such as Cormac McCarthy's *The Road* (2006), Margaret Atwood's *The Year of the Flood* (2009), or Maggie Gee's *The Ice People* (1999). Post-pastoral dystopias, utopias, and pre or postapocalyptic texts all raise questions of ethics, sustenance, and sustainability that might exemplify Marx's vision of the pastoral needing to find new forms in the face of new conditions. Marx will not have been surprised to witness the explosion of what might be called "the prefix-pastoral," which would have to include the post-pastoral. William Empson might be said to have begun this redefinition of the pastoral with his "proletarian pastoral," but urban pastoral soon followed, together with radical pastoral (from Gerrard himself in 1996),[37] postmodern pastoral, gay pastoral, hard pastoral, soft pastoral, Buell's revolutionary lesbian feminist pastoral, black pastoral, ghetto pastoral, frontier pastoral, militarized pastoral, domestic pastoral, and, most recently, a specifically "Irish pastoral" in Donna Potts' *Contemporary Irish Poetry and the Pastoral Tradition* (2011). Much of this represents the contemporary need of environmental criticism to both draw from and redefine the pastoral as, in Buell's words quoted earlier, "a species of cultural equipment that western thought has for more than two millennia been unable to do without."[38]

NOTES

1 Greg Garrard, *Ecocriticism*, 2nd ed. (Abingdon, UK: Routledge, 2011), p. 65.
2 Lawrence Buell, *The Environmental Imagination* (Cambridge, MA: Harvard University Press, 1995), p. 32.
3 Leo Marx, "Does Pastoral Have a Future?," in John Dixon Hunt (ed.), *The Pastoral Landscape* (Washington, DC: National Gallery of Art, 1992), p. 222.
4 Paul Alpers, *What Is Pastoral?* (Chicago: University of Chicago Press, 1993), p. 93.
5 See Timothy Morton, *Ecology without Nature* (Cambridge, MA: Harvard University Press, 2007).
6 See Catriona Sandilands, "Landscape, Memory, and Forgetting: Thinking through (My Mother's) Bodies and Places," in Stacy Alaimo and Susan Hekman (eds.), *Material Feminisms* (Bloomington: Indiana University Press, 2008), pp. 344–373.
7 See Simon Estok's *Ecocriticism and Shakespeare: Reading Ecophobia* (New York: Palgrave Macmillan, 2011). For Early Modern pastoral see Todd Borlik, *Ecocriticism and Early Modern Literature: Green Pastures* (Abingdon, UK: Routledge, 2011) and for Renaissance pastoral ecocriticism see Ken Hiltner, *What Else Is Pastoral? Renaissance Literature and the Environment* (Ithaca, NY: Cornell University Press, 2011).
8 Hiltner, *Pastoral*, p. 67.
9 *Pope Poetical Works*, ed. Herbert Davies (Oxford: Oxford University Press, [1966] 1978), p. 44, lines 250–252; p. 50, line 434.
10 *Poems of Tennyson* (London: Henry Frowde, 1904), p. 389.
11 John Barrell and John Bull (eds.), *The Penguin Book of English Pastoral Verse* (London: Allen Lane, 1974).
12 F. R. Leavis, *New Bearings in English Poetry* (London: Chatto and Windus, 1932).

13 Raymond Williams, *The Country and the City* (London: Chatto and Windus, 1975).

14 Roger Sales, *English Literature in History 1780–1830: Pastoral and Politics* (London: Hutchinson, 1983), p. 17.

15 Barrell and Bull, *Pastoral Verse*, p. 386.

16 John Goodridge, *Eighteenth Century Labouring – Class Poets, Vol. 3, 1780–1800* (London: Pickering and Chatto, 2003), p. 53.

17 Theocritus, *Idylls*, translated by Robert Wells (London: Penguin, 1989), p. 71.

18 Barrell and Bull, *Pastoral Verse*, p. 401.

19 Barrell and Bull, *Pastoral Verse*, p. 413.

20 Barrell and Bull, *Pastoral Verse*, p. 312.

21 See especially their discussion of pastoral in V.S. Naipaul, *The Enigma of Arrival* (New York: Vintage, 1988) and Graham Huggan and Helen Tiffin, *Postcolonial Ecocriticism: Literature, Animals, Environment* (Abingdon, UK: Routledge, 2010), pp. 112–116.

22 Leo Marx per. com.

23 Leo Marx, *The Machine in the Garden: Technology and the Pastoral in America* (New York: Oxford University Press, 1964), p. 25.

24 Marx, *Machine in the Garden*, p. 25.

25 Marx, *Machine in the Garden*, p. 364.

26 Leo Marx, "Pastoralism in America," in Sacvan Bercovitch and Myra Jehlen (eds.), *Ideology and Classic American Literature* (Cambridge, MA: Cambridge University Press, 1986), p. 66.

27 Buell, *The Environmental Imagination*, p. 50.

28 Borlik, *Ecocriticism*, p. 209.

29 Marx, "Does Pastoral Have a Future?," p. 222.

30 See note 19 above.

31 See my discussion of *North* in *Green Voices: Understanding Contemporary Nature Poetry*, 2nd ed. (Nottingham, UK: CCC Press, 2011), pp. 115–116.

32 Gifford, "Gods of Mud: Ted Hughes and the Post-Pastoral," in Keith Sagar (ed.), *The Challenge of Ted Hughes* (London: Macmillan, 1994), pp. 129–141; Gifford, *Green Voices*, 2nd ed., p. 191; Gifford, *Pastoral*, pp. 146–174.

33 Sasha Matthewman, *Teaching Secondary English as if the Planet Matters* (Abingdon, UK: Routledge, 2011), p. 31.

34 Donna L. Potts, *Contemporary Irish Poetry and the Pastoral Tradition* (Columbia: University of Missouri Press, 2011), p. x.

35 Ted Hughes, *Collected Poems* (London: Faber and Faber, 2003), p. 62.

36 Terry Gifford (ed.), *John Muir: The Eight Wilderness-Discovery Books* (Seattle: The Mountaineers, 1992), pp. 248–249.

37 Greg Garrard, "Radical Pastoral," *Studies in Romanticism* 35:3 (1996), pp. 33–58.

38 Buell, *The Environmental Imagination*, p. 32.

2

ALFRED K. SIEWERS

The Green Otherworlds of Early Medieval Literature

Northrop Frye's 1948 theory of the "green world comedy" in early English literature provides a neglected key to reading medieval literature environmentally. Frye described the literary tradition of the green world in works such as *A Midsummer Night's Dream* as "largely medieval in origin," involving the "rhythmic movement from normal world to green world and back again" that "makes each world seem unreal when seen by light of the other." [1] He astutely identified this framework as a form of medieval comedy different from Dante's, given the allegorical *Commedia*'s inspiration from Scholasticism's more fixed and ethereal *analogia entis*. Frye's green world (as in William Shakespeare's Forest of Arden or the Wandering Woods of Edmund Spenser's fairyland) evoked a natural yet magical realm beyond that of everyday human conception, yet unlike Dante's allegorical universe, overlaid and entwined with actual geography and ecological life on the surface of Earth. The "green world" – akin to Paradise in medieval Christian geography, with its four named rivers identified both with actual waterways and the flow of virtues from Divine Wisdom [2] – suggested, Frye wrote, "an original golden age," with maternal associations, "the triumph of life over the waste land, the death and revival of the year impersonated by figures still human but once divine as well." [3] Its literary origins reach back to the so-called Celtic Otherworld in early Irish and Welsh texts, and the Arthurian romances that grew from them. In such medieval works, "green world" or Otherworld comedy evokes an overlay landscape, in which the world of everyday human constructions of reality interweaves an imaginative dimension of larger natural contexts. Landscape features such as overgrown Neolithic mounds (in Irish *síde*, in Welsh *gorseddau*), rivers, wells, countryside, forest, islands, or the sea itself, prove portals into this metanatural dimension. In such literary works, Frye wrote, "The conception of a second world bursts the boundaries of Menandrine [social] comedy [in] no world of eternal forms," but "a wonderful contrapuntal mingling of two orders of existence." [4]

It took almost fifty years to highlight the significance of Frye's model for ecocriticism, beginning with a foundational article in cyber studies by Paul N. Edwards. Edwards contrasted the "closed world" of the military-industrial origins of cyberspace (and by extension its largely corporatized state today) with Frye's literary "green world" of the past. The latter, he wrote, imaged forth

> an unbounded natural setting such as a forest, meadow, or glade … frequently affected by magic and mysterious natural events (think of A *Midsummer Night's Dream* or *The Tempest*). The green world is indeed an "open" space where the limits of law and rationality are transcended, but this does not mean that anything goes. Rather, the opposition is between a human-centered, inner, psychological logic and a magical, natural, transcendent one.[5]

The poet Simon Armitage, a translator of the classic medieval example of the green-world trope, *Sir Gawain and the Green Knight*, recently made an environmental reading of this narrative tradition of overlay landscape more explicit.

> The *Gawain* poet had never heard of climate change and was not a prophet anticipating the onset of global warming. But medieval society lived hand in hand with nature, and nature was as much an enemy as a friend. … Gawain must negotiate a deal with a man who wears the colors of the leaves and the fields. He must strike an honest bargain with this manifestation of nature, and his future depends on it.[6]

By the end of the *Gawain* poem, written in the fourteenth century, today's ecocritical reader is struck by an inversion of realities, natural versus socio-political. The geography of the supernatural "green world," in the "wild" cultural periphery of West Britain's Celtic Fringe, stands out more realistically than the geography and setting of the supposedly "real" and "historical" court of King Arthur. The latter are described in terms suited to the Norman French feudal regime dominating the metropolis. This structure of the Otherworld/"green world" model for storytelling evokes for readers an experience of what today can be understood in terms of environmental phenomenology.

Literary Otherworlds and Early Environmental Phenomenology

Edwards' commentary on environmental aspects of the "green world," and Armitage's commentary on their effects in *Sir Gawain and the Green Knight*, suggest how the framework of Otherworld overlay landscape (embodied in the Green Knight) gives agency to the reciprocity and intersubjectivity of nature, as now understood in environmental humanities. The literary tradition highlighted a type of iconographic landscape perspective. Resistant to objectification and "the gaze" by the dynamic interrelation of narrative to physical geography, it encourages a sense of landscape looking out at us. This provides a textual analogue to the "pop out" visual perspective of Byzantine iconography of the same period, paralleled in some respects by early Insular illuminated manuscripts, exemplified by the Book of Kells. The green world highlighted a sense of the "other side" of nature, which humans, themselves embedded in nature, cannot fully know or control.[7] In writing of the likely twelfth-century Welsh *Mabinogi*'s overlay landscape (also to be examined in more detail later), the Celticist John K. Bollard observes that it is "hard to differentiate at times whether the countryside is an embodiment of these tales or the tales are an explanation of the land itself."[8] E. G. Van Hamel long ago noted that the trope "tends towards the central notion of the preservation and protection of the land, both from inside and outside."[9]

Such landscape-narratives tended to resist cultural domination and colonization, by personalizing landscape as a relationship, rather than an object, suggesting the kind of connections between environmental and social justice explored in ecocriticism today. Key texts in the medieval tradition of overlay landscape (such as the *Táin Bó Cúailnge* and the *Mabinogi*) emerged at times of Norman colonial pressure on native Christian cultures in Ireland and Wales in the twelfth century, while the Norse sagas (which also reflect aspects of the overlay landscape frame) emerged as literature in the thirteenth-century era of monarchical pressure on the Icelandic republic from the Continent. Foundational English poetry such as *Sir Gawain and the Green Knight*, also in the fourteenth century, asserted itself against an old Norman-French colonial feudal regime. The latter tottered amid social turmoil in the wake of the Black Death, which led into the Wars of the Roses, the era of *Le Morte Darthur*. Looking back to the earliest Irish Otherworld texts, dating to traditions before *c.* 800, the Celticist John Carey describes a process of "the baptism of the gods," by which native traditions of a spiritual dimension in the landscape seem to have melded with Judeo-Christian ideas of Paradise, as incarnational desert asceticism – itself in a sense resisting imperial Rome – adapted to Atlantic islands.[10]

Two influential postmodern critics of neocolonialism, Gilles Deleuze and Félix Guattari, indeed have celebrated the liberating effect of non-modern art in which "the landscape *sees*," while apparently unaware of the greenworld medieval tradition.[11] Deleuze scholar Philip Goodchild explicated their view: "The work of art opens thought onto the body and landscape, so as to give a voice to the body before all words," granting "from perception of the object and states of the perceiving subject ... a percept that belongs to matter itself ... moments of vision that constitute the world."[12] Medieval texts of the Otherworld exemplified this more poetically, in the contexts of agrarian cultures synthesizing native and Christian traditions. With greater clarity than Deleuze and Guattari, the environmental phenomenologist Erazim Kohák drew on medieval and Czech traditions of nature to explain the overlay-landscape effect:

In meaningful interaction with our world, we are reading the text of nature:

> encountering in it its meaningful presence. Its meaning is not an "essence" in our usual naïve sense, a mysterious internal component. Nor is it merely an idea in our minds, picked at random and applied arbitrarily, by trial and error. It is an intermediate reality: the text has or is endowed with a meaning of its own.[13]

The ecosemiotic scholar Timo Maran expanded this notion of "the text of nature," to suggest a model of "nature-text," formed in overlapping contexts of environment, text, author, and reader, combining to shape meaningful landscape.[14] The ecocritic Louise Westling follows Maran by explicating Maurice Merleau-Ponty's view (in his *Visible and Invisible*) that "literary works 'gesture' and thus open these dimensions [of earth] that can never be closed." She writes,

> this language is the human voicing of immanent meanings in the world ... literary works achieve this witnessing within a larger network of animal articulations ... the yearning for articulation of every being, ... the profound synergies that link living creatures together on the planet. Human efforts are part of a larger tapestry of animal expression and aesthetic creation.[15]

In symbolizing this, the overlay-landscape trope of the literary Otherworld or green world also highlights the semiotics of Charles S. Peirce. Peirce, the nineteenth-century grandfather of environmental semiotics, suggested that we live *in* our thoughts (our environmental sign-relations), rather than *having* thoughts.[16] This supports Jakob von Uexküll's biological model of *Umwelt*, or meaningful environment of an organism or species, which Juri Lotman and Jesper Hoffmeyer forged into the notion of a semiosphere – an intersubjective, reciprocal eco-community of meaning, in which numerous *Umwelten* overlap.[17]

Peirce drew partly on medieval apophatic philosophy for his model of our environment as a living landscape of communicative process, rather than objectified essence. Such early philosophy, as adapted by German Idealism and Romanticism, undoubtedly affected von Uexküll indirectly as well. But while Frye identified some types of traditional comedy with the influence of specific philosophers – New Comedy with Aristotle, Old Comedy with Plato, Dante's *commedia* with Aquinas – he concluded that it was hard to do the same for green-world comedy, given that its subject is a meaningful "verbal universe."[18] Yet that last observation in itself points to an often neglected early "Celtic" philosopher of nature, namely John Scottus Eriugena, as the Aquinas of the green world.[19]

Eriugena's pre-Scholastic approach to nature in the ninth century drew heavily both on the process-centered and anti-essentialist apophatic theology of the Christian Dionysian texts, and on Maximus the Confessor's explication of Creation as communicative, the Logos' *logoi*, which Maximus identified with energies of God. Eriugena's *Periphyseon* synthesized such nuanced Greek Christian approaches to nature (adapting biblical and classical emphases to incarnational theology) with Augustine's writings, and with Eriugena's own background in the monastic communities of early Ireland. The latter had transplanted the asceticism of the desert fathers to the archipelago of the European Atlantic. In Eriugena's philosophy of nature, physical Creation is a continuum from primordial causes that he described as divine to theophanies and their physical effects. The result is a physical world sparkling with divine energies or meaning, in which dialectic and metonym and hermeneutics iconographically become incarnational processes. The ruling principle of being is not the *analogia entis* of Aquinas (which took poetic form in Dante's worlds), but a kind of *theophania entis* or (in the terms of the Byzantine theological doctrine of the uncreated energies of God in nature) *energeia entis* – emphasizing the energy and theophany of being, rather than the analogy of being. Eriugena began the *Periphyseon* with an arresting and paradoxical definition of nature, which could serve as the basis for the contemporary Irish Otherworld literary tradition: "Nature, then, is the general name, as we said, for all things, for those that are and those that are not."[20] The five-part *Periphyseon* devotes much of Book I to a lengthy discussion of place as an immersive envelope of life, rather than a quality of body, and later Book IV offers a lengthy exegesis of the biblical Paradise, as in effect a spiritual overlay of Earth. The latter's opening focus includes an image of the "ocean of divinity" in which all creatures live.

In Eriugena's work, the incarnational emphases of patristic Greek and Syriac Christianity, embodied in a desert asceticism whose writings often seem almost Zen-like today, intersected native Irish traditions of an ancestral spiritual dimension to the natural landscape. The result, in effect, offers a philosophical model for the pre-Scholastic origins of the Otherworld, and for derivative green worlds of later English literature. Writing in the ninth century, shortly after the first flourishing of Otherworld stories in his native Ireland and the heyday of illuminated manuscripts such as the Book of Kells, which visually suggest the cultural milieu of the Otherworld, Eriugena crystallized a way of experiencing the world that was already deeply embedded in literary cultures around the Irish Sea.

Celtic Otherworlds as Roots of Literary Green Worlds

What Eriugena called "the ocean of divinity" finds typological expression in *Immram Brain*, an Irish story dating back perhaps to the eighth century.[21] In it, the legendary Bran Mac Febail, a supposedly historical ruler of a realm around Lough Foyle (near modern-day Derry), hears mysterious sweet music that ultimately connects to a woman visitor from the Otherworld, who has brought him a silver branch from an apple tree there. He sails off to find the island of which she sang, and encounters Manannán Mac Lir, a god of the sea. Manannán shows Bran the Otherworld in the sea, which is not an empty deathless and hostile space, but teeming with life – an analogue to Eriugena's "ocean of divinity," or image of the cosmos as infused with divine energies. Manannán tells Bran:

> An extraordinary beauty it is for Bran in his coracle across the clear sea: but to me in my chariot from a distance it is a flowery. ... Speckled salmon leap from the womb of the shining sea, on which you look; they are calves, beautifully colored lambs at peace without strife ... The expanse of the plain, the number of the host, beauties shining with bright quality ... A pleasant game, most delightful, they play in fair contention, men and gentle women under a bush, without sin, without crime. Along the top of a wood has floated your coracle across ridges, there is a beautiful wood with fruit under the prow of your little boat. A wood with blossom and fruit, on which is the vine's true fragrance, a wood without decay, without defect, on which are leaves of golden hue. We are from the beginning of creation without age, without decay of earth-freshness. We do not expect weakness from decline. The sin has not come to us.[22]

The sea here seems to include a parallel reality, but the parallel reality also seems to include the sea. Both adjoin and envelope Bran's home country, which itself in Irish tradition was associated with an ancient flood that had overwhelmed the lands of Lough Foyle. This whole cosmic landscape thus evokes an antediluvian Paradise with biblical associations, but also pagan analogues associated with familiar native geography. Other verses in the story link the birth of Manannán's son, Mongán, a legendary ruler in Ulster during its early Christian era, to the Incarnation of Christ. Elsewhere in Irish tradition, Mongán is identified with the legendary green-world outlaw Finn, a kind of personification of the wild areas of the Irish countryside, extending the ocean Otherworld to the forests as well.

Another early Irish Otherworld tale, *Tochmarc Étaíne*, roughly contemporary to Eriugena's philosophy of nature, articulated an overlay landscape of the countryside via Ireland's network of overgrown Neolithic mounds. *Tochmarc Étaíne* forms a satellite tale of a larger overlay landscape of stories known as the Ulster Cycle, which boasts as its core the *Táin Bó Cúailnge*. Travelers can trace the route of the cosmic cattle raid of the latter story, across the Irish landscape, on the *Táin* Trail, via car, bicycle, or on foot. They also can visit mound-portals featured in *Tochmarc Étaíne*, which explains how a breach of contract between the high king and the Otherworld produced chaos among the ancient realms of Ireland, leading to the war in the longer *Táin*. Both works involve an otherworldly dimension entwined with the physical geography of Ireland. The twin mounds of Emain Macha, a home base for the warriors of the Ulster Cycle, were named for the goddess Macha's twin children according to the stories, by some accounts transformed into the cosmic otherworldly bulls of the *Táin*. There, the hyper-masculine hosts of pagan Ireland are destroyed shortly before the birth of Christ, as they seek to possess the dark and light bulls, which kill each another in one account. Emain Macha itself becomes twinned geographically and in story with nearby Ard Marcha, the heights of Macha or Armagh the storied seat of Christianity in Ireland.

As a prequel to the *Táin*, *Tochmarc Étaíne* focuses on a network of portals to the Otherworld, centered around the Bruig na Bóinde mound of the goddess Bóand. In it, the god Dagda sires a son with the goddess, the divine youth Óengus. Óengus, with help from his father, gains control of Bruig na Bóinde by magical cosmic law. He then arranges for his foster father Midir to marry Étaín, a royal daughter of the warrior realm of Ulster. Yet Midir's other, druidically trained, wife receives her rival Étaín badly, transforming her into a magical fly. As a result, Étaín is reborn a thousand years later, near the time of Christ. Midir follows her from the past, through the otherworldly landscape, and recites verses to her near the royal mounds at Temair (Tara), where she lives with her husband the high king of Ireland. In them, Midir reminds Étaín, whom he calls by her Otherworld name, Bé Find, of life in the secret folds of the landscape:

> Bé Find will you go with me to a strange land where there is harmony? ...
> Neither mine nor yours there; white tooth, dark brow;
> The troop of our hosts gladdens the eye – color of foxglove on each cheek. ...
> Miraculous of lands, the land of which I tell: youth not leading to ancientness there.
> Warm, sweet currents over the land, choicest of mead and wine;
> Outstanding human beings, not disfigured, procreation without sin or illegality.
> We see each one on every side, and no one sees us;
> The shadow of Adam's sin prevents our being reckoned right.[23]

Midir's song juxtaposes place names with both physical and fantasy associations, shaping the reader's sense of an imaginary geography of a nonetheless actual Ireland, while also highlighting its connections with the biblical Paradise. As the story unfolds, action moves between the portals at Midir's home mound of Bri Leith in Leinster to Étain's apparently otherworldly home at a mound in Munster, to Temair in Meath. Étain's human husband-king, Eochaid Airem, tries to excavate mounds to find her, after she and Midir transform into swans to escape Temair. The Otherworld portals form part of an interconnected network of the hidden side of the landscape. Eochaid's attempt to force his rule as king on that Otherworld leads him via enchantment to commit incest with their daughter. This in turn becomes part of a chain of events leading in sequel stories to the collapse of the high kingship, which enables the chaos of the apocalyptic cattle raid in the *Táin Bó Cúailnge*. The structure and themes of *Tochmarc Étaíne* resist central control or conceptualization of the landscape, and suggest symbolically the Irish tradition of hierogamic marriage as an alternative to objectification, figuring a personalization of the land to come in Christ and His mother.[24] It offers pre-Christian tradition, of the sovereignty goddess of the land whom the king must engage respectfully, as a typology fulfilled in medieval Christian iconography. The latter includes both the marriage of Christ and His Church, and the figure of Mary, identified with the Earth, as mystically both Bride and Mother of God.[25]

Early Irish literary monastics had reason to favor a personal contractual model of the environment, rather than a centralized objectifying one, given their position as cultural brokers among decentralized overlapping social networks, and their practice of Christian "desert" asceticism. In the process, they bequeathed to environmental readers, in the different contexts of our era, a literary model of a landscape as relationship.

Perhaps the most significant part of Midir's verse about the Otherworld in *Tochmarc Étaíne* is its biblical connection: "The shadow of Adam's sin prevents us from being reckoned right." That element of the overlay landscape from the biblical Paradise, suggested too in *Immram Brain*, also expresses itself in the Otherworld of the Welsh *Mabinogi*. Probably compiled in final literary form in the early twelfth century at a native monastic community, the *Mabinogi* incorporates earlier influences from Ireland, which had been the dominant early Insular Christian literary culture.[26] The *Mabinogi*'s Four Branches (as the intertwined stories in the cycle are called, in tree-like fashion) move from south to north Wales, and back again, evoking the landscape as central character of the cycle. Written as the Normans were taking over Wales and erasing its native monasteries, the stories weave into the Welsh landscape strands of both early medieval

Christian and native pre-Christian symbolism. These include the biblical tetramorph of four animal symbols and related virtues, as interpreted by Gregory the Great and others, as a totemic framework for the four tales.[27] Among its many memorable scenes, in a non-linear *tour de force* of narrative landscape, is the encounter of Pwyll, prince of Dyfed, with the goddess figure Rhiannon at the mound of Arberth, whose etymology suggests a sacred place, "at the grove." Pwyll's need to respect Rhiannon highlights the theme of marriage as a symbol of bringing the mutual Otherworlds of human and nonhuman together in partnership, but within a framework of the aforementioned Christian tetrarchal structure. The text expresses cosmic typology, in the birth of a child associated both with a native god and the birth of Christ, while warning against objectification of the native land. It does so in the contemporary context in Wales of the Norman Conquest, whose main landscape narrative by contrast was the utilitarian *Domesday Book*.

Middle English Green Worlds

Sir Gawain and the Green Knight, written by an unknown author in a borderland between Welsh-speaking and English-speaking regions of Britain, shows a distinctive conjunction of themes from the First Branch of the *Mabinogi*. These include an overlay landscape associated with a mysterious annual ritual contest. But there is also in both texts an otherworldly temptress with natural associations and surprising guises. A suggested identification of the wife of the Otherworld ruler Arawn in the *Mabinogi* with the earth-goddess figure Rhiannon, for example, would also parallel Bertilak's wife's situation in *Sir Gawain* as counterpart to the "goddess" Morgan who directs the Green Knight.[28] Both stories involve a mound-like portal to the hidden landscape of the countryside. In *Sir Gawain* the portal is described as a cave-like "Green Chapel," to which Gawain comes to be sacrificed. There, however, he encounters redemptory absolution, after a surprising uncovering of his own limitations, which leads him to a kind of breakdown. The agent for redemption is the Green Knight, living in the wilds of lands that Gawain reaches by traveling through the indigenous cultural realms of Wales, from a Frenchified Arthurian court in the unspecified Anglo-Norman space of Camelot. The poem carefully tracks Gawain's geographical route to the realm of the Green Knight, through west Britain. Medievalists have identified sites whose place names and folklore, in the probable region of the poem's composition, likely contributed to the setting of the Green Chapel in the poem. But where, by contrast, is the actual geography of metropolitan Camelot, with its Norman ways?

The Arthurian framework on which *Sir Gawain* drew, and in which both the pivotal characters of Gawain and Morgan (the Green Knight's ruler) are embedded, itself emerged from the Otherworld traditions of Ireland and Wales. We see this connection in Middle English green-world terms in Thomas Malory's fifteenth-century *Le Morte Darthur*. Amid the final historical collapse of the centralized system of medieval feudalism in England, Malory's narrative evokes a plexity of time involving an indigenous sense of eternity, identified with the roots of Arthurian tradition in the Celtic Otherworld. He in effect reinserts the Arthurian cycle into British history, as an overlay of actual events, with a more prosaic down-to-earth style than the French romances. Yet in the text a green-world context continually intersects and subverts linear history and centralized control of the landscape. Geraldine Heng notes the feminine nature of this otherworldly subtext, embodied by the Ladies of the Lake and of Avalon, and Morgan le Fay.[29] Irish tradition sometimes called the Otherworld "the land of women," which featured feminine associations centered on the goddess of the land or of sovereignty, already mentioned. Even the quest for the Sangreal arguably became a sign of this feminine disruption, and for healing of a hyper-masculinized and objectified political landscape. It brings a relational sense of a more natural landscape as divine, paralleling Celtic and Christian traditions of a Mother figure identified with the earth. Such aspects conjoin, in Malory's work, in the complex multiplex landscape of Christian Glastonbury, also known as the native-otherworldly Avalon.[30]

Toward the end of Malory's cycle, the Sangreal departs to heaven, and Joseph of Arimathea reappears, as if to reopen the connection of the Arthurian realms to Glastonbury that is also Avalon, the hidden landscape immanent in England. The Round Table begins to collapse. Fatally wounded, Arthur tells Bedivere, in a major epiphany of the work, "in me is no truste for to truste in, for I will into the Vale of Auylyon to hele me of my greuous wounde." Otherworldly queens, including Morgan, take Arthur to Avalon for healing, while his sword returns to the waters.[31] The survivors of the traumatic end of Arthurian Britain then converge on the green world of forests at or near Glastonbury. Bedivere encounters the exiled Bishop of Canterbury in the woods at a Glastonbury hermitage, where Lancelot likewise arrives after parting from Guenever.[32] When Guenever dies at a convent not far away, Lancelot and other refugee knights bring her body back to be buried with Arthur's, although the certainty of his death remains questioned.[33] After Lancelot's death, the remaining knights gather at Glastonbury for a month before scattering to live as holy men, presumably as hermits in the woods like those hermits and damsels from the green world who had assisted and harried them in the past.[34] Avalon remains an unobjectifiable if phenomenologically real "other side" of nature, intersecting history in the dynamic landscape of Glastonbury and its imagined surrounding primeval forest of hermitages.

Paradoxically, perhaps the most popular example of green-world writing in English literary tradition is the least obvious, because its very prominence in canonical literary studies has hidden its ecocritical meaning in the tradition outlined in this chapter. Geoffrey Chaucer's *The Canterbury Tales* illustrates the difference drawn by Frye between Dante's Scholastic comedy and green-world types of comedy, by inscribing an otherworldly yet incarnate landscape of stories – told by a ragtag carnivalesque band on pilgrimage – across a traceable geography in the English countryside. The pilgrims ride from commercial London and Southwark on an old Roman road to the spiritual shrine of Canterbury, never reaching their goal, always in process, the poem in the Ellesmere manuscript ending with the incarnationally grounded, ascetically penitential Parson's Tale. This contrasts with Dante's all-virtual geography (in Edwards' terms) of a closed world, centered on one individual's subjective reaching of a heaven outside of earth. Chaucer's work famously begins:

> Whan that Aprill with his shoures soote
> The droghte of March hath perced to the roote,
> And bathed every veine in swich licour
> Of which vertu engendred is the flour;
> Whan Zephirus eek with his sweete breeth
> Inspired hath in every holt and heeth
> The tendre croppes, and the yonge sonne
> Hath in the Ram his halve cours yronne,
> And smale foweles maken melodye,
> That slepen al the nyght with open eye,
> So priketh hem nature in hir corages,
> Thanne longen folk to goon on pilgrimages.[35]

The line "so pricketh him nature in her corages," can be read as "nature sparkles in their hearts so," referencing the whole ecopoetically meaningful landscape. This is no interiorized virtual reality modeled on a Gothic Cathedral. The road trip remains always in motion through the natural world, realizing self in dialogues and external connectivity. Weather, wind, vegetation, celestial bodies, birds, people, and spiritual mentors, all form part of this landscape. These cosmic connections reappear in The Knight's Tale's satire of chivalric subjectivity, with its description of the senseless destruction of the green world of the grove. In its Prologue and throughout, the poem often validates characters who are grounded in that connective landscape, sparing them from irony reserved for those who set themselves up as at odds against it. Chaucer associates the Otherworld analogue of "elvishness" with the symbolism of marriage in both the Wife of Bath's Tale (a derivative of the old Celtic sovereignty myth) and The Man of Law's Tale (hearkening back to early Insular Christianity). These suggest landscapes of partnership as alternatives to both the objectified courtly love and mistreatment of the land in The Knight's Tale, and to the unbridled materialism of the so-called "bawdy tales." The medievalist Rory McTurk suggests that Chaucer's overlay landscape framework for *The Canterbury Tales* as a whole borrowed that of the most popular and longest late-medieval Irish narrative, the *Acallam na Senórach* ("Tales of the Elders"), which melded Otherworld landscape narratives featuring Finn with St. Patrick's travels. McTurk argues that Chaucer, in the service of the Earl of Ulster, likewise modeled his proto-iambic pentameter verse on Irish poetic tradition – even as the poem's beats echo Old English patterns blended with continental syllabic style, in a metrical overlay to match its layered landscape.[36] In any case, *The Canterbury Tales*, together with *Sir Gawain and the Green Knight* and *Le Morte Darthur* – all foundational texts for English literature – preserved and adapted the earlier Celtic tradition of the Otherworld overlay landscape, as if so many mythopoetic arks. Their green worlds in turn influenced the nature-writing of Anglo-American Romanticism and fantasy. Twenty-first-century ecocriticism has come to cherish these literary green worlds of the past as if literary nature preserves, sources of imaginative hope in our struggles with massive global environmental challenge today.

NOTES

1 Northrop Frye, "The Argument of Comedy," in D. A. Robertson, Jr. (ed.), *English Institute Essays – 1948*, (New York: Columbia University Press, 1949), pp. 58–73, at 67, 68, and 72.

2 See John Scottus Eriugena's ninth-century *Periphyseon* (*Patrologia Latina* 122), the exegesis on Paradise in Book IV; I. P. Sheldon-Williams (ed.) with John J. O'Meara, *Periphyseon (Division of Nature)* (Montreal: Bellarmin, and Washington, DC: Dumbarton Oaks, 1987).

3 Frye, "Argument of Comedy," pp. 71, 69, and 67.

4 Ibid., p. 70.

5 Paul N. Edwards, "Cyberpunks in Cyberspace," in Susan Leigh Star (ed.), *The Cultures of Computing* (Oxford: Blackwell Publishers/Sociological Review, 1995), pp. 69–84, at 72–73.

6 Simon Armitage, "Introduction," in Simon Armitage (trans.), *Sir Gawain and the Green Knight* (New York: W. W. Norton, 2007), pp. 9–16, at 12.

7 Bruce V. Foltz, "Nature's Other Side: The Demise of Nature and the Phenomenology of Givenness," in Bruce V. Foltz and Robert Frodeman (eds.), *Rethinking Nature: Essays in the Environmental Philosophy*, Bloomington: Indiana University Press, pp. 330–341.

8 John K. Bollard, *The Mabinogi, Legend and Landscape of Wales* (Llandylsul, UK: Gomer, 2006), p. 15.

9 A. G. Van Hamel, *Aspects of Celtic Mythology*, Proceedings of the British Academy 20 (London: Humphrey Milford Amen House, 1934), p. 18.

10 Title of the first chapter in John Carey, *A Single Ray of the Sun: Religious Speculation in Early Ireland* (Andover, MA, and Aberystwyth, UK: Celtic Studies Publications, 1999).

11 Gilles Deleuze and Félix Guattari, *What is Philosophy?*, trans. Hugh Tomlinson and Graham Burchell (New York: Columbia University Press, 1994), p. 169; emphasis in the original.

12 Philip Goodchild, *Deleuze and Guattari: An Introduction to the Politics of Desire* (London: SAGA Publications, 1996), p. 190.

13 Erazim Kohák, *The Embers and the Stars: A Philosophical Inquiry into the Moral Sense of Nature* (Chicago: University of Chicago Press, 1984), p. 69.

14 Timo Maran, "Towards an integrated methodology of ecosemiotics: The concept of nature-text," *Sign Systems Studies* 35 (2007), 269–294.

15 Louise Westling, *The Logos of the Living World* (New York: Fordham University Press, forthcoming), chapter 3.

16 See James Hoopes, "Introduction," in Charles S. Peirce, *Peirce on Signs: Writing on Semiotic*, ed. James Hoopes (Chapel Hill: University of North Carolina Press, 1991), pp. 1–13.

17 Thus Peirce noted: "The entire universe is perfused with signs, if not composed exclusively of signs." (Charles S. Peirce, "The Basis of Pragmaticism in the Normative Sciences," in The Peirce Edition Project (ed.), *The Essential Peirce, Selected Philosophical Writings*, vol. 2 (1893–1913) (Bloomington: University of Indiana Press), pp. 360–397, at 394. On *Umwelt* and semiosphere, see Yuri M. Lotman, "On the semiosphere," trans. Wilma Clark, *Sign Systems Studies* 33 (2005), 205–227.

18 Northrop Frye, "The Argument of Comedy," p. 70.

19 See my *Strange Beauty: Ecocritical Approaches to Early Medieval Landscape* (New York: Palgrave Macmillan, 2009).

20 *Periphyseon* 1.1, 441A. Translations are from I. P. Sheldon-Williams (ed.), revised by John J. O'Meara, *Periphyseon (Division of Nature)*, (Montreal: Bellarmin, and Washington, DC: Dumbarton Oakes, 1987), here, p. 1.

21 Modern use of the English term Otherworld is queried and discussed in Patrick Sims-Williams, "Some Celtic Otherworld Terms," in A. T. E. Matonis and Daniel F. Melia (eds.), *Celtic Language, Celtic Culture, A Festschrift for Eric P. Hamp* (Belmont, MA: Ford & Bailie, 1990), pp. 57–81; and John Carey, "The Irish 'Otherworld': Hiberno-Latin Perspectives," *Éigse* 25 (1991), 154–159.

22 The translation is mine, based on the Old Irish edition of Séamus Mac Mathúna (ed. and trans.), *Immram Brain, Bran's Journey to the Land of the Women: An Edition of the Old Irish Tale with Linguistic Analysis, Notes and Commentary* (Tübingen: Max Niemeyer Verlag, 1985), pp. 39–40. I rely heavily on Kuno Meyer (ed. and trans.), *The Voyage of Bran Son of Febal to the Land of the Living*, vol. 1 (1895, repr. New York: AMS, 1972), pp. 16–22; sec. 33–38, 40–44; and on Mac Mathúna.

23 See Osborn Bergin and R. I. Best, "Tochmarc Étaine," *Ériu* 12 (1938), 180–181, at 137–196; John Carey (trans.), *Tochmarc Étaíne, in The Celtic Heroic Age:*

Literary Sources for Ancient Celtic Europe and Early Ireland and Wales, John T. Koch (ed.) with John Carey (Malden, MA: Celtic Studies Publications, 1995), p. 149; Jeffrey Gantz (trans.), *Early Irish Myths and Sagas* (London: Penguin, 1981), pp. 55–56; and Bergin and Best, "Tochmarc Étaine," p. 181. On its ninth-century dating, see Rudolf Thurneysen, *Die irische Helden- und Königssage bis zum siebzehnten Jahrhundret* (Halle: M. Niemeyer, 1921), pp. 47, 77, 78. Others place its origins perhaps in the eighth century, although its surviving forms are from later manuscripts.

24 On issues of sovereignty and landscape in early Ireland, see, Roseanne Schot, Conor Newman, and Edel Bhreathnach (eds.), *Landscapes of Cult and Kingship* (Dublin: Four Courts Press, 2011); and Máire Herbert, "Goddess and King: The Sacred Marriage in Early Ireland," in Louise Olga Fradenburg (ed.), *Women and Sovereignty,* (Edinburgh: University of Edinburgh Press, 1992), pp. 265–275.

25 On distinctive Marian devotion in early Ireland, see Christina Harrington, *Women in a Celtic Church, Ireland 450–1150* (Oxford: Oxford University Press, 2002), pp. 280–282. On Christian-pagan analogies, see Dean A. Miller, "Byzantine Sovereignties and Feminine Potencies," in Louise Olga Fradenburg (ed.), *Women and Sovereignty* (Edinburgh: Edinburgh University Press, 1992), pp. 250–263.

26 John Carey, *Ireland and the Grail* (Aberystwyth, UK: Celtic Studies Publications, 2007).

27 See my *Strange Beauty,* pp. 56–65, and my "Writing an Icon of the Land: The *Mabinogi* as a Mystagogy of Landscape," *Peritia* 19 (2005), 193–228.

28 Patrick Ford, "Prolegomena to a Reading of the *Mabinogi,*" in C. W. Sullivan III (ed.), *The Mabinogi: A Book of Essays* (New York: Routledge, 1996), pp. 197–216, at 210.

29 Geraldine Heng, "Enchanted Ground: The Feminine Subtext in Malory," in Stephen H. A. Shepherd (ed.), *Sir Thomas Malory, Le Morte Darthur* (New York: W. W. Norton, 2004), pp. 835–849.

30 See my "Gildas and Glastonbury: Revisiting the Origins of Glastonbury Abbey," in Thomas Hall, Thomas Hill, and Charles D. Wright (eds.), *Via Crucis: Essays on Early Medieval Sources and Ideas in Memory of J. E. Cross* (Morgantown: West Virginia University Press, 2002), pp. 423–432.

31 Thomas Malory, *Caxton's Malory: A New Edition of Sir Thomas Malory's Le Morte Darthur,* ed. John W. Spisak and William Matthews (Berkeley: University of California Press, 1983), p. 591.

32 Ibid., pp. 592–593, 595.

33 Ibid., p. 592.

34 Ibid., p. 599.

35 Chaucer, Geoffrey, *The Riverside Chaucer,* 3rd ed., ed. Larry D. Benson (Oxford: Oxford University Press, 1988), p. 23, pp. 1–18.

36 Rory McTurk, *Chaucer and the Norse and Celtic Worlds,* p. 181.

3

SHARI HUHNDORF

"Mapping by Words": The Politics of Land in Native American Literature

In the scene that opens *Wind from an Enemy Sky* (1977), D'Arcy McNickle's novel about the entwined political, cultural, and material dimensions of conquest in the early twentieth century, controversy over a dam calls attention to the centrality of land in indigenous colonial contexts. The story commences when Bull, leader of the fictional Little Elk tribe, encounters the dam for the first time, and his reaction initiates events that illuminate the dynamics of colonization and ultimately drive the narrative to a tragic conclusion. Built at the behest of white farmers, the dam was intended to "make the land rich" by irrigating the arid valley,[1] an area previously occupied by the tribe. As the dam enriches the farmers' land, it diverts water away from the territory where the Little Elk people now reside. In this and other ways, it represents the latest episode in a long history of dispossession. Its construction follows in the aftermath of the General Allotment Act, the 1887 policy that divided collectively held reservation land into private property and opened "surplus" lands for white settlement. In the novel, these lands fall to the white farmers who initiate the dam project.

As the context of Allotment situates the dam in the history of land loss, it sheds light on the connection between dispossession and assimilation policies enacted around the turn of the twentieth century, the time frame of the novel. Because Allotment imposed private property ownership and agricultural economies on Native communities, it counts, along with boarding school education and missionization, among the most significant policies designed to assimilate Native peoples into the colonizing society. The "deep meaning" of assimilation, contends David Wallace Adams, was the transfer of Native territory into white hands: "The Protestant ideology, the civilization-savagism paradigm, and the White hunger for Indian land were all mutually reinforcing and hopelessly intertwined as factors influencing the ... campaign to assimilate the Indian. ... As the Indian is pushed off the canvas of American life, the land remains for the taking."[2] So it is in *Wind*, and when Bull encounters the dam, he naturally reacts angrily. Castigating those who had "killed the water," he futilely shoots at the structure in an act that signifies the violence of its construction and portends the story's tragic end.

Wind, in other words, tells a story in which the myriad dimensions of colonization converge in a contest over land. The novel thus underscores the crucial importance of territorial conflicts in colonial struggles, and it also demonstrates the significance of land in Native American literature. Although contemporary scholarship frequently overlooks the centrality of territorial conflicts, argues Cole Harris, the "experienced materiality of colonialism is grounded ... in dispossessions and repossessions of land." Consequently, he insists, any critique of colonial power must start "not with texts, language, and strategies of representation, but with the dispossession of colonized peoples of their land."³ While this is true in *Wind*, the novel, *pace* Harris, also takes up the integral connections among attitudes, linguistic and cultural practices, and the material dimensions of dispossession. "The problem is communication," reflects the well-meaning reservation agent Rafferty, and "the answer, obviously, is that we do not speak to each other – and language is only a part of it. Perhaps it is intention, or purpose, the map of the mind we follow."⁴ Indeed, in the story, conflicts over territory emerge as much from opposing material interests as from differences between colonial and traditional indigenous "maps of the mind," especially as they are expressed in cultural understandings and representations of land. *Wind* draws out the disastrous effects of colonial epistemologies and representations, and it brings to light suppressed indigenous understandings and the material practices that follow from them.

A scene when the character Adam Pell (whose company built the dam) surveys the reservation exemplifies the colonial spatiality criticized by the novel: "From the vantage point of the hilltop it was possible to see a large expanse of valley, all of it cut into squares and rectangles by fence lines. Only the irrigation canals had a way of their own and followed contour lines without regard for geometrical symmetry."⁵ This notion of land as abstract, geometrical space, devoid of history and reduced to exchange value, is what Henri Lefebvre describes as the homogeneous space of capital, the "subordination [of land] to the unifying but abstract principle of property" antithetical to the sacred and to "lived experience."⁶ Not incidentally, this notion of space emerged with the so-called age of discovery, when Europe staked its first imperial claims across the globe, and it coincided with the earliest commercial uses of land as property.⁷ *Wind* clarifies the link between such colonial spatialities and European expansion: the "settlement of the Great Plains," opines Adam, "was responsible for the monstrous custom of applying straight lines and right angles to the earth."⁸ In this scene, the novel also invokes the biblical creation story in which Adam is given dominion over the earth. It thus underscores the connections between culture and material practices as it condemns the collusion of the state, the capital, and the church in the colonial project.

By undertaking a critique of colonization that centers on conflicting meanings and uses of land, *Wind* illuminates the political engagement of Native American literature more broadly. Published in 1978, *Wind* appeared at the height of the outpouring of creative expression that critics have labeled the Native American Renaissance. This era also marked the resurgence of indigenous activism that took the form of calls for the sovereignty, or political autonomy, for Native communities as well as global indigenous land rights movements. Scholars have demonstrated the convergences between Native literature and the politics of sovereignty, but little attention has been devoted to the connections between contemporary Native literature and land claims. Throughout the colonized world, indigenous land claims have hinged not only on legal agreements such as treaties but also on histories of long-term occupation, the basis of the common law doctrine of aboriginal title.[9] Traditional indigenous cultural expressions established community histories on the land and served as legal documents in territorial disputes.[10] In my reading, contemporary texts like *Wind* similarly provide counterhistories to dominant narratives that erase Native people, as they lend moral weight to Native claims by depicting the obscured violence of colonization. At the same time, I argue, these texts represent indigenous senses of space that dispute colonial claims and capitalist exploitation.

Wind contests the practices of dispossession recounted by the novel in part by exposing their colonial motivations and drawing out their disastrous effects. "Indian lands had been taken because they would be put to a higher order of use, because they would contribute to the advancement of a higher order of society," but actually such plans, realizes Adam, "were well and ingeniously considered as devices to exploit the Indians."[11] The novel thus undoes the colonial logic of progress that justifies dispossession, and it condemns assimilation and affirms Bull's rejection of the colonizing society. "If it hadn't been for him," in one character's words, "more of this Indian land would be in white ownership."[12] This is true not only because Bull opposes colonial power, but also, as his reaction to the dam suggests, because he holds traditional knowledge that the novel sets against colonial spatialities. Rather than an inert site available for exploitation, the dam is situated on sacred space to be treated with respect: "Be careful what you do here," Bull's grandson Antoine learns, "This is a place of power. Be careful what you think. Keep your thoughts good." These beliefs contest the logic of capitalist development and instead understand the dam as "an unnatural disruption of a functioning universe, a kind of crime against life."[13] Nevertheless, the protests of the Little Elk people go unheeded, and the opening scene when Bull shoots the dam presages the novel's tragic conclusion. Rendered hopeless by relentless assaults on the tribe and its territory, Bull fires at Pell and Rafferty, major colonial figures in the story, and then succumbs to the retaliatory shot he knew would end his own life.

As *Wind* exemplifies the engagement of Native literature with indigenous land conflicts, its themes and publication history trace relationships among different eras of Native writing and politics. McNickle is a prominent figure in Native literature and politics: his earlier work *The Surrounded* (1936) is often identified as the foundational modern Native novel, and he was key in the movement toward Native self-determination in the 1930s. He commenced writing *Wind* in the 1940s, inspired in part by turn-of-the-century colonial politics, a lasting theme of his writing, as well as by new dam projects that, in the early twentieth century, had begun to decimate Native reservations. The novel was finally published in 1978, the year following his death. *Wind* shows twentieth-century events such as dam building as emerging from nineteenth-century histories, the period that supposedly marked the end of conquest.

But at the same time, the novel registers shifts among these eras, particularly with regard to strategies of political engagement and cultural representation. In the land rights movements that emerged in the 1960s, forming one critical context for *Wind*, maps became essential tools for staking indigenous claims to territories by representing Native histories on and understandings of the land. Because of their entwined cultural, historical, and social dimensions, Native maps have taken narrative as well as graphic forms in a process that indigenous geographer Margaret Wickens Pearce labels "mapping by words":

> We have historically constructed an absence of native mapping ... by examining the artifacts which, by definition, were designed to erase native landscapes and render Indians invisible ... To locate native mapping, then, we must look beyond the printed maps of colonial narratives and into the realm of daily mapping activities. ... Maps are representations that facilitate a spatial understanding, and mapping is the process of creating and interpreting these representations.[14]

While, in McNickle's novel, "maps of the mind" is a metaphor for examining the connections between epistemologies and political practices in territorial disputes, other literature of this era, in my reading, complements the emergence of new indigenous cartographies by engaging in parallel projects of "mapping by words."

To consider these connections between literature and cartography, I analyze two contemporary novels: Linda Hogan's *Solar Storms* (1997) and Leslie Marmon Silko's *Almanac of the Dead* (1991). *Solar Storms* takes up a recent conflict that, like McNickle's *Wind*, centers on a dam: the James Bay Hydroelectric Project in Quebec, which began in the 1970s and flooded vast traditional territories of Cree and Inuit communities. The novel scrutinizes the role that cartography has played in conquest, and it engages in a project of "mapping by words" that illuminates indigenous histories and spatialities to support indigenous territorial claims. Silko's *Almanac* also takes up issues of land claims, in this case through a narrative in which the 500-year history of the Americas renders inevitable an indigenous revolution to reclaim indigenous territories. Like *Solar Storms*, *Almanac* scrutinizes colonial uses of cartography, but it also draws on indigenous traditions to turn maps into tools for indigenous land claims. Together these three novels illustrate the political significance of land in Native literature, and they trace a history of ongoing dispossession that shows territorial disputes as the enduring center of indigenous politics.

Cartography and Conquest in Linda Hogan's *Solar Storms*

Like *Wind from an Enemy Sky*, *Solar Storms* tells a story about a dam that sheds light on the broader dynamics of colonization. At the novel's beginning, the teenaged character Angel Wing returns to her childhood home in Adam's Rib after traumatic years spent in foster homes. Tumultuous events begin to unfold shortly after she arrives: the ancient Dora-Rouge, Angel's great-great-grandmother, announces her wish to return to her home community in the North (Inuit territory) to die, and messengers from that area arrive to warn that flooding from newly constructed dams will soon devastate the land. The story is a fictional rewriting of the catastrophe that ensued when, in the early 1970s, the Quebec government diverted rivers flowing into James Bay to construct a hydroelectric plant. The dams flooded traditional territories of Cree and Inuit communities, igniting a struggle between indigenous groups and the Canadian government that raged for decades. In the novel's rendering, this conflict extends a history of conquest and dispossession that commenced with the arrival of European explorers, and it brings into focus connections among various dimensions of ongoing colonization, including land conflicts and assimilation policies. The anticolonial critique in *Solar Storms* extends to gender, exposing environmental devastation and sexual violence as twin forms of colonial destruction. In the story, three women characters – Angel, Agnes (Dora-Rouge's daughter), and Bush (Angel's adoptive grandmother) – accompany Dora-Rouge on her return to her birthplace. Their journey North becomes, in one sense, a journey back in time that retraces European explorers' routes and exposes the devastation that ensued from them, the place of the dam in this history, and the colonial spatiality that underlies these endeavors. At the same time, the novel discloses an indigenous spatiality expressed through traditional knowledge that counters colonial discourses that at once subordinate indigenous women and land. By unraveling narratives that cast conquest as progress and redemption, and by relating suppressed Native spatialities and histories, *Solar Storms* supports indigenous claims to land in the story and the James Bay conflict that inspired it.

Solar Storms accomplishes this political work in part through figures of maps. In the conquest of the Americas, contends J. B. Harley, maps have historically served "as statements of territorial appropriation" and "devices by which a Native American presence could be silenced."[15] Through "the destruction of [indigenous] names" and "the redescription of an anciently settled landscape," they constitute "part of a wider colonial discourse, one that helped to render Indian peoples invisible in their own land."[16] Such maps, as we have already seen, reduce land to two-dimensional space devoid of history and cultural meanings, and they reflect the Enlightenment preoccupation with scientific rationalism. During this era, shifts in geographical thought, explains R. D. K. Herman, entailed "the removal of any 'spiritual' aspect of the world – that is, a reduction of the world into pure mechanistic materiality," and this "bifurcation of humanity and nature poses a conceptual distance and detachment that allows for the commodification of the material world essential for capitalism."[17] In *Solar Storms*, when Angel, Dora-Rouge, Agnes, and Bush commence their journey North, they follow ancient maps created by European explorers that clarify these connections between cartography and conquest. One bears an image of a sinking boat, its Indian passengers chained together as slaves bound for Europe.[18] These are "incredible topographies, the territories and tricks and lies of history," created by "men possessed with the spoils of this land" whose legacy was "the removal of spirit from everything." As such, these maps overlook "people [and] animal lives" as well as "the carnage" brought about by European settlement and the establishment of the fur trade.[19] Three hundred years later, the hydroelectric proposal similarly represents land through "their figures, their measurements, and ledgers" as a "flat, two-dimensional world."[20] These correspondences between historical and contemporary cartographic renderings of space and the resulting exploitation define the hydroelectric project as the latest episode of a conquest that commenced with European exploration.

As the women follow the ancient routes and maps of explorers, their story unravels the colonial myths and spatialities that rationalize European claims to territory. "We were undoing the routes of explorers," ruminates Angel, "taking apart the advance of commerce, narrowing down and distilling the truth out of history." While European maps suppress history to depict land as available for appropriation, "the waterways," in the novel's account, "had a history."²¹ Often carried in oral narratives rather than official documents, this history testifies to an ongoing indigenous presence as well as to the material enactments of power on indigenous land and bodies that fall outside of colonial discourses. Angel recalls, for instance, the story of the indigenous woman who first encountered white men in the territory and saw "the wind-filled sails of [their] graceful boat of death," a "tormented world ... its true cargo." Little did she know then that because of their arrival "beloved children would be mutilated, women cut open and torn, that strong, brave men would die, and that even their gods would be massacred."²² Just as this story inverts the conventional encounter narrative, indigenous place names render conquest legible from an indigenous perspective. Poison Road, the main street in Angel's hometown, recalls the slaughter of wild animals to make room for European settlers, while Bone Island holds the remains of victims of epidemics that annihilated entire tribes.²³ By exposing these histories, the journey contests colonial narratives that erase indigenous peoples and cast colonization as progress.

In *Solar Storms*, land and women's bodies are intersecting sites of colonization, a conjunction that signals integral connections among patriarchy, dispossession, and conquest. Like *Wind, Solar Storms* implicates Christianity in colonial destruction by calling up the biblical creation story. The place name Adam's Rib invokes how Adam gains dominion over the earth and over Eve, and connects it to the history of that town, its houses built by missionaries and its main street (Poison Road) named for the violence of dispossession. Like the landscape, women's bodies are physically marked by violence. Agnes tells Angel about meeting the young Loretta, who would become Angel's grandmother and whose body, like the land, was scarred and poisoned:

> Loretta smelled of something sweet, an almond odor that I couldn't place until years later. ... When I finally placed the odor, when I knew it was cyanide, I knew who she was, what people she came from. She came from the Elk Islanders, the people who became so hungry they ate the poisoned carcasses of deer that the settlers left out for the wolves ... The curse on that poor girl's life came from watching the desperate people of her tribe die ... After that, when she was still a girl, she'd been taken and used by men who fed her and beat her and forced her.²⁴

Because of this torture, Loretta becomes "the one who hurt others,"[25] and the story of her daughter Hannah (another biblical name) repeats that of her mother. When Hannah appears as a young child at Adam's Rib, she too exudes the smell of cyanide, a smell "deeper than skin … blood-deep … history-deep," and "her skin was a garment of scars," of "burns and incisions," the "signatures of torturers."[26] Her body, in Bush's words, is "a battleground," a place where "time and history and genocide" meet – a description that resonates with the disputed territory in the story.[27] Angel's body too is "marked" and scarred, some of the wounds inflicted by Hannah.

By condemning these entangled forms of colonial violence, *Solar Storms* disputes colonial narratives that use gender to justify dispossession and, conversely, use dispossession to subordinate indigenous women. Land in imperial discourse, contends Peter Hulme, "is named as female in passive counterpoint to the masculine thrust of European technology," a patriarchal convention that constructs "virgin land" as sexualized space available for appropriation.[28] At the same time, dominant narratives erase indigenous women or depict them as collaborators in conquest, thus obscuring colonial violence. Stories about Pocahontas, Sacajawea, and La Malinche – the best-known among the few Native women who find a place in American histories – affirm European superiority and suggest Native assent to dispossession: the "passive indigenous woman" facilitated "a gendered and sexualized reading that saw the land as a woman … open to the embrace and penetration of Europe," writes Pamela Scully, while the narrative of Europeans who bore children with Native women "symbolically affirms the fathers' right to the soil."[29] Such narratives about indigenous women's betrayals and their ostensible role in dispossession recall the story of the biblical Eve's transgression, which leads to another displacement (expulsion from the Garden of Eden) and, like the creation story, legitimates patriarchy. But the novel, by contrast, invokes the story of Eve to condemn colonization. "Loretta wasn't the original sin," explains Agnes, and Angel realizes that "my beginning was Hannah's beginning, one of broken lives, gone animals, trees felled … Our beginnings were intricately bound up in the history of the land … in the nooks of America."[30] These accounts of violence undercut myths of female passivity and consent that depict land and women's bodies as available for appropriation.

As the journey unfolds, the novel engages in twin projects of remapping the land and redefining the place of indigenous women in territorial conflicts. The explorers' map crumbles in Bush's hand, and the women uncover "a deeper map," the "map inside ourselves" drawn from "the old ways, the way we used to live."[31] Their journey repeats and undoes European journeys of exploration by returning to the "old ways" remembered by Dora-Rouge.

This alternative spatiality revives the "ancient pact ... humans had once made with animals" and recognizes land as alive, changing, and multidimensional, "refus[ing] to be shaped by the makers of maps."[32] Such understandings and the long histories of occupation they reflect carry political implications for the territorial disputes in the novel. "Defiant land" with "its own will ... made it difficult for [Europeans] to claim title," while the histories recounted by the novel contest the claims of the government agents, who "insisted the people had no legal right to the land," by establishing that "[Angel's] own people ... had lived there forever, for more than ten thousand years, and had been sustained by these lands that were now being called empty and useless."[33]

The story not only presents an alternative spatiality that disputes claims of capital and the state, but it also marks out a central place for indigenous women in territorial conflicts. Dora-Rouge holds superior knowledge of the waterways that supersedes that of European explorers, and she also remembers traditional uses of plants. This knowledge resonates with cartographic endeavors by indigenous groups beginning in the 1970s, the time frame of the novel, to establish legal claims to land. During this era, the Canadian government commenced "use and occupancy studies" to establish the legitimacy of aboriginal title. Most often, including in the context of the James Bay dispute, these took shape as mapping projects that documented the relationship of indigenous communities to their territories by representing histories, place names, and subsistence and cultural practices. Such mapping projects, observes Mac Chapin, have provided "a powerful tool for indigenous peoples in their struggles to defend and claim their ancestral lands ... and preserve their cultures." Yet, a key shortcoming, he points out, has been that women remain "weakly represented" in indigenous mapping.[34] *Solar Storms* extends these projects through a story that establishes women's histories on – and thus claims to – indigenous landscapes. The novel further counters colonial narratives and erasures by making Angel, Bush, and Dora-Rouge (who survives until after her return home, though Agnes dies along the journey) the leaders in the fight that, as in the James Bay dispute, halts construction of the dams.

While *Wind from an Enemy Sky* tells the story of unmitigated colonial destruction, *Solar Storms* is a narrative of political and social regeneration that centers on women. Hogan's novel follows in the path of earlier novels such as *Wind* by engaging an ongoing territorial conflict, but its concern with gender and its optimism emerge from the political climate of the post-1960s era, when Native communities achieved major gains in sovereignty rights and (especially in Canada) land claims. Silko's monumental novel *Almanac of the Dead*, too, reflects the hopefulness of the contemporary era through a story about revolutionary women. Although it remains rooted in actual histories of conquest, *Almanac* tells a story about indigenous land claims in the future of the Americas, and it establishes these claims by turning mapping into an instrument of indigenous resistance.

Countermapping in Silko's Almanac of the Dead

Like *Solar Storms*, *Almanac of the Dead* recalls the role of maps in European expansion, but while Hogan's novel carries out its projects of critique and remapping through narrative, *Almanac* reworks the visual conventions of cartography to draw out its political possibilities for indigenous land claims. Published in 1991, the year before the Columbus quincentennial celebrations, *Almanac* recasts Europe's "discovery" and settlement of the Americas as brutal violence and theft. Drawing on actual events, the novel narrates the slaughter, enslavement, and dispossession of indigenous peoples that commenced with Columbus's arrival, continued through the Spanish conquests and the Indian Wars, and persists in the present. "Sixty million Native Americans died between 1500 and 1600," reads the frontispiece, and "the Indian Wars have never ended in the Americas." As conquest remains ongoing, so too do "the defiance and resistance to things European continue unabated" as Native Americans "seek nothing less than the return of all tribal lands." Entwining historical events and fictional episodes, *Almanac* follows in the path of *Wind* and *Solar Storms* by creating a story of unbroken conquest that centers on land, but on a broader historical and geographical scale. In *Almanac* as well, clashes over land invoke conflicting colonial and indigenous conceptions of space. Among the emblematic colonial figures in the novel are a real estate developer, an architect, and a geologist, each of whom regards land as an object to be owned and exploited. "Some nights Leah [the developer] would lie with her eyes closed and imagine that the city limits of Tucson and the surrounding Pima County were a gridwork of colored squares" as she planned her aqueous dream city of Venice, Arizona, a scheme for which she ruthlessly circumvents both Indian water rights and environmental protections.[35] By contrast, the indigenous revolutionaries in the story dispute the notion of land as private property and source of material wealth, as they seek the return of tribal territories.

These conflicting conceptions of space and claims to territory find expression on the "five hundred year map" that opens *Almanac*. The map draws on European and indigenous cartographic traditions to expose the role of cartography in colonial power and to support the indigenous land claims project of the novel. Europe's "discovery" of the Americas, the subject of *Almanac*'s critique, coincided, as we have already seen, with shifts in conceptions of geographical space. This era also gave rise to new forms of representation that privileged visuality and facilitated the depiction of land as Euclidean space, reduced to surfaces and organized as a geometric grid. "This new 'scopic regime,'" argues J. B. Harley,

> was undoubtedly an increment to the technology of the European power in its first great age of expansion into the overseas world. It offered opportunities ... for its conquest, appropriation, subdivision, commodification, and surveillance. As David Harvey puts it, "it seemed as if space, though infinite, was conquerable and containable for purposes of human occupancy and action. It could be appropriated in imagination according to mathematical principles."[36]

Such maps represented land as available for appropriation and exploitation, and they erased all evidence of Native presence and claims to territory, thus creating the "virgin land" of the colonial imaginary.

Almanac's "five hundred year map" draws upon these cartographic conventions to reflect colonial appropriations and reorganizations of space. The map employs European toponyms and geographical scale (roughly, at least) to represent the land as two-dimensional space, and the U.S.-Mexico border, a colonial demarcation of territory, is its central image. But while colonial maps obscure colonial violence to support European claims to territory, Silko's map, by contrast, exposes the power relations that come to bear on land. Its legends recall the slaughter of conquest ("sixty million Native Americans died between 1500 and 1600"), and the map makes visible the presence and attempted erasure of indigenous peoples by naming characters and storylines from the novel that depict histories of indigenous occupation and European brutality (histories recounted in the narrative itself). These recollections of violence challenge the political authority of colonial nation-states named on the map – "Only a bastard government/Occupies stolen land!," intones the poet/lawyer Wilson Weasel Tail near the novel's end[37] – as they also unsettle their claims to territory. The "five hundred year map" thus employs European cartographic conventions against themselves to engage in what Sherene Razack, citing Richard Phillips, labels "unmapping," or the effort "to denaturalize geography by asking how spaces come to be but also 'to undermine world views that rest upon it.'"[38]

At the same time, Silko's map draws on indigenous cartographic traditions to represent an alternative geography that supports Native claims to land. While colonial maps render land as "blank space," Native cartographies, by contrast, emerge from the histories, social relations, and cultural beliefs that constitute landscape in traditional indigenous contexts. In Mesoamerican traditions, a key subject of *Almanac*, the cartographic structuring device, explains Barbara Mundy, is social: physical geographies take shape through depictions of the political organization of particular communities, the ways those have communities occupied spaces, and the historical events that have transpired in particular places.[39] Such indigenous "alternative cartographies," in Harley's words, constituted a "conscious strategy of resistance" to European claims to territory that provided a "record of past ownership" and thus "a challenge to appropriation by the colonists."[40] Although cartographic practices changed as the conquest unfolded, they continued to serve the explicitly political goal of creating community identities through shared histories, social practices, and spatial relations that supported Indian land claims after the invasion. In this later period, indigenous maps, Gordon Brotherston explains, typically appeared as title pages in the *teoaxoxtli*, literary accounts that, like Silko's novel, represent historical and cosmic dimensions of Native experience while they "construct political space and anchor historical continuity."[41] Because they establish histories and boundaries of Native occupation of the land, they constitute "political statements to defend land and home," and they have been used as legal instruments to establish Native land title throughout the twentieth century.[42]

Similarly, the "five hundred year map" brings into play these cartographic traditions to support *Almanac*'s broader project of indigenous land claims by inscribing indigenous histories and contemporary social relations on the land. Countering the "blank spaces" and atemporality of colonial cartography, the map recalls the long indigenous occupation of the Americas: "when Europeans arrived," reads one legend, "the Maya, Azteca, Inca cultures had already built great cities and vast networks of roads," while the storylines and character names point to the ongoing colonial conflicts developed throughout the rest of the novel. Together, these constitute a continuous history of indigenous occupation and ongoing resistance to conquest. In these ways, the map represents the social dimensions of space that gain political meanings in colonial territorial disputes, the histories on the land of indigenous occupation that undo the abstraction of capitalist space and underlie Native claims to territory both within and outside of the novel.

But the "five hundred year map" traces a geography that is not only retrospective but also anticipatory, engaging in what Matthew Sparke labels the "proleptic effects of mapping," or "the ways maps contribute to the construction of spaces that later they seem only to represent."[43] Likewise, in the novel, memory of conquest facilitates political consciousness and revolt – "The powers who controlled the United States didn't want the people to know their history ... If the people knew their history, they would realize they must rise up"[44] – and the map gestures to a future when indigenous people retake their land. Although the U.S.-Mexico border is the most prominent image, lines trace the characters' incessant movements across borders, exposing those boundaries as a colonial conceit. Reversing the colonial narrative of indigenous disappearance, the United States goes unnamed, signaling the instability not only of the border but also of the colonial nation-state itself. The legends make explicit this connection between past and future, rendering visible the impending revolution at the novel's end: while "ancient prophecies foretold the arrival of Europeans in the Americas" they also "foretell the disappearance of all things European." Although maps have historically served as "weapons of imperialism," as both discourses and practical tools in the processes of "acquisition and dispossession that lie at the heart of colonialism,"[45] *Almanac* nevertheless turns cartography against its original purposes to counter colonial power and to establish indigenous authority and rights to territory. As it thus reflects the concerns and optimism of the 1960s era, it marks continuities in Native literature and politics and the enduring significance of land in ongoing colonial conflicts.

NOTES

1 D'Arcy McNickle, *Wind from an Enemy Sky* (Albuquerque: University of New Mexico Press, 1988), p. 169.
2 David Wallace Adams, "Fundamental Considerations: The Deep Meaning of Native American Schooling, 1880–1900," *Harvard Educational Review* 58, 1 (February 1988), 21, 23.
3 Cole Harris, "How Did Colonialism Dispossess? Comments from an Edge of Empire," *Annals of the Association of American Geographers* 94, 1 (March 2004), 167–168.
4 McNickle, *Wind from an Enemy Sky*, p. 125.
5 McNickle, *Wind from an Enemy Sky*, p. 229.
6 Henri Lefebvre, *The Production of Space*, trans. Donald Nicholson-Smith (Oxford: Blackwell, 1991), p. 252.
7 See, for example, Denis Cosgrove, "Prospect, Perspective and the Evolution of the Landscape Idea," *Transactions of the Institute of British Geographers* 10, 1 (1985), 45–62.
8 McNickle, *Wind from an Enemy Sky*, p. 229.
9 See Felix Cohen, *The Legal Conscience, Selected Papers* (New Haven, CT: Yale University Press, 1960), pp. 274, 278.
10 Gordon Brotherston, *Book of the Fourth World: Reading the Native Americas through their Literature* (Cambridge: Cambridge University Press, 1992), p. 83.
11 McNickle, *Wind from an Enemy Sky*, pp. 190, 193.
12 McNickle, *Wind from an Enemy Sky*, p. 121.
13 McNickle, *Wind from an Enemy Sky*, p. 5, 210.
14 Margaret Wickens Pearce, "Native Mapping in Southern New England Indian Deeds," in G. W. Lewis, ed., *Cartographic Encounters: Perspectives on Native American Mapmaking and Map Use* (Chicago: University of Chicago Press, 1998), pp. 172, 158–159.
15 J. B. Harley, "Rereading the Maps of the Columbian Encounter," *Annals of the Association of American Geographers* 82, 3 (September 1992), 522.

16 J. B. Harley, *The New Nature of Maps: Essays in the History of Cartography*, Paul Laxton, ed. (Baltimore: The Johns Hopkins University Press, 2001), pp. 181, 188.
17 R. D. K. Herman, "Reflections on the Importance of Indigenous Geography," *American Indian Culture and Research Journal* 32, 3 (1988), 74.
18 Linda Hogan, *Solar Storms* (New York: Scribner, 1997), p. 131.
19 Hogan, *Solar Storms*, pp. 122–123, 180.
20 Hogan, *Solar Storms*, p. 279.
21 Hogan, *Solar Storms*, pp. 176, 21.
22 Hogan, *Solar Storms*, p. 168.
23 Hogan, *Solar Storms*, pp. 24, 196.
24 Hogan, *Solar Storms*, pp. 38–39.
25 Hogan, *Solar Storms*, p. 39.
26 Hogan, *Solar Storms*, pp. 40, 99.
27 Hogan, *Solar Storms*, pp. 99, 101.
28 Peter Hulme, "Polytropic Man: Tropes of Sexuality and Mobility in Early Colonial Discourse," in Francis Barker, Peter Hulme, Margaret Iversen, and Diana Loxley, eds., *Europe and Its Others: Proceedings of the Essex Conference on the Sociology of Literature, July 1984, vol. 2* (Colchester, UK: University of Essex, 1985), p. 18.
29 Pamela Scully, "Malintzin, Pocahontas, and Krotoa: Indigenous Women and Myth Models of the Atlantic World," *Journal of Colonialism and Colonial History* 6, 3 (2005), 4, 13.
30 Hogan, *Solar Storms*, pp. 39, 96.
31 Hogan, *Solar Storms*, pp. 123, 17.
32 Hogan, *Solar Storms*, pp. 22, 123.
33 Hogan, *Solar Storms*, pp. 57–58.
34 Mac Chapin, Zachary Lamb, and Bill Threlkeld, "Mapping Indigenous Lands," *Annual Review of Anthropology* 34 (2005), 630.
35 Leslie Marmon Silko, *Almanac of the Dead: A Novel* (New York: Simon and Schuster, 1991), pp. 369, 376.
36 Harley, "Rereading the Maps of the Columbian Encounter," 524.
37 Silko, *Almanac of the Dead*, pp. 714–715.
38 Sherene H. Razack, "When Place Becomes Race," in Sherene H. Razack, ed., *Race, Space, and the Law: Unmapping a White Settler Society*, (Toronto: Between the Lines, 2002), p. 5.
39 Barbara E. Mundy, *The Mapping of New Spain: Indigenous Cartography and the Maps of the Relaciones Geográficas* (Chicago: University of Chicago Press, 1996), pp. xiv–xvi.
40 Harley, "Rereading the Maps of the Columbian Encounter," p. 528.
41 Brotherston, *Book of the Fourth World*, p. 4.
42 Brotherston, *Book of the Fourth World*, pp. 90, 83.
43 Matthew Sparke, "A Map That Roared and an Original Atlas: Canada, Cartography, and the Narration of Nation," *Annals of the Association of American Geographers* 88, 3 (1998), 466.
44 Silko, *Almanac of the Dead*, p. 431.
45 Harley, *The New Nature of Maps*, pp. 57, 195.

PART II

Theories

4

AXEL GOODBODY

Ecocritical Theory: Romantic Roots and Impulses from Twentieth-Century European Thinkers

Ecocritical *practitioners* typically examine literary, filmic, and other cultural representations of nature, and subject to critical analysis the understandings about humankind's relationship with other species and the natural environment, which they encapsulate. But the task of ecocritical *theorists* is less self-evident. It might reasonably be regarded as to reflect on how ecocriticism is practiced, on the scope and limitations of its various manifestations, and the normative assumptions underpinning them. Much ecocritical theory consists, however, of a broader engagement with environmental philosophy – especially ethics and aesthetics, but also epistemology, the philosophy of science, and the philosophy of language. Eco-theorists are sometimes also concerned with theory and practice in the natural sciences, anthropology, social theory, and other branches of knowledge, which relate to the nature/culture and human/nonhuman relationships. Eco-theory thus goes beyond the mapping of developments and trends in cultural representations that constitutes the central focus of the work of cultural historians, to question inherited ideas of nature, consider alternatives, and evaluate both, in terms of their ability to help us meet the environmental challenges of the present and the future. On the one hand, it reflects on the harmonious and antagonistic conceptions of the human relationship with the natural world, which coexist in western thought, and how these are related to understandings of personhood, what defines the good life, and the meaning of our existence. And on the other, it is concerned with the relationship between representation and reality, the real and the imagined, and with the part played by writers, filmmakers, and artists in shaping our perception of the world and ultimately influencing social behavior.

This chapter reviews key currents in theorizing the human/nature relationship (and in theorizing the part played by literature and culture in critiquing the status quo and articulating alternatives), which have fed into critical practice since the emergence of ecocriticism as a self-conscious

61

movement in the early 1990s. It has become commonplace to say that eco-criticism was originally conceived as an act of resistance in a scholarly community dominated by the theoretical fields of cultural studies, post-structuralism, and postmodernism. Seeking to redirect attention from quasi-autonomous textual structures to the outside world, it focused on mimetic texts such as nonfiction nature writing. Accusations that early studies of literary critiques of modernity and its impact on the natural environment were overly reverential, and that even sophisticated accounts like Jonathan Bate's *Romantic Ecology* (1991) and Lawrence Buell's *The Environmental Imagination* (1995) lacked robust theoretical underpinning, then led a sec-ond wave of ecocritical scholars to reengage with theory – at the same time approaching hitherto neglected questions of environmental justice, and broadening the thematic focus of the movement to include texts on urban as well as rural environments. This is, of course, an oversimplifica-tion. As Buell himself writes, looking back in his chapter on the emergence of ecocriticism in *The Future of Environmental Criticism*, "literature-and-environment studies have striven almost from the start to define their posi-tion on the critical map analytically as well as through narrative practice," and the "first-second wave distinction" should not "be taken as implying a tidy, distinct succession."[1] Buell alludes to early work by Verena Conley that explores links between French post-structuralism and ecology, and by Dominic Head on ecocriticism and postmodernism: he might equally have cited Patrick Murphy's exploration of Mikhail Bakhtin's relevance for the ecocritic.[2]

Bakhtin is only one of a series of twentieth-century European thinkers who have been increasingly referenced. Bate, for instance, in his ecological readings of English literature in *The Song of the Earth* (2000), draws on Martin Heidegger and Michel Serres when discussing the idea of dwelling, on Gaston Bachelard in commenting on space and place, and on Theodor W. Adorno when writing on nature sensibility and aesthetics. For all the indi-vidual differences it encompasses, much modern European thinking on the environment can be regarded as a critical engagement with the Romantic conception of nature. The chapter therefore starts with an outline of the legacy of Romanticism, before going on to examine the respective contribu-tions of phenomenology (Heidegger, Merleau-Ponty), Marxism (Adorno), theories of spatiality (Deleuze, Westphal), thinking on the part played by literature in shaping our perception of the environment (Zapf, Böhme), and posthumanism (Uexküll, Agamben). European thinkers have, of course, also contributed to other ecocritical approaches such as eco-postmodernism and ecofeminism.[3] Coverage, however, of these and other less significant areas would exceed the scope of the chapter.

The Romantic Legacy

Romanticism's formative influence on thinking about nature has been enormous, and its potential legacy is by no means exhausted. Its central idea, the unity of matter and spirit, and the integration of human beings in the cosmos, can be traced through nineteenth-century monism and early twentieth-century notions of organic community down to the Australian eco-philosopher Freya Mathews's contemporary revival of panpsychism. It profoundly influenced the philosophy of deep ecology, which has under-pinned much of the modern environmental movement. In the late eighteenth century, Romanticism drew attention to the losses incurred in the Enlightenment project of the conquest of nature, and the triumph of reason over intuition and the emotions. As the natural environment in Europe became increasingly domesticated and rationally exploited, "untouched" or "wild" nature acquired connotations of the pure and sacral. It is no coincidence that "Mother Nature" was a poetic product of the age of the steam engine. Externally, Romantic writers such as Rousseau, Goethe, Schiller, Novalis, Blake, Coleridge, Shelley, and Wordsworth drew attention to the (as yet local) environmental pollution resulting from industrialization. Internally, they lamented the impoverishment of people's lives through the fragmentation of the personality arising out of the division of labor.

Their vision of a lost state of psychic balance, rooted in intimacy between man and nature, served as a spur to overcome present disharmony. Art was seen as facilitating redemption of the blighted present through its intimations and modelings of a life of individual self-realization, in utopian alignment with the natural world and human society. Generic romanticism embraces a range of continuing modes of thought that oppose modern industrial society with nature and the natural, as norms of health, vitality, and beauty. As the "other side" of modernity, this romanticism with a small "r" has, as Timothy Clark notes in his *Cambridge Introduction to Literature and the Environment*, been a powerful feature of mainstream culture, as well as being at the heart of numerous countercultural movements.[4] Romantic ideas have been adapted and reformulated throughout the nineteenth century, and in both conservative and leftist thinking in the twentieth. They can be traced in phenomenology, in currents of Marxism taking up the vision of communism as the simultaneous liberation of humanity and nature in Marx's early writings, and in philosophical holism (which seeks to overcome the separation of matter and mind, nature and culture in modernity), but perhaps most patently in deep ecology.

Norwegian philosopher Arne Naess coined the term "deep ecology" in a conference paper in 1972[5] in which he analyzed the principles underlying different currents within the nascent environmental movement. Inspired by the ecology of Rachel Carson, the nonviolence of Mahatma Gandhi, and the pantheist metaphysics of the seventeenth-century Jewish-Dutch philosopher, Baruch Spinoza, Neass's philosophy was a response on the one hand to the cornucopian conception of nature as inexhaustible, and on the other to reform environmentalism's belief that prudent management of resources can suffice to avoid environmental disaster and societal collapse. He argued that we should see ourselves not as atomistic individuals, treating the world as a resource for consumption and self-assertion, but as part of a greater living community. Human demands must therefore be weighed against the needs of other species and the integrity of place. Deep ecology thus distances itself from the anthropocentrism and individualism inherent in romantic ecology's aesthetic consumption of landscapes by solitary individuals. Its very understanding of "nature" as essentially places unaffected by human activity, however, paradoxically perpetuates a dualistic world view, in which humanity is condemned to denaturalize and destroy an exoticized natural "other."

Patrick Murphy, Dana Phillips, Timothy Morton, and Timothy Clark have therefore argued that ingrained romantic thought patterns and proximity to deep ecology have restricted the intellectual scope of ecocriticism. They do this by focusing on texts that simplistically oppose organic growth to the mechanical, unity of mind and nature to dualism, intuition and feeling to the tyranny of rationalism, and intrinsic value to instrumentalization, and which adopt strategies such as the personification and resacralization of nature. Rather than rejecting romanticism outright, it is, however, through reformulating the romantic vision of a lost way of life harmoniously in tune with the natural world so as to take cognizance of the tensions in our relationship with nature and the processes of change within ecosystems, that some of twentieth-century Europe's most important thinkers have contributed to ecocritical theorizing. They may be located in schools of thought according to which of the fundamental dualisms identified by romanticism they see as lying at the root of our environmental problems: while phenomenology emphasizes the disjunction of modern man from corporeal experience, Marxism puts the blame on class relations and estrangement from work. Whereas feminism blames gender inequalities, posthumanism sees the problem originating in belief in human uniqueness and our exaggeratedly hierarchical relationship with other species.

The thinkers discussed in the following generally show critical awareness of romantic assumptions and seek to build their critiques of modernity on other foundations. Heidegger grounds his reflections on the "problem of technology" in phenomenology and a distinction between the unique mode of being of humans and that of all other animals, plants, and things. A direct line may be traced from Adorno's natural aesthetic back to the Romantics, but his vision of the redemptive power of nature is characteristically couched in oblique and hypothetical terms. In their concern with the special role played by literature and art in environmental discourse, the writings of Bertrand Westphal, Hartmut Böhme, and Hubert Zapf echo romantic conceptions of aesthetic education, but their formulations of how this may work open up new perspectives capable of informing innovative ecocritical studies. Derrida and Agamben probably move furthest in the direction of an anti-romantic posthumanism, emphasizing the embeddedness and entanglement of the human in all that it is not.

Phenomenology

"Heideggerian ecophilosophy" is the final one of the six key philosophical positions that Greg Garrard's influential introduction to the field, *Ecocriticism*, identifies as both providing the basis for a distinct approach in environmental writing associated with specific forms and themes, and inspiring ecocritics.[6] Phenomenology is concerned with the "phenomena," which Immanuel Kant distinguished as objects interpreted by human sensibility and understanding, from "nouomena," or objects as things in themselves, which humans cannot directly experience. Premised on our *experience* of places and situations, as embodied human beings, and our *lived worlds*, it challenges the notion that pure (scientific) objectivity is possible in our consideration of them. Edmund Husserl, founder of this school of thought at the turn of the twentieth century, distinguished between *Lebenswelt* (the locus of intentional activities of human beings) and *Umwelt* (the framework within which these activities are carried out). His focus on the former had implications for how we should live and dwell in the world.

Husserl's ideas were taken further by Heidegger in a sustained critique of modernity and technology. Heidegger's starting point is the difference between mere material existence and a mode of being in which things are disclosed, or reveal their thingness. This requires human consciousness, as the space in which disclosure takes place. Human "being" is conversely only fully realized through the act of disclosing things, that is, through the "letting be" of things in the space of our consciousness. Responsible human beings have a duty to let things disclose themselves in their own way, rather than forcing them into meanings and identities that suit their own instrumental values, for instance by treating the forest as a mere "standing reservoir" of timber. Heidegger's word for this human mode of being, which he associates with "saving" the Earth, is "dwelling."[7]

Heidegger was also concerned with the articulation in texts of the experience of nature, and its reproduction in images. Poetry is for him a crucial mode of letting be. Its oblique and often archaic language, read meditatively, models for us the act of disclosure, and stands in contrast to everyday language, which "enframes" things, by treating them as resources on call for our use. Poetic language is therefore a "house of Being," which acknowledges the autonomy and resistance of things to our purposes, and teaches us how to engage with things while letting them be.[8]

Heidegger is a controversial thinker, not merely because of the eccentricity of his language and the fancifulness of his thinking in more mystical passages, but also as a result of the political tainting of his thinking on dwelling through his association with German fascism in the early 1930s. However, major ecocritical studies such as Robert Pogue Harrison's *Forests: The Shadow of Civilization* and many minor ones are indebted to Heidegger. Examining great works of literature since the Gilgamesh epic, Harrison maps out the different ways in which the dichotomies of civilized/wild, human/animal, and legal/outlaw have been conceived in medieval, Renaissance, Romantic, and modern times. He is, however, careful to avoid the philosopher's agrarian rootedness and conservative politics. Jonathan Bate, Kate Rigby, and others have similarly engaged in detailed revisions and adaptations of Heidegger's concepts and arguments. His philosophy remains particularly attractive to ecocritics because of the pivotal role he assigns to the work of art in "saving the Earth."[9]

Like Husserl and Heidegger, Maurice Merleau-Ponty, Gaston Bachelard, and contemporary thinkers in the phenomenological tradition such as Gernot Böhme[10] see the problem at the basis of environmental destruction as one of alienation from the body and our feelings. Heidegger described humans as uniquely capable of acting as "shepherds of Being," and insisted on an essential difference between the human and animal body. Especially in his late writing, Merleau-Ponty sought to overcome this residual anthropocentrism of Heidegger's. He wrote of the kinship of all living organisms through coevolution, and of humans being enmeshed in the "wild realm" of the actual world as "flesh of its flesh." While language is unique to man in Heidegger, Merleau-Ponty holds that it is born out of our bodily participation in a landscape that "speaks" to us through sensory experience, and stresses its gestural, emotionally expressive qualities. In *The Spell of the Sensuous*, David Abram has developed and popularized this idea of a protolanguage of bodily perception shared by all creatures, implying the existence of a benign life spirit through concepts such as the "animate earth," and "more-than-human natural world."[11] More broadly, Merleau-Ponty's philosophy has encouraged ecocritics such as Leonard

Scigaj to highlight the sensuous pleasure of encounters with the "flesh of the world," as opposed to the Puritan self-denial often associated with environmentalism.[12]

Marxism

The rich tradition of Marxist literary and cultural theory offers a second alternative to deep ecology's embrace of the wild and moralizing aesthetic, one working on the materialist premise that it is not consciousness that determines our actions, but social being that dictates our self-understanding. Marxism depicts humans as inextricably connected to nature, and "nature" as socially mediated and constructed. It posits human self-realization through "metabolic" interaction with the natural environment, and critiques the capitalist structures leading to inequality as responsible for environmental destruction. For our environmental problems to be solved, capitalist production for the accumulation of wealth must be replaced by meeting people's real needs.

The publication of Karl Marx's *Economic and Philosophic Manuscripts of 1844* in the late 1920s, which explored the estrangement (or alienation) of wageworkers from their own lives under the conditions of modern industrial societies (as opposed to Marx's later works, which are more concerned with his structural conception of capitalist society), led a series of theorists to develop the vision they articulate of a future in which all members of a classless society can enjoy unalienated work and indulge in experience of an environment in a "natural" state. Impulses from Walter Benjamin's critiques of the ideology of domination of nature, from Adorno's conception of nature as harboring utopian conditions, from Ernst Bloch's utopian Marxism, and from more recent Marxist theorists such as Raymond Williams and Jacques Rancière have already been drawn on by ecocritics, and have the potential to further inform their work.

In his *Aesthetic Theory*, Adorno points out that the freedom, autonomy, and dignity of the subject established in Kant's philosophy were achieved at the expense of nature, animals, and women. While rejecting the idea that is possible to "go back to" nature, he sees the work of art as performing a crucial function in reconciling humanity with it. He describes images of untouched nature or a simply harmonious relationship between nature and human culture as deeply problematic, because they serve as a "deceiving phantasm" and an alibi for further exploitation. However, he sees unique value in depictions of European "culturescape" (cultivated landscape) as a product of the humanization of nature, which reflects the traces of the damage inflicted on it, yet at the same time harbors a utopian potential. If Marxism in general is the ideological basis of the work of one of Germany's two best-known first wave ecocritics, Jost Hermand, the thinking and formulations of the Frankfurt School, and Adorno in particular, have been drawn on extensively by the other, Hartmut Böhme.[13]

The Spatial Turn and Geocriticism

Theories of the social and cultural construction of space and place play an important role in readings of environmental writing. The spatial turn has constituted one of the most significant developments in critical theory since the 1980s. Bringing to an end the domination of a discourse of time, history, and teleological development, it coincided with the displacement of the modernist aesthetic that enshrined the temporal by a postmodern, space-oriented aesthetic, which has had the effect of generating heightened awareness of the natural and urban environment, and the relationships between places.

Literary topography is based on the idea that representations of spaces complement geography by recording the experience of places and interrogating it, a process that includes exploring their cultural meanings. It finds its most developed form in Bertrand Westphal's *Geocriticism: Real and Fictional Spaces* (French original 2007). Although Westphal is not directly concerned with environmental change and crisis, geocriticism is akin to ecocriticism in a number of ways. First of all, it shifts the focus of attention away from the human subject in the examination of texts. Place is the organizing principle in a study in which Westphal has examined narratives of the city of Alexandria, by its inhabitants and travellers who visit it. Secondly, while not going so far as to decenter the human being in relation to other species, Westphal makes plurality of perspective a guiding principle. Multifocalization gives insight into the range of properties and full identity of the place, acknowledging contingency, change, and the plurality of systems of reference involved in its perception. Further, he limits the domination of the visual by foregrounding polysensory corporeality in the texts. Westphal juxtaposes historical and travel writing with images, fiction, and even myth. But literary texts occupy a privileged place in his corpus of writing because of their reversal of the normal hierarchy of the senses. The often discreet unfolding of haptic, gustatory, and olfactory landscapes in literary texts brings places nearer to us, redresses the domination present in the gaze, and helps overcome the split between self and environment.[14]

Of the many variants of spatial theory relevant to ecocriticism, one of the earliest was Henri Lefebvre's study, *The Production of Space* (French original 1974). Space is here understood not as something objective or given, but as a social product and a dynamic means of control and domination. Distinguishing it from the "perceived" space of everyday encounter, and the maps and plans of "conceived" space, Lefebvre developed a suggestive conception of "lived space" as the spatial imaginary of a particular society. Shaped by images and symbols, "lived space" acts as a bridge between "perceived" and "conceived" space, and is, as a heterogenous, socially open site of resistance to social control, the key to potential social transformation.[15] This emancipatory thrust is paralleled in Michel Foucault's concept of the "heterotopia" as a locus of alternative social order, a free sphere of intimacy resisting codification, and a counter-site where other places are represented, contested, and reversed. It is equally present in Homi Bhabha's conception of "third space" as a utopian, transgressive, liminal site inhabited by hybrid individuals and borderline cultures.[16] Inspired by such thinking, Westphal, who regards literature as an "experimental field of alternative realities," "laboratory of the possible," and "a vector of counterhegemonic speech,"[17] conceives geocriticism not least as the quest for an imagined, emancipatory other in literary texts on place.

A highly syncretic theorist, he also incorporates ideas from the postmodern theories of Deleuze and Guattari, including their distinction between "striated" and "smooth" space in *A Thousand Plateaus* (French original 1980). Striated space is divided up by walls, enclosures, and roads. A sedentary space, it is home to the state apparatus, the *polis*, politics, and the police. Opposed to it is the smooth space of the *nomos*, home to the nomad, or mobile dweller. Deleuze and Guattari began an inventory of smooth spaces (the sea, the desert, ice fields), and saw it as constantly threatened by the striating, which settled civilization imposes.[18]

"Literature can act on the real world," Westphal asserts, "conferring an ethical responsibility on those who produce it."[19] Toward the end of *Geocriticism*, where he writes of the need for a new realism, and quotes the author Michel Butor on settling in place in such a way "as to serve it,"[20] he appears to look, like many ecocritics, to literature and literary study as ways of overcoming our alienation from the natural environment and the resulting indifference to ecological damage. There are parallels between Westphal's view of literature's transgressive social function and both Hartmut Böhme's conception of it as an archive from which traces of an alternative relationship with nature may be drawn, and Hubert Zapf's theory of literature as cultural ecology.

Literature as Archive of Alternatives and Cultural Ecology

Hartmut Böhme's conception of premodern science, nature philosophy, and literary and artistic tradition as an archive or reservoir of alternative understandings of nature builds on his brother Gernot's ecological aesthetics. Gernot Böhme argues in *Für eine ökologische Naturästhetik* that natural beauty is not the projection of a mode of seeing derived from art, but rather an objective presence, which is registered by the human body as itself part of nature. Perception of nature as beautiful is an appreciation of the order of the manifold in its unity, by means of feelings and sensual reactions to the environment. Poetic language has a special ability to reconnect with nature, by evoking the same sensual responses in a sort of translation of the aesthetic-corporeal language of nature. Hartmut Böhme writes of the cultural archive as a key source of strategies of renaturalization, which is necessary to save humankind from self-extinction.

Hubert Zapf draws on ideas and arguments of the literary anthropologist Wolfgang Iser, who explained the cultural function of fiction as dramatizing our relationship with nature, confronting everyday experiences with possible alternatives, and staging attempts to understand the other and fashion the self. He describes literature and other forms of cultural imagination in analogy with ecological processes as necessary to restore continually the richness and diversity of the cultural ecosystems of modern humans, which are threatened by impoverishment.[21] The internal landscapes produced by modern culture and consciousness are as important for human beings as their external environments. Literature's power to innovate and promote cultural self-renewal derives from a threefold dynamic: it serves as an imaginative counterdiscourse, a reintegrative interdiscourse, and a cultural-critical metadiscourse. As a textual form, literature breaks up ossified social structures and ideologies, empowers the marginalized symbolically, and reconnects what is culturally separated. In these ways, and by critiquing nonliterary discourses of nature, it counteracts economic, political, and pragmatic interpretations and forces instrumentalizing human life.

Symbolically reconnecting nature and culture, mind and body, human and nonhuman life is for Zapf one of the prime forms of literary knowledge production and a vital social function of literature. Representations of animals are an important part of this reconnection of the human and the nonhuman. In our conception of the animal we simultaneously formulate a self-understanding of what it means to be human, and how humans should relate to the natural world. The last part of this chapter is therefore devoted to the reconfiguration of this conception in the second half of the twentieth century, in what has become known as "posthumanism."

Posthumanism

René Descartes's exaggerated distinction in the seventeenth century between (mechanistic) animals and (ensouled, rational) human beings, possessing language and self-reflexive consciousness, is commonly cited in critiques of humanism as a key source of the "hyperseparation" of the two, which denies the real relationship of the superior to the inferior, and simultaneously polarizes mind and body, reason and emotion. A series of twentieth-century philosophers have worked to revise this anthropocentric worldview, decentering humanity, acknowledging our human animality, and evoking reconciliation with animals. The zoologist and biophilosopher Jakob von Uexküll was a founder of ecology, and a forcrunner of biosemiotics and ethology, who influenced Heidegger, Deleuze, and the development of posthumanism with his writings on animal cognition and subjecthoods. His conception of *Umwelt* (the perceptual world of an individual creature) stripped humanity of its superiority over other animals, and provided a model for understanding how humans interact with and destroy their environments.[22] Where classical science saw a single world comprising hierarchically ordered species, Uexküll proposed an infinite variety of perceptual worlds that, despite being uncommunicating and mutually exclusive, are equally perfect. *Umwelt*, the environing world, is constituted by *Bedeutungsträger* (elements bearing significance) and *Merkmalträger* (elements with marked features). These are the only things that interest the animal.

Deleuze and Guattari have played a significant role in exploring the cultural implications of Uexküll's findings, decentering the human by coupling it to other orders of being. In *A Thousand Plateaus*, they develop the concept of "becoming animal," a letting-go of the illusory fixity of conventional human standpoints, and an opening up to otherwise unimagined modes of perception and sense.[23] Formal and linguistic experimentation presenting assemblages of coordinations and impulses can make the text a space of identification between the human and nonhuman. Deleuze writes similarly in his theory of cinema of the duty of film to make visible modes of seeing other than those of an embodied human eye, and to reflect the different experience of time and space of other species.

The philosopher Jacques Derrida made a further much-cited contribution to posthumanism in his essay "The Animal That Therefore I Am" (French original "L'Animal que donc je suis (à suivre)," 1999). Its very title counters Descartes' grounding of human existence in the mind rather than the body, and suggests that the human follows the animal rather than enjoying precedence and superiority. He challenges the notion of "animal" as a word that humans have invented to set themselves apart from the community of living creatures. The insuperable line it draws between humans and animals needs to be replaced by a proliferation of differences in a scheme of unfixed hierarchies, with radical implications for the entire nature/culture dualism.[24]

Giorgio Agamben's book, *The Open: Man and Animal* has also attracted the interest of ecocritics. It opens with the description of a startling illustration in a thirteenth-century religious manuscript depicting the righteous on the Day of Judgment – with animal heads. The artist appears to be suggesting that the relations between animals and men in paradise will take on a new form: man will be reconciled with his animal nature. Throughout the book, Agamben examines how the "human" has traditionally been distinguished from the "animal," and imaginings of a reconciliation of the two. The reasoning with which we distinguish ourselves from animals, for which he adopts the Deleuzian term "anthropological machine," presupposes what it seeks to discover. Wild men, slaves, barbarians, foreigners, and more recently the Jews, have all been regarded as animals in human form, and excluded from social life. We need to understand traditional and modern mechanisms, "so that we might, eventually, be able to stop them."[25]

In our day, Agamben argues at the end of *The Open*, the preservation of biological life has become the supreme political task, and this demands assumption of the burden of the animality of man. If, as Serenella Iovino has proposed in her contribution to a recent *ISLE* "Special Forum on Ecocriticism and Theory," it is the task of ecotheory to provide a theoretical framework for the practice of ecocriticism as a discourse of cultural change and social hope, interpreting and promoting literature's enhancement of ethical awareness and political inclusivity,[26] then the critical engagement with Romanticism by such European thinkers must surely have a part to play in it.

NOTES

1 Lawrence Buell, *The Future of Environmental Criticism: Environmental Crisis and Literary Imagination* (Malden, MA: Blackwell, 2005), 9, 17.

2 See Verena Conley, *Ecopolitics: The Environment in Poststructuralist Thought* (London: Routledge, 1997); Dominic Head, "The (Im)possibility of Ecocriticism," *Writing the Environment: Ecocriticism and Literature*, Richard Kerridge and Neil Sammells (eds.) (London: Zed Books, 1998); Patrick D. Murphy, *Literature, Nature, and Other: Ecofeminist Critiques* (Albany: State University Press of New York, 1995). Bakhtin's conception of literature's "dialogicity," that is, its openness to different standpoints and its staging of engagement between different perspectives (including nonhuman perspectives) is identified by Murphy as a model for contemporary notions of ecological aesthetics, which attribute to literature the culturally regenerative principles of openness and complexity. At the same time he found in Bakhtin's concepts of answerability to others, and "anotherness" (that is, self-constitution through being "other" to others) a form of ecological ethic.

3   On postmodernism see Phillips, "Ecocriticism, Literary Theory, and the Truth
    of Ecology," *New Literary History* 30 (1999), 577–602; Serpil Oppermann,
    "Rethinking Ecocriticism in an Ecological Postmodern Framework: Mangled
    Matter, Meaning, and Agency," *Literature, Ecology, Ethics: Recent Trends
    in Ecocriticism*, Timo Müller and Micahjel Sauter (eds.) (Heidelberg:
    Universitätsverlag, 2012), 35–50. On ecofeminism see Barbara T. Gates, "A
    Root of Ecofeminism: *Écofeminisme*," *Ecofeminist Literary Criticism: Theory,
    Interpretation, Pedagogy*, Greta Gaard and Patrick D. Murphy (eds.) (Urbana:
    University of Illinois Press, 1998), 15–22; and Christopher Cohoon, "The
    Ecological Irigaray," Axel Goodbody and Kate Rigby (eds.) *Ecocritical Theory:
    New European Approaches* (Charlottesville: University of Virginia Press, 2011),
    206–214.
4   Timothy Clark, *The Cambridge Introduction to Literature and the Environment*
    (Cambridge, UK: Cambridge University Press, 2011), 13.
5   Arne Naess, "The Shallow and the Deep, Long-Range Ecology Movement: A
    Summary," *Inquiry* 16 (1973), 95–100.
6   Greg Garrard, *Ecocriticism* (2nd ed. London: Routledge, 2012), 34–36.
7   See Martin Heidegger, "Building, Dwelling, Thinking," *Basic Writings*, David
    Farrell Krell (ed.) (San Francisco: HarperSanFrancisco, 1977), 319–339.
8   See, for example, "Letter on Humanism" and "The Question Concerning
    Technology," *Basic Writings*, David Farrell Krell (ed.) (San Francisco:
    HarperSanFrancisco, 1977), 193–213 and 283–317.
9   Robert Pogue Harrison, *Forests: The Shadow of Civilization* (Chicago: University
    of Chicago Press, 1992).
10 Maurice Merleau-Ponty, *Phenomenology of Perception* (French original 1945,
    trans. Donald A. Landes, London: Routledge, 2012); Gaston Bachelard, *The
    Poetics of Space* (French original 1958, trans. Maria Jolas, New York: Orion
    Press, 1964); and Gernot Böhme, "An Aesthetic Theory of Nature: An Interim
    Report" (trans. John Farrell), *Thesis Eleven* 32 (1992), 90–102; and *Für eine
    ökologische Naturästhetik* (Frankfurt am Main: Suhrkamp, 1989).
11 David Abram, *The Spell of the Sensuous: Perception and Language in a More-
    Than-Human World* (New York: Pantheon, 1966).
12 Leonard Scigaj, *Sustainable Poetry: Four American Ecopoets* (Lexington:
    University of Kentucky Press, 1999). See also Louise Westling, "Merleau-Ponty's
    Ecophenomenology," *Ecocritical Theory: New European Approaches*, Axel
    Goodbody and Kate Rigby (eds.) (Charlottesville: University of Virginia Press,
    2011), 126–138.
13 See Teodor W. Adorno, *Aesthetic Theory*, Gretel Adorno and Rolf Tiedemann
    (eds.) (trans. Robert Hullot-Kentor) (Minneapolis: University of Minnesota
    Press, 1997); Jost Hermand, *Grüne Utopien in Deutschland: Zur Geschichte des
    Ökologischen Bewusstseins* (Frankfurt am Main: Fischer, 1991); and Hartmut
    Böhme, *Natur und Subjekt* (Frankfurt am Main: Suhrkamp, 1988).
14 Bertrand Westphal, *Geocriticism: Real and Fictional Spaces* (trans. Robert T.
    Tally, Jr.) (New York: Palgrave Macmillan, 2011), 131–136.
15 Henri Lefebvre, *The Production of Space* (trans. Donald Nicholson-Smith)
    (Oxford: Blackwell, 1991).
16 Michel Foucault, "Of Other Spaces," French original 1967, *Diacritics* 16 (1986),
    22–27; Homi Bhabha, *The Location of Culture* (London: Routledge, 1994).

17 Westphal, *Geocriticism*, 59, 63, 116.
18 Gilles Deleuze and Felix Guattari, *A Thousand Plateaus: Capitalism and Schizophrenia* (trans. Brian Massumi) (Minneapolis: University of Minnesota Press, 1987). On the ecocritical significance of smooth space see Goodbody, "The Nomad."
19 Westphal, *Geocriticism*, 98.
20 Ibid., 163.
21 Hubert Zapf, "Literary Ecology and the Ethics of Texts," *Ecozon@* 1 (2010), 136–147.
22 See Jakob von Uexküll, *A Foray into the Worlds of Animals and Humans, with a Theory of Meaning* (trans. Joseph D. O'Neil) (Minneapolis: University of Minnesota Press, 2010).
23 Deleuze and Guattari, *A Thousand Plateaus*, 233–309.
24 Jacques Derrida, "The Animal That Therefore I Am (More to Follow)" (trans. David Wills), *Critical Inquiry* 28 (2002), 369–418.
25 Giorgio Agamben, *The Open: Man and Animal* (trans. Kevin Attell) (Stanford, CA: Stanford University Press, 2004), 38.
26 Serenella Iovino, "Ecocriticism, Ecology of Mind, and Narrative Ethics: A Theoretical Ground for Ecocriticism as Educational Practice," in "A Special Forum on Ecocriticism and Theory," *Interdisciplinary Studies in Literature and Environment* 17 (2010), 759–671.

5

TIMOTHY CLARK

Nature, Post Nature

Introduction

Even as the global environmental crisis intensifies, the inherited language with which it is often addressed has become more fragile. Urgent protesting appeals to "nature" and to "the natural" as what is being destroyed, eroded, or under threat have awkwardly coincided with a time of forceful arguments against the coherence or the implicit cultural politics of inherited concepts of "nature."

To say that something is "natural" or is "naturally" x or y is to use a word that seems to validate itself as a matter of course, "naturally." One crucial but dubious function of the concept of nature has been to lend seemingly unchallengeable foundations to very contestable political claims. Western history has been plagued by kinds of dogmatic politics in which some appeal to nature or to what is natural for a human being was central, as, for instance, in assertions about hierarchy, ethnicity, or about some same sex relationships ("it's not natural"). In the modern humanities nature has now become a term pulling in opposite directions at once: "either nature is something to be passionately defended against capitalist predations," or "'nature' can always be revealed as an ideological mask for oppressive social relations."[1] Nature is a word so laden with history and with cultural politics that it is often easy to agree with Timothy Morton that environmental debates would be addressed more rationally if the term were dropped altogether.[2]

With so slippery a term, some preliminary clarifications are unavoidable.[3] Simplifying, one can say that three basic meanings of the term circulate in English. Firstly, nature names the totality of the material universe. It embraces everything, barring the allegedly supernatural. This is the nature studied by physics. Secondly, there is nature understood as the other of culture, that which arises of itself without human agency. It may be reverenced as wilderness or pristine animality, or feared as the bestial and cruelly inhuman. Looser variants of this sense use nature to name the biosphere, or, more casually, a certain idea of the rural as opposed to the urban. Lastly, there is nature in the sense of a defining characteristic, as in "the nature of politics," "human nature," or "the nature of a problem."

Clearly, it is nature in the second sense that is the concern of environmental politics, that which is being damaged or destroyed by human activity. The defining problem becomes that of the antagonistic opposition of culture and nature. At the same time, the nature/culture distinction has been breaking down in numerous areas, physically, as in issues such as climate change, and, intellectually, in categories of thought increasingly recognized as incoherent or as having never really worked.

Nature as a Foundational Concept in Politics

In Western thinking, concepts of nature as the correlative of culture have often served a foundational role. Nature functions deceptively as the essentially political notion of a condition prior to politics. This has been especially marked in various social and artistic uses of the theory of evolution by natural selection. For instance, in Jack London's *The Call of the Wild* or Frank Norris's *The Octopus*,[4] the view that all life is essentially a competition/struggle for existence feeds into views that have little to do with biology and more to do with Herbert Spencer's "social Darwinism" or with the ruthlessly baronial American capitalism of the time (with *The Octopus* presenting the building of a railroad as something as inevitable as a force of nature).[5] In forms of racism and eugenics, certain concepts of nature and the natural have been used to underwrite the most terrible crimes.

To use nature as a founding concept is a widespread gesture in theories of the state. For a political theorist, faced with the need to justify certain conceptions of law, of property, or of right, reference to something not contrived by humanity but given and unalterable ("nature") offers what seems a secure starting point for argument. Nature thus operates as a basic reference on whose foundations everything else in human affairs may be conceived, whether this be, for Thomas Hobbes in the seventeenth century, a sense that political institutions need to exist to override and neutralize the brutal, chaotic condition of the "state of nature" or, for Jean-Jacques Rousseau in the eighteenth century, the need to criticize such institutions for distorting some lost ideal of natural humanity.[6] What is depicted as a "state of nature" in Hobbes, or, to very different implication, in Rousseau, are essentially tendentious postulates serving to underwrite a particular view of the political, not the innocent references to some pre-cultural condition they claim to be (even assuming, as one should not, that the notion of the pre-cultural actually makes much sense applied to the human species, or even to many now extinct hominids).

Much environmental politics works in exactly the same way, characterized as it is by a broadly diagnostic stance focused on concepts of nature. The destruction of the wild, the extermination of other species, the threat to future generations, are understood to be the result of political or social systems built upon questionable constructions of nature. In his *Political Nature*, John M. Meyer traces two main arguments in such environmentalist diagnostics. For many thinkers, the ultimate source of humanity's destructive relation to the natural world is *dualism* – the assumption that humans and nature are quite separate, that the human is radically divided in kind from the rest of creation. This diagnosis is found in such diverse thinkers as Val Plumwood, Arne Naess, and Max Oelschlaeger. At the same time, many other environmentalist thinkers (e.g., Carolyn Merchant, Lewis Mumford) trace environmental degradation to attitudes to nature associated with the mechanistic or "scientific" world that arose in the seventeenth century.[7] A supposed disenchantment of the natural world is seen as having been intensified by the rapacious successes of industrial technology. In both cases, however, the same political implication underlies the diagnosis – change the dominant conception of nature, make it something more genuinely "ecological" in its recognition of human finitude, of natural interconnectedness and dependence, and so forth, and then social and political conceptions and practices will all change accordingly.

Might this, however, imply too simplistic an understanding of the relation of human politics to conceptions of nature? It repeats that sleight in much political theory of using nature as a foundational element on whose basis everything else must somehow follow. Yet, "[A]n ecological conception of nature, like any conception, has the potential to inspire a number of diverse and potentially contradictory positions."[8] If it is a matter of rendering human society more ecological, is not some kind of eco-fascism as plausibly natural a condition for the human polity, as, say, anarchism, or either as plausible as forms of socialism?

To trace environmental degradation to a false worldview is also to ascribe an implausible amount of power to cultural representations, as if these and these alone had sole and decisive agency in how people live and act, produce food, use resources, and so forth. In many European countries the incoherence of this stance is now daily apparent. Thanks to increasing environmental awareness, the dominant public conception of nature is now loosely ecological, and notions of "biodiversity" and the "eco-friendly" are ubiquitous truisms. At the same time forms of environmental degradation continue to accelerate. Much modern fiction and film casts its protagonists within various landscapes of environmental collapse, not as something presented apocalyptically but as a kind of almost taken-for-granted, post-disaster world, one developing even its own neo-Gothic aesthetic.[9]

Nature and Romantic Humanism

For a long time it was a general assumption in environmental politics that to be ecological or to be deeply engaged with the natural world was some sort of act of retrieval, to be living or at least thinking in ways that predate some sort of human fall,[10] whether that be the invention of agriculture, urbanism, or the industrial revolution. A kind of messianic essentialism about the human and the natural has pervaded ecocritical writing and much environmental politics. Correspondingly, as ecocriticism emerged as a recognized school in the early 1990s, many critics often saw themselves as attacking the artificial distortions of industrial society and, on their own turf, of a literary culture dominated by "theory." Ecocritics put into a practice a romantic counterprogram of affirming certain kinds of writing as enacting modes of thought or culture that are supposedly less antagonistic to or oblivious of the natural world.

Such arguments committed themselves to the claim that some forms of language are more in tune with the natural/real than others, or at least more open to a sense of the limits of the cultural, as in Lawrence Buell's defense of environmental nonfiction as enacting the realist practice of a discipline of extrospection (Thoreau, Wendell, Berry, et al.). There have also been numerous defenses of the imaginative, the mythic, the metaphorical, and so forth, as modes of thought and language supposedly more natural than the abstract and often instrumentalist literalism of "scientific" or economic discourse.[11] The nature engaged and celebrated in such texts was usually a concept of the non-artificial, the uncontrived (with all the moral overtones of those terms), one associated with sites of minimum or only benign cultural interference, with wilderness and the wild, or the landscapes of premodern forms of agriculture.

Jonathan Bate's *Romantic Ecology* and *The Song of the Earth*[12] are exemplary of the romantic humanism of this kind of ecocriticism, celebrating engagement with the wild, either immediately or in literature, as the recuperation of some supposed natural part of a human identity seen as suppressed by the effects of abstraction, instrumentalist rationality, urban culture, and so forth. In effect, concepts of nonhuman nature in this context are often actually secondary, the projected counterpart of a romantic *humanism*.

Environmental politics more generally also often portrays itself as a kind of corrective, striving to address cultural forces that are seen as distorting a more natural or lost relation of humanity to its environment. It is increasingly coming to be recognized, however, that a concept of nature can no longer function in this kind of archaeological/teleological way. What, for instance, as the evidence suggests, if the exploitative and opportunistically destructive had always been characteristic of the species and its hominid predecessors, that there is no irenic natural human norm to be restored?[13] In retrospect, for ecocritics to ascribe such a redemptive power to writing that supposedly transmits nature as the other of culture may seem more of an escapist than a critical gesture.

This may seem unjust to the deep political commitment of so many environmental writers and ecocritics. Nevertheless, confronted with numerous television documentaries in which images of unspoiled nature now rarely appear without background music of heavenly choirs, it becomes hard not to think that green romantic humanism has now been thoroughly commodified.

The Anthropocene

Let us turn to Bill McKibben's book *Eaarth* – the title is not misspelled but indexes by a kind of snarl that the planet has now become something needing a different name. What is really at issue is the crossing of a threshold into the Anthropocene. To be standing in the remotest desert or ocean is now, in a sense, still to be breathing the enclosed air of a vast human crowd. This concern is actually very different, one might say, from the kind of wilderness-fixated sacralization of a lost nature of his earlier *The End of Nature*[14]:

> The planet on which our civilization evolved no longer exists. The stability that produced that civilization has vanished; epic changes have begun. ... We *may*, with commitment and luck, yet be able to maintain a planet that will sustain *some kind* of civilization, but it won't be the same planet, and hence it can't be the same civilization. The earth that we knew – the only earth that we ever knew – is gone.[15]

The major irony of the Anthropocene is that, although named as that era in the planet's natural history in which humanity becomes a decisive geological and climatological force, it manifests itself to us primarily through the natural becoming, as it were, dangerously out of bounds, in extreme or unprecedented weather events, ecosystems being simplified, die-back, or collapse. Natural events may now take on an opaque or debatable element of "meaning." The Anthropocene brings to an unavoidable point of stress the question of the nature of nature and of the human. In Bronsilaw Szersynski's words: "the very notion of the Anthropocene contains an element of indecision: is this the epoch of the apotheosis, or of the erasure, of the human as the master and end of nature?"[16]

If one considers the degree to which so much ecocriticism has evaded such intractable and truly global issues as climate change and overpopulation, the simplicity of the kinds of broad cultural diagnoses offered by green thinkers becomes increasingly questionable. What was once the nature/culture distinction becomes the incalculable interaction of imponderable contaminated, hybrid elements with unpredictable emergent effects. The nature/culture dichotomy seems too crude a tool to think issues such as the carbon emissions and food miles at issue in, say, a Danish pork sausage being eaten in Dublin, or a world where many such seeming trivialities become subject to the incalculable multiplier effect of growing population numbers and the uncertainty of unknown ecological tipping points.

In the Anthropocene, defense of nonhuman nature can also no longer be fully assimilated without evasion to kinds of ecocriticism modeled upon the pervasive liberal-progressive oppositional stance long dominant in the modern humanities, as in forms of social ecology and ecofeminism. The depredations of international, patriarchal capitalism must surely remain a main antagonist of environmental politics, but the emergence of humanity as a dangerous geological force also involves such factors as increased longevity, more prosperity, and the trivia of daily energy use and infrastructure design, largely innocent things that now become politicized in imponderable ways. Things have become at least as "political" as people. A new car in San Francisco or Shanghai must also be considered, however minutely, as a threat to the snow line in Nepal or Spitsbergen. Is this a "cultural" or a "natural" phenomenon? It is obviously both at once, cutting across received ways of thinking, dissonantly embracing such things as notions of lifestyle, prosperity, and individual "right" with the unknown qualities of various carbon sinks, thresholds for the melting of tundra, and so on. For Bruno Latour the importance of radical environmentalist arguments (what he calls "political ecology") lies not on their own terms, those of the protection or reaffirmation of the natural, but in the way environmental issues destabilize in practice basic distinctions between science and politics, nature and culture, fact and value.[17] "The Anthropocene," understood beyond its strictly geological reference, becomes one name perhaps for this slow but massive shift in the tectonic plates of human self-conceptions.

What emerges is a sense of the plurality, multiple agency and unpredictability, and compromised condition of the natural world. New terms emerge for the nature/culture that we inhabit, or are, such as Morton's "the mesh"[18] or Stacy Alaimo's "transcorporeality."[19] These express the fact of an incalculable connection between bodies, human and nonhuman, across and within the biosphere (food, water, nutrients but also toxins and viruses), with a sense of both holism and, increasingly, entrapment.

Nature and the Question of Literary Representation

What then of literary representation in the Anthropocene? A survey of eco-criticism to date reinforces the need to give up arguments that some forms of writing are more natural than others. Even some conceptions of eco-poetry, modeling notions of poetic form on an understanding of the multiple linkages that make up a healthy ecosystem, have to acknowledge their essential mode of being as that of a human artifact, symbolic only of a particular *idea* of an ecosystem.[20]

The twenty-first century has seen numerous works of travel literature depicting degrading landscapes (such as Sara Wheeler's *The Magnetic North: Notes from the Arctic Circle*),[21] but the main artistic implication of trying to represent the Anthropocene must be a deep suspicion of any traditionally realist aesthetic. With its bizarre kinds of action-at-a-distance, its imponderable scale, the collapse of distinctions between the trivial and the disastrous, nature and culture, and the proliferation of forces that cannot be directly perceived, the Anthropocene becomes deeply counterintuitive. It may find its analogue in modes of the fantastic, new forms of magic realism or science fiction, or texts in which distinctions between "character" and "environment" become fragile or break down, or in which the thoughts and desires of an individual are not intelligible in themselves but only as the epiphenomenal sign of entrapment in some larger and not necessarily benign dynamic. Thus some forms of gothic, myth, or science fiction may well seem more interesting than a new novel displaying the latest subtleties of nuance in psychological or social observation, confining itself, that is, to the anthropocentric and arguably illusory world of conventional realism.

Do you understand or represent nature better by changing your scale? For instance, John Keats's "To Autumn"[22] may convey in three middle-sized stanzas the two-month unfolding of a southern English autumn, but even such an artificially speeded time frame would be inadequate to represent the time and space dimensions of global climate change. This is easier to envisage being done by the use of quasi mythic, or perhaps allegorical figures, such as appear in Gary Snyder's *Mountains and Rivers without End*,[23] which tries to encompass a view of human life from the Pleistocene until the late twentieth century. Donna Haraway's use of the old indigenous figure of "Coyote" the trickster as a preferred term for non-human nature represents a similar solution.[24] There is also the advantage here that her knowingly mythic term serves to highlight the provisional, finite mode of our knowledge of these forces and scales.

The philosopher David Wood writes of one facet of the current global situation as the *loss of externality*. One of the traditional functions of the concept of nature has been to name a space of supposed externality, not just as the other of culture, but more literally its outside:

> Now there is no outside, no space for expansion, no more *terra nullius*, no *Lebensraum* no slack, no "out" or "away" as when we throw something "out" or "away." ... Yet so much of our making sense, let alone the intelligibility of our actions, still rests on being able to export, exclude, externalize what we do not want to consider. When that externality is no longer available, we are in trouble.[25]

Several such externalities have been the sea, the atmosphere, people outside the "developed countries," and, above all, the future. The end of "externality" means that the consequences of human action do not go away anymore. To live in a space in which illusions of externality have dissolved is to see the slow erosion of the distinction between the distant waste dump and the housing estate, between the air and a sewer, between the open road and a car park, and between the self-satisfied affluence of a Sydney suburb and a drowning village in Bangladesh.

Let us turn here to Will Self's first short story collection, *The Quantity Theory of Insanity*.[26] The seemingly fantastic elements of Self's texts read as magnifications of that logic of both entrapment and yet disavowed externality that largely defines the so-called developed world. Take, for instance, "The North London Book of the Dead."[27] Here the narrator describes the painful scenes of his mother's death from cancer, his subsequent denial, grief, and a period of gradual acceptance until, one day, he simply meets his mother again, walking toward him down a street in a very ordinary suburb of London. What, then, is death? Death, it turns out, is a meaningless recycling scheme:

> I wrung it out of her eventually. It went something like this: when you die you move to another part of London where you resume pretty much the same kind of life you had before you died. There are lots of dead people in London and quite a few dead businesses. When you've been dead for a few years you're encouraged to move to the provinces.[28]

This particular afterlife resolves none of the big questions: it merely collapses nature and culture upon each other as part of the same depthless and insignificant conveyor belt or moving walkway, in a crowded world that no one ever leaves. Self's title story "The Quantity Theory of Insanity"[29] repeats the basic trope of a closed realm operating according to its own, often bizarre, laws. In this case the "quantity theory" of the title states that in any social grouping there is only so much sanity to go around. Thus, if x number of people in a distinct group are mentally sound then there must be a y number in that group who are mentally sick (or vice versa). This "sanity quotient" will find expression in differing ratios of normal and deviant pathologies existing – or deliberately created – in each respective group. The satirical implications of this hyperreal world soon become clear, and another sense of the Anthropocene becomes readable, the implications, that is, of living in a world without "externality": "If you decrease the number of social class 2 anorexics you necessarily increase the numbers of valium abusers in social class 4," or "[Australians] lived in a society where constant rates of sanity had been achieved by the creation of a racial underclass which was killing itself with alcoholism."[30]

Lorrie Moore's story "Like Life"[31] has more familiar elements of dystopian satire. ("That year was the first in which it became illegal – for those who lived in apartments or houses – not to have a television.")[32] Set in a contemporary or near future New York, it dramatizes intentions and the malaise of the central character Mamie, a would-be writer of history books for children. With something described as precancer in her throat, she is regularly dropping off a jar with a sample of saliva to a clinic. A sense of the permeability of the body is directly linked to a suspicion of one's most spontaneous thoughts or words as not one's own (whatever "one's own" might now mean):

> Mamie lost sleep. She began to distrust things, even her own words; too much had moved in. Objects implanted in your body – fillings, earrings, contraceptives – like satellite dishes, could be picking up messages, substituting their words for yours, feeding you lines. You never knew. Open your mouth, it might betray you with lies, with lackadaise, with moods and speak not your own. The things you were saying might be old radio programmes bounced off the foil of your molars, or taxi calls fielded by the mussely glove of your ear. What you described as real might be only a picture, something from *Life* magazine you were forced to live out, after the photography, in imitation.[33]

The implications of illness with chronic psychic effects may be that it no longer makes adequate sense to judge a character by inherited moral categories or any kind of familiar ethics. For instance, the story culminates in a scene in which Mamie comes across a crowd watching a cornered mass murderer preparing to commit suicide by jumping from a bridge. For some reason she mistakes him for her husband Rudy, and climbs up in a failed effort to save him. The disturbing thing is the peculiar assumption that mass murderer of women was one role her husband could easily inhabit. Furthermore, the text of the children's storybook Mamie is composing is a fictional narrative by a Native American at the time of the northern continent's first colonization by Europeans, who wonders why so many of his own people are dying of disease, while the English are not. Just as Self's characters are less individuals than the epiphenomenal psychic manifestations of obscure nature/cultural forms of action-at-a-distance, so Moore's cancer-ridden New York finds an ironic analogue in the monstrous biological accident at the basis of modern North America (differing disease resistance to European pathogens).

Nature becomes the biological/ecological machine in which we are constituted and the Enlightenment goal of a rational overview of the human condition may come to seem unachievable, even arrogant: "We are all strangers to ourselves, ... occupying worlds in which our own roles are beyond the reach of even the most advanced Enlightenment modes of inquiry."[34] In the past, nature may have seemed to offer a stable frame to give basic structure to human life, as with the immediate cultural overtones of the seasons in the temperate zone (love as spring-like; winter as a time of unhappiness, source of images of cruelty; summer as passion, luxury, and excess; autumn as fruition and decline). A sense of entrapment, unpredictability, and fragility becomes dominant now.

The Evasion of "Human Nature"

In fact, it is extremely easy to think of scenarios that avoid the disasters of the Anthropocene. One can suggest: an organized equitable redistribution of wealth, the full representation of future generations and nonhumans in all significant political and economic decisions, the delegitimation of the drive to immediate profit as the overriding motor in human society. These are not hard to suggest – the obstacle, for want of a better phrase, is not nature, or even conceptions of nature, but human nature. Too often treated as a separate issue, it is arguably various notions or norms of human nature that have utterly determined conceptions of nature.

For years even to assert that human beings, like other species, have a specific nature of some kind was to be seen as already halfway toward an endorsement of racist and other forms of biological determinism. In 1975 the leading naturalist Edward O. Wilson suddenly found himself at the center of such a controversy. His book *Sociobiology: The New Synthesis*[35] followed established Darwinian principles in the enlightenment tradition to study the biological bases of all social behavior in animals. Innocently and logically, Wilson included a last chapter on how biology must ultimately underpin human social behavior. Presenting a paper at a conference, he suddenly found himself being yelled at by self-righteous protesters and having a pitcher of water tipped over his head ("Racist Wilson you can't hide, we charge you with genocide").[36]

The Anthropocene, however, makes further evasion of the question of human nature irresponsible. Alf Hornborg argues:

> The natural scientists need to understand the specificity of the human species. Why do humans, of all species, pose such a threat to biodiversity? Biologists are not equipped to understand the driving forces of environmental degradation e.g. in culture, politics, and economy. Conversely, social scientists trained to think in terms of "social constructions of nature" are ill equipped to visualize a biophysical environment objectively endangered by human activity.[37]

Is the Anthropocene to be no more than a time in which humanity en masse must confront its own inadequacy, even its self-destructive pettiness? Currently, this seems all too plausible. Take given and emerging scenarios for the regulation of greenhouse gases, for example. No sooner might the competing interest of national groups be accounted for by being embedded in some sort of carbon market or system of carbon credits, than individuals in the group will seek to evade the restrictions on their own activities. Conversely, groups compete to shift the costs to others, making claims for the supposed carbon-absorbing powers of their national forests or population policy. Some may even deliberately synthesize stores of a potent greenhouse gas in order to secure the credits for not releasing it. Bolivian activist Rosa Maria Ruiz observes despondently, in relation to those romanticized icons, the indigenous Indians of the rainforest, "people who used to hop down trees and hunt in the forest only for their own needs now use machines and guns and sell the forests resources as far away as China."[38] It would be dishonest to deny just how unsurprising this all is as a picture of human behavior.

The point here is not to be cynical, but to underline a lacuna in ecocriticism. Studies that seem sharply analytical of inherited concepts of nature become far less secure as soon as one tries to pin down what conception of the nature of a human being is at issue in their proposed remedies. Even someone as astute as Tim Morton can seem unrealistic here, advocating what may seem too implausible a shift in human cultures: to "truly love nature," he urges, "would be to love what is non-identical to us," to love the monstrous, the automaton, as such, without romantic illusion.[39] The evasion of the question of human nature makes many ecocritical exhortations to some vast revolution in cultural attitudes seem on a par with fantasies that pigs might fly. In effect, ecocritical arguments, whether romantic humanist, eco-justice oriented, or post-nature like Morton's, still circle repetitively around competing and in some ways anachronistic political/ethical *norms* of human nature, and less around any increasing engagement with *understandings* of it.

The Anthropocene represents, for the first time, the demand made upon a species consciously to consider its impact, as a whole and as a natural/physical force, upon the whole planet – the advent of a kind of new, totalizing reflexivity as a species. Individual acts of generosity, cultural change, national achievement, and so on, now become something that must be conceived at this higher, unprecedented level of self-reflection.

Above all, considered at this planetary scale, the Anthropocene undermines the nature/culture distinction itself, the difference between natural history and human history. A term often heard in philosophical and scientific accounts of human agency is "folk psychology."[40] It is usually mentioned in contradistinction to the challenge of the scientific worldview that all human psychology and behavior ultimately be explained naturalistically, as instantiations of physical laws, the workings of the evolved brain, and so forth. "Folk psychology" names the "manifest image,"[41] which we have of ourselves as people, of what being a person means – that common sense philosophy of mind according to which human beings are relatively free agents, and that what they do can be explained by reference to such posited entities as inner thoughts, decisions, desires, projects, and intentions, each held to be directing meaningful sequences of action and goal-oriented behavior. This common sense internal human self-image and model of mind has emerged over the millennia as seeming to provide a reliable framework in which to conceive of ourselves and our interactions. It has always worked.

What, however, if one implication of the Anthropocene were that our immediate sense of what being a person is, its scale of reference, its intentional contours, must now also emerge as having become itself an "environmental problem"? While evolutionary explanations of human behavior are often held in suspicion it still seems fairly safe to assume that the environment in which the manifest image of personhood emerged was not one on the scale of a whole planet. One unusually cold winter in Britain and newspaper headlines there start mocking the very idea of global warming. There is a blatant mismatch between the scale of our most basic self-conceptions, the horizons of our personhood, the arena of our meaningful engagements, and the centuries-wide planetary context in which they must now operate. Environmental history also suggests that the agency of the human is far more circumscribed and saturated with illusion than one might suppose. Human beings, regarded on global scale, may now even appear as zombies bent on the destruction of their own conditions of existence. What seems reasonable, commonsensical, rational self-interest and purposiveness on the scale of an individual life may present the picture, en masse, of humanity as an unprecedented primate superorganism, which acts out ultimately destructive laws of ecology and population dynamics that both result from and in many ways override the myriad seemingly free decisions of people's day-to-day affairs of life within the individual horizon of the "manifest image." In sum, the distinction between nature as the correlative of culture and nature in the more fundamental sense of physical systems and their laws, object of natural science, comes to breakdown in the Anthropocene. Ecocritics continue to press, harder and harder, the worn button named cultural change (whether it be for some more intimate understanding of one's local bioregion, or for a planetary cosmopolitanism), to almost no effect. More productive of real change may be the frightening, visible, year by year erosion of any comfortable nature/culture distinction. In response, human beings will, as they always have, continue to act on a stage dominated by unpredictable nonhuman agency, but this time increasingly divested of illusions of sovereignty.

NOTES

1　Andrew Biro, *Denaturalizing Ecological Politics: Alienation from Nature from Rousseau to the Frankfurt School and Beyond* (Toronto: University of Toronto Press, 2005), p. 8.

2　Timothy Morton, *Ecology without Nature: Rethinking Environmental Aesthetics* (Cambridge, MA: Harvard University Press, 2007).

3　For useful overviews see Kate Soper, *What is Nature?* (Oxford: Blackwell, 1995); Raymond Williams, "Ideas of Nature," in Williams, *Problems in Materialism and Culture: Selected Essays* (London: Verso, 1980), pp. 67–85, 75.

4　Earle Labor and Robert C. Leitz III (eds.), *The Call of the Wild, White Fang, and Other Stories* (Oxford World's Classics) (Oxford: Oxford University Press, 1998); Kevin Starr (ed.), *The Octopus: The Epic of Wheat v. 1: A Story of California* (Penguin Twentieth Century Classics) (London: Penguin, 1998).

5　See Michael Ruse, *Defining Darwin: Essays on the History and Philosophy of Evolutionary Biology* (New York: Prometheus Books, 2009), pp. 153–170.

6　For Hobbes and Rousseau in this respect see John M. Meyer, *Political Nature: Environmentalism and the Interpretation of Western Thought* (Boston: MIT, 2001).

7　Meyer, *Political Nature.*

8　Meyer, *Political Nature*, p. 22.

9　See Frederick Buell, *From Apocalypse to Way of Life: Environmental Crisis in the American Century* (New York: Routledge, 2004).

10　See Dana Phillips, *The Truth of Ecology: Nature, Ecology, and Literature in America* (Oxford: Oxford University Press, 2003), p. 183.

11　For an overview of such arguments see my *The Cambridge Introduction to Literature and the Environment* (Cambridge: Cambridge University Press, 2011), pp. 19–21, 47–48.

12　Jonathan Bate, *Romantic Ecology: Wordsworth and the Environmental Tradition* (London: Routledge, 1991); *The Song of the Earth* (London: Picador, 2000).

13 For prehuman species, see Chris Stringer, *Origin of Our Species* (London: Penguin, 2011).

14 Bill McKibben, *The End of Nature: Humanity, Climate Change and the Natural World*, revised edition (London: Bloomsbury, 2003).

15 Bill McKibben, *Eaarth: Making a Life on a Tough New Planet* (New York: St. Martin's Griffin, 2010), p. 27.

16 Bronsilaw Szersynski, "Reading and Writing the Weather: Climate Technics and the Moment of Responsibility," *Theory, Culture & Society* 27 (2010), pp. 9–30, 16.

17 Bruno Latour, *Politics of Nature: How to Bring the Sciences into Democracy*, translated by Catherine Porter (Cambridge, MA: Harvard University Press, 2004), p. 4.

18 Timothy Morton, *The Ecological Thought* (Cambridge, MA: Harvard University Press, 2010), p. 28ff.

19 Stacy Alaimo, *Bodily Natures: Science, Environment and the Material Self* (Bloomington: Indiana University Press, 2010), pp. 2–4.

20 For "eco-poetry" see Clark, *The Cambridge Introduction to Literature and the Environment*, pp. 139–140.

21 Sara Wheeler, *The Magnetic North: Notes from the Arctic Circle* (London: Jonathan Cape, 2009).

22 Jack Stillinger (ed.), *The Poems of John Keats* (London: Heinemann, 1978), p. 249.

23 Gary Snyder, *Mountains and Rivers without End* (New York: Counterpoint, 1996).

24 See Donna Haraway's "Cyborgs, Coyotes, and Dogs: A Kinship of Feminist Figurations" in Haraway, *The Haraway Reader* (London: Routledge, 2004), pp. 321–332.

25 David Wood, *The Step Back: Ethics and Politics after Deconstruction* (Albany, NY: SUNY Press, 2005), pp. 172–173

26 Will Self, *The Quantity Theory of Insanity* (1991; London: Penguin Books, 1994).

27 Self, *The Quantity Theory of Insanity*, pp. 1–15.

28 Self, *The Quantity Theory of Insanity*, p. 11.

29 Self, *The Quantity Theory of Insanity*, pp. 95–150.

30 Self, *The Quantity Theory of Insanity*, p. 127; p. 141.

31 Lorrie Moore, *The Collected Stories* (London: Faber and Faber, 2008), pp. 453–478.

32 Moore, *The Collected Stories*, p. 454.

33 Moore, *The Collected Stories*.

34 Braden R. Allenby and Daniel Sarewitz, *The Techno-Human Condition* (Cambridge, MA: MIT, 2011), p. 189.

35 Edward O. Wilson, *Sociobiology: The New Synthesis* (Cambridge, MA: Harvard University Press, 1975).

36 See Ullica Segerstråle, *Defenders of the Truth: The Sociobiology Debate* (Oxford: Oxford University Press, 2000), p. 23.

37 Quoted in Adam Robbert, "Six Problems in Thinking Nature-Culture Interactions," http://knowledge-ecology.com/six-problems-in-nature-culture-interactions/

38 Rosa Maria Ruiz, "Trials of the Amazon Activist," *New Scientist* 22, 1 (2011), pp. 28–29.

39 Morton, *Ecology without Nature*, p. 185.

40 See, for instance, Daniel Dennett, *Consciousness Explained* (London: Penguin, 1991), pp. 313–319.

41 See Sellars, "Philosophy and the Scientific Image of Man," in Robert Colodny (ed.), *Frontiers of Science and Philosophy* (Pittsburgh: University of Pittsburgh Press, 1962), pp. 35–78.

6

Violent Affinities: Sex, Gender, and Species in *Cereus Blooms at Night*

Violence

Shani Mootoo's novel *Cereus Blooms at Night* is an exquisitely painful rendering of gender, colonial, species, and especially sexual violences.[1] It is also a strangely beautiful work that includes moments of breathtaking attention to the riches of interhuman and multispecies encounters. The novel is sensual, immediate, and plays at the boundary between the real and the surreal: both violences and *jouissances* are intensified as time is slowed down and rearranged; as minuscule encounters are made large; as dissociative fantasies become parts of the common world; and as humans, invertebrates, and plants respond to another's needs and desires in complex interminglings of possibilities. As a result, the book is sometimes difficult to read, and certainly difficult to write about; Mootoo has produced such an extraordinary universe of pain and pleasure, of repulsion and cherishing, that extends far beyond anthropogenic interactions, that it is hard to know how to unravel, for the sake of an ecocritical essay, the communicative, affective, and biotic webs that are the novel's scaffolding. But I attempt to do so, here, in order to address a question that is, I think, particularly important at the current conjuncture of feminist, queer, materialist, and ecocritical thought: how to address the relations between the violences of the present socio-ecological moment (colonial, gendered, sexual, interspecies) and the promises of renewed ontological connection offered in the multispecies, multiagential universe of some recent feminist materialist writings?

Mootoo writes with particular attention to violence. Set on the fictional island of Lantanacamara in the town of Paradise, the novel centrally concerns the life of Mala, to whom we are introduced as she enters the lifeworld of Tyler, a genderqueer nurse at the Paradise Alms House.[2] Mala, long since the local "crazy lady," has been accused of killing her father, but as there is no direct evidence of any crime (the site of the supposed murder has been destroyed), she is, instead of being sent to prison, consigned to the care of a geriatric residence in which Tyler is a new and nervous employee (he is the first man to be educated as a nurse in the Shivering Northern Wetlands and to return to Lantanacamara; he is also exploring what it might mean to be queer at home). Mala does not speak; Tyler instead listens to her in the ways she chooses to communicate. He notices that she mimics the calls of birds and insects with exceptional fluency; he begins to understand that she is speaking with other species in ways that he cannot interpret. And so he continues to listen, to develop Mala's trust, and to begin to understand the words with which she begins to pepper the conversation, especially "where Asha (her sister)?"[3]

Through Tyler's investigations and pieced-together knowledges, we begin to understand Mala's story. She is the child of Chandin Ramchandin, who was chosen by the local missionary to be the (brown) poster boy for Christian proselytizing on the island; as his desires confront the limits of colonial and racial possibility, his love-interest (the missionary's daughter, Lavinia) is revealed to actually love his wife, Sarah. Lavinia and Sarah escape, but they leave behind Mala (Pohpoh, her childhood name) and Asha in a scene of intense conflict. Chandin, already fallen from missionary grace, is broken by this loss, and he descends into the worst possible self-pity; he drinks heavily, brutally controls his daughters' behavior, and begins to "mistake Mala for his wife," as the local gossip puts it. Mala substitutes her body for Asha's in an attempt to protect her younger sister from the traumas of his drunken sexual molestations; Asha eventually runs away. And his traumas inflect Mala's; she cares for him and suffers his ongoing sexual, emotional, and physical abuses because she excuses his violence in light of his distress, and because she really doesn't have anyone (the residents of Paradise have expelled her from consideration, as if the abuse were her stain) in whom to confide.

Throughout her life, Mala/Pohpoh has cared for nonhuman animals and plants: they are her confidantes, creatures to whom she relates viscerally. In childhood, with her one friend Boyie (Ambrose), she rescues garden snails from the schoolyard so that they will not get squashed and destroyed in the midst of bullies' games (she and Asha are also squashed and destroyed in these games); Lavinia once told her that protecting a living snail would cause it to remember and protect her when it dies, and that if she "displays [naturally-emptied shells] so they can be spotted by the floating souls of the snails that once occupied them … everyone whom you love will be ensured the fullest protection of the benevolent forces of the universe."[4] Pohpoh knows the story to be a harmless fantasy; it is, however, because she runs back into the house to retrieve a bag of shells (and a clipping from a cereus plant, to which I will return) that Pohpoh is caught by her father as the women and girls are attempting to escape. And yet, years later, when Mala has barricaded herself in her garden and withdrawn from all human company (and human speech), she plants snail shells in neat rows in her lush but reeking garden as part of her ritual attentions to other species' lives and deaths. The snails may have failed to protect her in the manner promised by a fairy story (a lie akin to the one Lavinia told when she assured Sarah that they would never leave the children behind), but their contributions to Mala's rituals, to the complex ecology of her garden, and especially to the miasma of decomposition that keeps most human visitors away, are certainly part of a network of protection in which Mala becomes involved once it is clear that that no human being is going to step up to defend her: including Ambrose.

Because we learn the story in pieces woven back into Tyler and Mala's blooming friendship – which comes to include the affections of an older Ambrose and his daughter-turned-son, Otoh – it is not until much later in the novel that we come to understand the full extent of Mala's experiences of violence. Ambrose, then a young man, returns to Paradise after being educated as an entomologist in the Shivering Northern Wetlands (it was Pohpoh who inspired his interest in insects). Ambrose and Mala, then a young woman, begin courting behind Chandin's back; Ambrose does not know about the abuse, and Mala worries about how and when to tell him. He includes her in his plan to develop a spider silk business; she takes risks to cook for and spend time with him; he brings her a gramophone, and they dance; they fall in love, a new and more intense kindling of their childhood friendship, and Mala begins to consider the possibility of a life away from Chandin.

The day that Ambrose and Mala first have (adult) sex, perhaps unsurprisingly, inaugurates the most intensely violent passage in the novel. At the moment Mala breathes in Ambrose's scent and he touches his lips to her hair, Chandin feels a tightness in his chest as he sits drinking in a rum shop. As Mala and Ambrose make love, "his first time, and her first time with someone of her own choice,"[5] Chandin experiences intense pain "like a thick metal chain being yanked around his torso"[6] and he decides to go home. He reaches the gate just as Ambrose is leaving the house. Chandin, unseen, watches him go; he enters the kitchen where Mala, terrified, pretends that nothing is out of the ordinary. He smells Ambrose on her hands; he dissolves into rage, smashing the furniture, tearing up her clothes, destroying the gramophone, beating her viciously, and raping her multiple times over the course of the night.[7] The next morning, Chandin quietly eats and leaves (he stations himself out of sight to witness Ambrose's arrival); Mala latches the back door, hoping that Ambrose will go away so that he doesn't see her pain and bruising (she blames herself for "cheating on her father"). Ambrose arrives and enters by the front door, sees the destroyed house, imagines (in a last moment of denial) that they have been robbed, finally finds Mala visibly battered and sobbing, and the light goes on: "your father?"[8] Chandin enters – "So what are you going to do about it?"[9] – and threatens Ambrose and Mala with the cleaver; Mala's fury takes over, she lunges at Chandin, struggles with him over the cleaver, bites his wrist, and draws blood. As he writhes on the floor, Ambrose flees the room, in so doing bashing Chandin in the head with the heavy door. And, at this moment, Ambrose commits his own, unforgivable violence against Mala: he feels a shame "as though he had been *betrayed by Mala*,"[10] he distances himself from her and, despite her cries and distress, he runs out of the house. Mala is absolutely alone; again, she remembers her father's response to her mother's flight. She waits for Ambrose, who does not return, and for everyone else who has left her: Sarah, Lavinia, Boyie, Asha. She returns to her unconscious father in the bedroom; she smashes his head with the door several more times, then drags him through the house and pushes him down the stairs, locking him (alive) into the dark sewing room at the bottom.

Other than the sheer brutality of this story, part of its horror is that there is a bond of *empathy* between Chandin and Mala: abuse forms, here, a truly repulsive connective tissue as he feels her desire for Ambrose and as she feels her loss of Ambrose from the same place as Chandin felt his loss of Sarah and Lavinia.[11] Indeed, empathy and affinity are a constant texture of the novel as a whole, but as this passage reminds us most forcefully, *all* of these relations are the products of different forms of violence: Tyler is able to understand Mala because he understands gender and sexual ridicule himself; Mr. Hector (the Alms House gardener) is able to accept Tyler (and Otoh, with whom Tyler eventually becomes romantically involved) because his own brother was also genderqueer and abused by their father; Mala is able to communicate with the more-than-human beings with whom she shares her garden, both before and especially after other humans have been expelled from it, because they are all threatened together. As she gives up human speech beginning in the moment of Ambrose's betrayal, she develops the ability to talk to "the garden's birds, insects, snails and reptiles."[12] And it is in this language that Tyler first hears her speak.

These relationships are part of the complex web of violent affinities that meshes the novel together. Affections cannot be separated from the brutalities that gave rise to them, and sensual enjoyments become abusive opportunities in an instant; people and others shape-shift and reveal themselves to be things other than the ones we thought they were, and extraordinary beauty arises in scenes of repulsive decay, passages attenuated by the novel's exaggerations of ordinary reality and possibility. One final example, then, of the ways these becomings are arrayed: as the police enter into the sewing room years after Chandin's disappearance, they encounter, in the midst of a nauseating stench, his decomposing body. One officer attempts to lift the sheet that covers it, and as he does so the sheet begins to move: "It hovered, then broke apart in a flurry of activity. Thousands of tiny white moths had so tightly packed themselves side by side that the tiny hooks on the edges of their wings had locked together, linking them to form a heavy sheet that was slowly devouring the corpse underneath."[13] The inanimate becomes animate; that which shelters devours; the intricate beauty of the shimmering moths is enabled by Chandin's loathsome death, and in turn by the chain of horrors that preceded it.

Affinity

There are many ways *Cereus Blooms at Night* can be brought into conversation with other ecological feminist texts. One could, with Elizabeth Grosz, consider its depiction of the enabling and disciplining complexities of power: both of a multiplicity of relations of force at work to create a specific local topology of intersecting oppressions (racialized, gendered, colonial, sexual, interspecies), and also of the ways in which power works by demanding and producing these cohesions of identity in the first place (i.e., the require-ment to enact identity itself is part of the way in which power operates). As Grosz writes, a utopian feminist project could concern itself with *difference* instead of identity; rather than focus on creating the conditions in which certain named modes of identity (e.g., woman, trans person, person of color, peekoplat, mudra tree, snail) can potentially appear outside of power or within justice, we could "understand difference as the generative focus of the world, the force that enacts materiality (and not just its representation), the movement of difference that marks the very energies of existence before and beyond any lived or imputed identity."[14] By imagining ourselves beyond our identities – indeed, as *sharing an experience of difference*, as the novel has us do – we may come to "understand that this multiplicity configures in unique ways for each individual yet enables shared patterns to be discerned for those who share certain social positions [without confusing] these acts for a latent order or, worse, for a coercive system."[15]

One could also consider, with Karen Barad, the ways in which the novel powerfully depicts the relationality of ontology, how both identities and materialities are more a matter of becoming than they are of being, and in which *relationships* are key to any understanding of both human and more-than-human constitution. The moths are but one example: as Barad writes, "all bodies, not merely 'human' bodies, come to matter through the world's iterative intra-activity – its performativity."[16] That the moths are mistaken for the blanket underscores the fact that they have *become* the blanket, and that they are also *becoming* the corpse (and the corpse the moths) as they devour it. At different points, Otoh (short for *otoh botoh*, meaning "on the one hand/on the other") becomes a man, and then becomes his father, in ways that are matters of fact/facts of matter for the people (Ambrose, Tyler, Mala) with whom he interacts. Chandin "mistakes Mala for his wife" (not all indeterminate becomings are life-affirming) and Mala also becomes Asha for him; Mala becomes the birds and crickets whose sounds she emulates, as she is also transformed by practicing forms of ritual attention to the snails and insects in her fetid garden, in which creatures of all kinds are constantly in the process of both becoming alive and becoming dead. Certainly, Mootoo points in the direction of a posthumanist performativity, in which different manners of materialization are revealed to be inseparable; as Barad notes, performativities are "not [only] human-based activities, but rather, specific material (re)configurings of the world through which the local determinations of boundaries, properties, and meanings are differently enacted. And matter is not a fixed essence; rather, matter is a substance in its intra-active becoming – not a thing but a doing, a congealing of agency."[17]

Of course, both of these points are important for ecological feminism, and for *Cereus Blooms at Night*: power relations work by intervening into, constraining, and appropriating – sometimes violently – multispecies and multiagential possibilities for difference and becoming. But as Mootoo emphasizes: things also happen specifically *from and in violence*. As Donna Haraway writes, famously, in "The Cyborg Manifesto," it is *because* of the deadly circuits of power inherent in industrial capitalism (and here, also colonialism) that corporeal capacities and individual/social desires are thrust together in specific ways that also reveal and proliferate affinities because they tear apart other arrangements of relating, which were neither better nor somehow more organic, and because newer configurations are also not better or more empowering of diversity.[18] Although Haraway is writing against the naturalizing and essentialist trends of some 1980s (eco)feminisms that countered power with a sort of organicist holism – and although I do not mean to suggest in any way that Grosz and Barad are inattentive to the generative effects of "the informatics of domination" (we are all writing after Haraway in this regard) – the fact remains that ecological feminisms must respond especially to the ways in which posthuman/multispecies identities, differences, relational performativities, and intercorporealities are enmeshed in both macro- and micro-political *violences*. Grosz formulates this dynamic clearly: "the acts that constitute oppressions also form the conditions under which other kinds of inventions, other kinds of acts, become possible."[19] But Mootoo insists more viscerally: violences haunt both our implications in, and our appreciations of, a multispecies universe, and affinities are sometimes painful, sometimes destructive, and sometimes even deadly because they are configured through and in the midst of proliferating brutalities. For feminists, there can be no innocent affinities, and recognition of biotic en-meshedness is inadequate without an understanding of both ontological and *political* connection.

Nancy Tuana writes that poverty is a "material-semiotic interaction" that "leaves its effects in the bodies and psyches of those it touches."[20] Through systemic inequalities in relations to nutrition, access to health care, proximity to environmental hazards, and capacities for resilience in the face of nature/cultural disasters such as Hurricane Katrina, poor people's bodies, livings, and desires are placed in different relations to specific multiagential assemblages (industrial food production, corporate health care, disaster planning, and response) than are those of the wealthy. Andrew Solomon documents that depression is a sociocultural/neurochemical assemblage that disproportionately affects women, poor people, and, in North America, aboriginal people on reserves, who are most likely to experience isolation, loneliness, and traumatic violence. Experiences of trauma are among the major causes of depression and, cruelly, depression writes itself iteratively on the body: although a precise understanding of the relations between neurotransmitters and clinical depression remains elusive, the working psychopharmacological consensus is that stress interferes with the body's ability to produce neurotransmitters, and that the human brain remembers this response and tends to follow it again in the face of subsequent stresses.[21] Dayna Scott argues that some aboriginal communities in North America are routinely subject to the effects of endocrine-disrupting chemicals that seem to produce a disproportionate number of girl in relation to boy babies, even as we might locate the harm of this imbalance in relation to experiences of community suffering rather than according to a predefined and normative notion of population gender dimorphism. In this case, cross-gender becomings are not primarily a question of transgressive resistance, even as it is both ontologically and politically important to imagine responses to these chemical violences in ways that do not accede to homophobic panics about so-called natural gender and sexual comportments in humans and other species.[22]

As Haraway reminds us, an ecological feminism responsive to such multiple trajectories of intercorporeal violence must recognize the ways in which our affinities are anything but innocent: to act responsibly in these conditions "means embracing the skilful task of reconstructing the boundaries of daily life, in partial connection with others, in communication with all our parts."[23] As Stacy Alaimo adds, "recognizing how the bodies of all living creatures intra-act with place – with the perpetual flows of water, nutrients, toxicants, and other substances – makes it imperative that we be account-able for our practices."[24] For Chris Cuomo, it is, then, this deeply *situated* interspecies interaction that grounds ecological feminist ethics. "Flourishing without purity," in her terms, requires conscious critical attention to the ways in which all ecological understandings are at once corporeal, rela-tional, compromised, and provisional:

> Flourishing on the boundaries of nature/culture is not just a matter of dwelling on the overlapping borders of identities, practices, and characteristics which are not supposed to occur within the same body – it requires *claiming* a space there: cultured animal, mutt, anti-feminine woman, race traitor, computer-enhanced forest-dweller. It also requires active opposition to unifying logics that aim to fix us, and that aimed, variously, to fix Others since time immemo-rial. [And it] ... also implies letting go of dreams of a purity of resistance. How do we transgress boundaries while maintaining, and acting from connected-ness, as complex and contradictory social, ecological beings?[25]

Cereus

For Mootoo, this problem of flourishing in the midst of violent contradic-tions is embodied acutely in, and pursued through, practices of gardening; the idea of what it means to *cultivate* connections in the midst of violence is an issue not only in humans' (especially Mala's) relations to plants, but also in humans' relations to each other (and to other animals) that proceed through plants.[26] Gardening is not in The Garden, here; indeed, the name of the fictional island is that of a species of verbena, *Lantana camara*, that is indigenous to the Caribbean but that has an especially unpleasant smell, a stench that always already permeates Paradise (it is also considered invasive in other tropical regions, is toxic to livestock, and is extremely fire-tolerant). To cultivate affinities in the midst of this stink, then, is not to restore some sweeter-smelling organic whole; it is to embrace the contradictions that are part of the sociobotanical relations of gardening, in which various forms of violence may thrust us together with plants in particular ways. What we do to cultivate each other's flourishing, however, involves making con-scious choices to take responsibility for our practices, including our own violences.

Mala's dead-snail-studded, stinking garden (which is also her bedroom and bathroom) is a perfect example. She has retreated to the garden because it is a relatively safe space, a liminal zone in between the violences of what lies outside the fence (ridicule, rejection, condemnation) and what lies inside the house (a legacy of rape and abuse, embodied in her now-comatose father rotting alive in the downstairs sewing room). But the garden is not Paradise (it is, perhaps ironically, a defense *against* Paradise); it is a miniature ecosystem that is fed on blood sacrifice, constantly in the process of decomposing, and – in Mootoo's emphasis – especially full of dead things, to which Mala actually pays more systematic attention than she does to growing ones. Her cultivation is neither tidy nor instrumental; instead, she allows things to flourish even when that flourishing means destruction:

> Fruit trees and hot pepper trees had sprung wherever birds and insects dropped their seeds. A patch of bright orange, sweet-smelling roses and a profusion of night-blooming cereus plants were the only ornamentals in the yard. The roots of the cereus, like desperate grasping fingers, had bored into the damp wood of the back wall of the house. It was no longer the wall that supported the succulent but rather the other way around. The yard was a jumble of different greens: the bright yellow of the lime trees, the silver of the eucalyptus, the dark blue of the mango.[27]

It is, of course, the cereus that is the central botanical character in the novel. *Selenicereus grandiflorus*, otherwise known as "Queen of the Night," is a species of cactus, indigenous to the Caribbean, Mexico, and Central America, that blooms spectacularly, once a year. We are introduced to the cereus before we are introduced to Mala: a cutting has been given to her by Ambrose and Otoh, was planted by Mr. Hector according to Tyler's wishes, and the plant is about to bloom. As we learn Mala's story, we learn about the parent plant that gave rise to this cutting: it was grown from specimens that Lavinia brought, one each, to Mala and Asha: "Cereus, she called them, pronounced like the bright, fuzzy star, a climbing succulent whose leaves and trunk were ragged and unsightly until they bloomed."[28] When Popoh overhears Lavinia and Sarah planning their escape, she snaps off a leaf, determined to see the blooms at some future, transplanted point; the leaf and the snail shells are, however, the contents of the bag that she rushes back to rescue from the house, and that cause her to be caught by her father, a decisive moment inaugurating the hell that is the rest of her childhood and early adulthood. She is, like the cereus plants, rooted in that place as Boyie, and then Asha, and then Ambrose also leave. But as the plants grow and become integrated with the structure of the house, their impenetrable and spiny tangle also shelters Mala and her secret: "the succulents, half a dozen plants in all, had raged over the side of the house, further concealing the boarded-up window of the room downstairs,"[29] the space containing Chandin's body. The climax of the story coincides with the annual blooming of the cereus: "as the night unwound she witnessed the slow dance of the huge, white cereus buds – she counted sixty-two – trembling as they unfolded against the wall, a choreography of petal and sepal opening together, sending dizzying scent high and wide into the air."[30] Otoh, attracted by the scent (which, for this one night, overpowers the stench of decomposition), wants to bring a girlfriend into Mala's yard (he is, like the moths, "drunk from the smell"[31]) but the evening is ruined by the girlfriend's confession that she had once tormented Mala; the next day, Otoh is determined to find the plant, and to find Mala, and he enters the forbidding yard alone.[32] He sees "the wall of cereus blossoms, every one of them completely wilted"; their sweet vanilla scent has also been replaced by "an even more startling one that seemed to emanate from the wall behind the blossoms."[33] Upon being shown, by Mala (she mistakes him for a young Ambrose), the source of the smell behind the wilted blooms, Otoh runs out, terrified, and collapses in the street; the police, hearing his rantings about a murder, investigate, and begin to hack away at the plants. Mala reluctantly shows them the body, and they take her into custody. Before they can prosecute her (but not before the Paradise hordes chop down the mudra tree and capture the peekoplats for profit, completely destroying the garden), Otoh discreetly sets fire to the house, destroying all evidence and rescuing only cereus clippings from the flames. It is one of these clippings that he and Ambrose bring to Mala at the beginning of the story. A year later, the flower is set to bloom again: the night will be the occasion of Tyler's and Otoh's first sex, and it is also the scent of the possibility of finding Asha: new possibilities for love and hope.

Of course, it is possible to read the cereus *as* Mala: it is *she* who blooms at night, *she* who begins the novel as a "ragged and unsightly" scrap of stem and grows toward flowering, sensually (if fleetingly), on the night promised at the end of the novel. Certainly, Mala has a great deal in common with the cereus: she cannot leave her father's house and, deprived of her more animal, bipedal mobility, develops other ways of resisting (like subtly poisoning Chandin by feeding him rotten pigeon flesh masquerading as chicken); she learns to detect plants in the ways plants often detect themselves, by smell and touch, "to name plants and insects with only their scent or a brush against them as clues";[34] and as Michael Marder might remind us, she simply *persists* in the place in the midst of her father's violences, growing new shoots from each fragment of her as her father tears her apart.[35] In addition, in several places we get glimmers – or more accurately, whiffs – of her distinct vegetality. Ambrose fantasizes about Mala's vagina as smelling like plants: "a place he imagined would exhale a hot mustiness with two very different scents – balsa wood from the silk cotton tree that he used to make spinners with, and the ripened fruit of the cannonball tree, a fearfully strong but very compelling odour."[36] And Tyler notes, as he takes his first breath of her, that Mala has "an aroma resembling rich vegetable compost."[37]

Although Mala's species identity is definitely questionable, I would argue that it is her embodied relation *to* plants, and not her metaphorical status *as* a plant, that is most important to the ecological feminist understanding developed in this novel. To put it differently, Mala's becoming-cereus is not primarily metaphorical, but both ontological and political, in that her taking on of plant qualities is part of the development of an *affinity* with plants that emerges from her participation in/recognition of their shared condition. Toward the beginning of the novel, Mr. Hector – who has heard of Mala's garden – picks a yellow gerbera flower to give her. Tyler explains that he cannot give her the flower because to do so would injure her: "I am beginning to understand some things about her and I think that she does not like things in nature to be hurt. To her, the flower and the plant would both be suffering because they are separated from each other."[38] Later, we find out that a teacher has taught her about plant suffering: Boyie reminds her that "teacher said plants respond to gentleness. He told us too that plants could show signs of trauma."[39] Mala has remembered this lesson, partly because she has also suffered such trauma; as she moves away from human language and into the communicative chirps, gurgles, and rustlings of other-than-humans, she brings gentleness into her botanical friendships: "She [and the garden's birds, insects, snails and reptiles] *and the foliage* gossiped among themselves. She listened intently. … She knelt on the ground and whispered to the grass and other young plants, encouraging them to grow, and then she listened as they stretched up to her."[40] Indeed, although Mr. Hector expertly categorizes the plants in Mala's garden according to their use (medicine, beauty, protection), he also admires her considerably more indiscriminate affections: "It look like she used to take care of it – useful, pretty, bad, whatever."[41] And then, of course: the cereus returns the favor, protecting Mala against the horrors inside the house, and the hordes outside it, without passing judgment on her actions.

It would be very difficult to read Mala's multispecies attentiveness according to a narrative of lost organic unity: her ability to identify with/as snails, insects, and plants is not so much an Edenic memory as a survival skill learned in the context of multiple, painful abuses and abandonments. Indeed, Mala's becomings-cereus can be understood as responses to her experiences of being denied the kinds of autonomy, speech, and mobility that are more often afforded to mammalian life forms (mostly, exclusively to humans): she discovers possibilities for growth, change, resistance, and movement in a small conspiracy of invertebrates and plants because she is treated like a mere snail or succulent in both intimate and public interpersonal encounters.

But at the same time, these violent affinities offer possibilities for a redrawn understanding of human and ecological community, for Mala and, eventually, for the people who come to understand her and relate to her story; as Cuomo insists, it is in these moments in which we *claim* particular dwellings in border-crossing ontologies that ecological feminist ethics and politics begin. If, with Grosz and Barad, we pay attention to the porous complexities of differences, ontologies, and becomings as central tenets of a feminist ecological politics, and if, with Haraway and others, we remember both the structural and the intimate violences in which these attendings and becomings *always* take place, then perhaps we can imagine, with Mootoo, new forms of relating that emerge in some very unlikely places.

NOTES

1 Shani Mootoo, *Cereus Blooms at Night* (Toronto: Press Gang, 1996).
2 As critics have noted, the novel is also a critique of the fantasy of the Caribbean as an exotic paradise: Paradise is scarred by colonial racism, sexism, homophobia, and the instrumentalization of other species, and the violences are ongoing.
3 There is, of course, a distinctly *queer* mode to Mala's and Tyler's connection: for example, Mala supports Tyler's gender transgressions, centering on a woman's nurse's uniform that she steals for him and in which he performs for her (and, later, Otoh). The queer politics of the novel have been amply explored; see John Corr, "Queer Nostalgia and Unnatural Disgust in Shani Mootoo's *Cereus Blooms at Night*," *Journal of West Indian Literature* 14:1/2 (2005), 67–95.
4 Mootoo, *Cereus Blooms*, 54.
5 Ibid., 218.
6 Ibid.
7 From the opening of this rampage in which Mala recognizes "the memory of her father when he discovered her mother gone" to the next morning in which she accounts for the different intensities of pain in her body (221–223), we experience very little of Mala's interiority, and about as much of Chandin's. Part of the power of the novel lies in the interplay between third-person narration (actually Tyler's voice) and the irruptions of different (sometimes impossible) interiorities into the story.
8 Ibid., 226.
9 Ibid.
10 Ibid., 227, emphasis added.
11 Ambrose's lack of empathy with Mala is shocking: as he acknowledges just before they have sex, he has been preoccupied with desiring his own desire, which has prevented him from really feeling Mala. Once he does "feel" her, he is overcome with remorse; he sleeps away most of the rest of his life to dissociate himself from his cowardice.
12 Ibid., 127.
13 Ibid., 184.
14 Elizabeth Grosz, *Becoming Undone: Darwinian Reflections on Life, Politics, and Art* (Durham, NC: Duke University Press, 2011), 91.

15 Ibid., 98.
16 Karen Barad, "Posthumanist Performativity: Toward an Understanding of How Matter Comes to Matter," in Stacy Alaimo and Susan Hekman (eds.), *Material Feminisms* (Bloomington: Indiana University Press, 2008), 141.
17 Ibid., 146.
18 Donna Haraway, "A Cyborg Manifesto: Science, Technology, and Socialist-Feminism in the Late Twentieth Century," in *Simians, Cyborgs, and Women: The Reinvention of Nature* (New York: Routledge, 1991), 149–181.
19 Grosz, *Becoming Undone*, 98.
20 Nancy Tuana, "Viscous Porosity: Witnessing Katrina," in Alaimo and Hekman (eds.), *Material Feminisms*, 203. See also Tanya Gulliver, "Broken Pieces, Shattered Lives: The Lasting Legacy of Hurricane Katrina," in L. Anders Sandberg and Tor Sandberg (eds.), *Climate Change – Who's Carrying the Burden? The Chilly Climates of the Global Environmental Dilemma* (Ottawa: Canadian Centre for Policy Alternatives, 2010), 173–183.
21 Andrew Solomon, *The Noonday Demon: An Atlas of Depression* (New York: Scribner, 2001); see also Elisabeth Wilson, "Organic Empathy: Feminism, Psychopharmaceuticals, and the Embodiment of Depression," in Alaimo and Hekman (eds.), *Material Feminisms*, 373–399.
22 Dayna N. Scott, "'Gender-Benders': Sex and Law in the Constitution of Polluted Bodies," *Feminist Legal Studies* 17:3 (2009), 241–265; see also Giovanna Di Chiro, "Polluted Politics? Confronting Toxic Discourse, Sex Panic, and Eco-Normativity," in Catriona Mortimer-Sandilands and Bruce Erickson (eds.), *Queer Ecologies: Sex, Nature, Politics, Desire* (Bloomington: Indiana University Press, 2010), 199–230.
23 Haraway, "Cyborg Manifesto," 181.
24 Stacy Alaimo, *Bodily Natures: Science, Environment, and the Material Self* (Bloomington: Indiana University Press, 2010), 158.
25 Chris J. Cuomo, *Feminism and Ecological Communities: An Ethic of Flourishing* (New York: Routledge, 1998), 88–89, emphasis in original.
26 See also Sarah Phillips Casteel, "New World Pastoral: The Caribbean Garden and Emplacement in Gisèle Pineau and Shani Mootoo," *Interventions* 5:1 (2003), 12–28.
27 Mootoo, *Cereus Blooms*, 115–116.
28 Ibid., 54.
29 Ibid., 130.
30 Ibid., 134.
31 The moth/cereus relationship is both erotic and violent: "by two o'clock in the morning, every moth was thirstily lapping sweet nectar, bruising and yellowing its body against the large stamens that waved from the flowers" (138).
32 The plot becomes complex during this climactic segment, involving two interesting becomings-Other. As Otoh dresses in his father's clothing to visit Mala, she dreams that she is Pohpoh, out on a forbidden nighttime adventure. Mala/Pohpoh become separate people, and Pohpoh's story is woven into the narrative of Otoh's impersonation of Ambrose, his discovery of the body, and the entry of the police into the house. Mala attempts to protect Pohpoh, as she would like to have been protected; she holds her and talks to her, and as the police move to restrain Mala, she sets Pohpoh free: "run, run fast, Pohpoh, run" (185).

33 Ibid., 154.
34 Ibid., 156.
35 See Michael Marder, "Resist Like a Plant! On the Vegetal Life of Political Movements," *Peace Studies Journal* 5:1 (2012), 24–32.
36 Mootoo, *Cereus Blooms*, 217.
37 Ibid., 11.
38 Ibid., 69.
39 Ibid., 91.
40 Ibid., 127–128, emphasis added.
41 Ibid., 68.

7

LEO MELLOR

The Lure of Wilderness

> What would the world be, once bereft
> Of wet and of wilderness? Let them be left,
> O let them be left, wildness and wet;
> Long live the weeds and the wilderness yet.[1]

This is the close of "Inversnaid," Gerard Manley Hopkins's 1881 poem of incantational mystification. Here is a formulation of feared loss – and, equal to that fear, a desire for communion with otherness; but where today can wilderness be "left" – and yet still be found? In a world of zoomable maps and satellite phones, what might such terrain look like? Perhaps we could peer into Lake Ellsworth in Antarctica, one of the subglacial lakes on that continent where life – in subzero conditions, with few nutrients, in complete darkness, and under intense pressure – may have evolved in isolation for at least 100,000 years. But here, as with everywhere else in every corner of the globe, this wilderness is conceived of as narratable.

The history of looking for wilderness, or fearing it, is inevitably accompanied by attempts to write about it – if only to designate it and keep it at bay. It has been central to Judeo-Christian culture as the *other* – somewhere defined by an opposition to the village, the dwelling, and the knowable zone of life – whether to be experienced as a place of biblical exile, or feared in Old English as "wilddeore" where beasts of all kinds, "deoren," lived beyond the human gaze. Beyond primordial old-growth woodland – for wilderness and wildwood are cognates in so much literature until the Renaissance – wilderness takes on multitudinous literary forms: desolate islands, rocky peaks, expanses of ocean, and zones of solitude. But until the eighteenth century these were nearly always negative, if not filled with rampant fear. Indeed one of the major genres in Western literature, the pastoral, was based upon a tamed landscape in which husbandry – and flirtation between shepherds and shepherdesses – could take place without the threat of deep woods or jagged peaks. But the growth of the Sublime as a philosophical category in the eighteenth century – from Edmund Burke through to the poetry of British Romanticism – enabled the awe and terror when looking at, and writing of, the natural world to be welcomed.

In William Wordsworth's *The Prelude* a view of Mont Blanc, a walk at night, and a mountainous cliff overhanging a lake, all cause both convulsive fear and acute wonder. But they also have a lasting effect, typified by this musing of how one external landscape – the terrifying cliff – subsequently impinged on consciousness: "After I had seen that spectacle, for many days, my brain / Work'd with a dim and undetermined sense / Of unknown modes of being."[2] Beyond such rumination the consequences of encounters with wilderness for writers include: elation, fear, despair, self-knowledge, a recalibration of self in the world – and indeed the universe. In North American literature varieties of wonder proliferate, such as in Henry Thoreau's snowy *Maine Woods*. This writer contemplates how "Nature was here something savage and awful, though beautiful," and he is thus transformed as he searches for meanings with an ecstatic edge of fear: "Contact! Contact! Who are we? Where are we?"[3] This tutelary role of the wilderness – a place that invites humans to ask the largest possible questions – also shapes the writings of John Muir.

His *My First Summer in the Sierra* of 1911, with its invocation of the natural sublime as a specifically American concept, is a travelogue that is totemic – both for nature writing and conservation advocacy; indeed preservation of wilderness was a key political justification for the designation of National Parks.

Yet all of these writers, and many others since, *construct* their wildernesses – and it is not oxymoronic to note it. They build experiences as they choose to see and walk along certain paths, and to ignore – or elide – forms of life that do not fit with the expected components of the wild: a grand scale, the absence of human life, some experiences of solitude and awe. Thus while the *idea* of wilderness continues to hold such a grip over the contemporary cultural imagination, it is also, usefully and pertinently, being questioned for what it leaves out and what it allows us to believe; indeed a recent essay captures well why the very term itself can be problematic:

> It is not a pristine sanctuary where the last remnant of an untouched, endangered, but still transcendent nature can for at least a little while longer be encountered without the contaminating taint of civilization. Instead, it's a product of that civilization, and could hardly be contaminated by the very stuff of which it is made.[4]

So this chapter tracks why rather different "wildernesses" have been found, and asks why layering this term on such varied terrains has been so rich – and problematic – for so many writers. Yet with such potential the chapter can become mimetic of many fears held about its subject: dissipating into trackless pages. Therefore pathways come in my parameters: the chapter concentrates upon prose (both fictional and nonfictional) and poetry; it is limited to Anglo-American traditions and focuses on the twentieth century. Differing traditions in British and American writing stem from, most obviously, the radically different scale of the landscapes, but also the dissimilar senses of the meaningfulness of wilderness in the respective cultures; but there are rhymes and parallels as well as chasms – so this chapter examines five propositions that draw on examples from both traditions: terrain, the limits of language, the erasure of the human, ruins, and small-scale wilderness.

Terrain

The idea of the "bioregion" – partly attributable to the thinking of Gary Snyder – is now a commonplace in environmental studies and literature. It gives a way of describing regions that exist beyond man-made divisions – but are rather unified around landmass characteristics with their related cultural and social features. In Nan Shepherd's *The Living Mountain* the bioregion is the windswept Cairngorms in Scotland, a granite mountain range – or rather, in her perceptive-altering view, an incised plateau. Shepherd was a modernist poet and novelist who worked as a teacher and lived in North East Scotland; written in the last years of the Second World War and unpublished until late in her life, *The Living Mountain* is a brief text – but one that transcends brief descriptions. It is a record of years spent walking in the mountains, detailing the landscape through geology and hydrology, plants and animals, and – crucially – the changes in selfhood that such exposure to a locale produces. The book consists of twelve chapters, interlocking and rhyming with each other through motifs and echoes, but it also consists of the narrated effort – the "toil" as she puts it – of walks she repeatedly took in the mountains. She swims in lochs, sleeps on moors, and revels in the particularity of description: whether of a field mouse or a stag, the shadow of a plane or "in the miniature size of the smallest willow, whose woolly fluff blows about the plateau as the silken hairs of the cotton grass blow about the bogs."[5]

Yet as Shepherd moves through the particularities of place she does not produce a definitive map or chart of her experiences. Rather than awe, the repeated nature of the project brings out a Keatsian negative capability, the knowledge that the mountains are unknowable. Her acceptance of "what the mountain has to give"[6] makes this a lyrical work, but with a steely belief in the power of perception:

The changing of focus in the eye, moving the eye itself when looking at things that do not move, deepens one's sense of outer reality. Then static things may be caught in the very act of becoming. By so simple a matter, too, as altering the position of one's head, a different kind of world may be made to appear. ... From the close-by sprigs of heather to the most distant folds of the land each detail stands erect in its own validity.[7]

Such observations make the world anew to the senses – and sensuality runs right through the work, or rather a knowledge that while wilderness is tutelary it teaches us how to think differently about the senses. In this move she is paralleled – in another part of the British Isles in the 1940s – by the Welsh reveries of Gwen Moffat, as she moves among an anarchic group of bohemian army deserters and mountain climbers, detailed in *Space Below My Feet* of 1961. For Shepherd though there is validation of aloneness above all – and with it a fierce understanding that fear and cold, danger and tiredness all are valid corporeal experiences as they bring "a sting of life is in its touch."[8] But how sensuality might be truly felt *only* because of the wilderness is in her language of sensations – which allows her, toward the close, to hymn: "I have walked out of my body and into the mountain. I am a manifestation of total life, as is the starry saxifrage or the white-winged ptarmigan."[9]

The terrain of Edward Abbey's novel *The Monkey Wrench Gang* is in the southwestern United States, a bioregion that comprises parts of "the canyon country, southeast Utah and northern Arizona."[10] These areas are only prescribed at the start of the sixth chapter as part of mapping where the four ill-matched characters will be moving through. But their business is not aesthetic appreciation, it rather requires:

> monkey wrenches, wrecking bars, heavy-duty wire cutters, bolt cutters, trenching tools, siphon hoses, sugar and syrups, oil and petrol, steel wedges, blasting caps, detonating cord, safety fuse, cap crimpers, fuse lighters and adequate quantities of Du Pont Straight and Du Pont Red Cross Extra.[11]
> [the latter both being types of explosives]

This list is needed because the novel tracks a guerrilla-war that the quartet, headed by an ex-Vietnam veteran named Hayduke, fights on behalf of the wilderness and against all those who would wreck, manage, or despoil it: mining companies, loggers, road builders, and the National Park itself. Hayduke muses toward the close of the novel, *in extremis*, whether he is "in 'Nam again with me as the last V.C. in the jungle. Or am I the first?"[12]; and this is a novel that has exerted a profound political – as well as aesthetic – influence: it is cited by Earth First!, who have waged a campaign of "eco-resistance" since the mid-1970s. Abbey's nonfictional *Desert Solitaire*, which recorded his year working for the Parks Service, gives a history to his anger – as it is a screed of rage against the "improvement" and "accessibility" of parks – but also gives a rationale for why one should fight for the land, as it is subtitled: "A Season in the Wilderness." Why one should fight comes from reverence, of knowing the insignificance of man in such a landscape:

> After the reconnoitring dust devils comes the real, the serious wind, the voice of the desert rising to a demented howl and blotting out sky and sun behind a yellow clouds of dust, sand, confusion, embattled birds, last year's scrub-oak leaves, pollen, the husks of locusts, bark of juniper.[13]

But in *The Monkey Wrench Gang* the reason to fight is considered further, especially with relation to a wider – American – ideal: "'The wilderness once offered men a plausible way of life,' the doctor said. 'Now it functions as a psychiatric refuge. Soon there will be no wilderness.' He sipped at his bourbon and ice. 'Soon there will be no place to go.'"[14] Against such despair Abbey's prose form is vital – in both senses; it is ripsnorting with energy as it marshals short sentences with lyric cries, invective with moments of transcendence. But it also stakes a claim for environmentalism as a form of individualism, the true spirit of the West – and adventure more generally: "the men locked wrists, a la Mallory and Irvine on Everest '24."[15] There is thus an urgency but also a pathos, a realization that, as Hayduke puts it: "My job is to save the fucking wilderness. I don't know anything else worth saving. That's simple, right?"[16]

Limits of Language

Testing whether any kind of language can respond to wilderness – or whether, in the face of terror humans should just be struck dumb – has preoccupied many writers from the eighteenth century onwards. But since the Second World War there have been numerous other pressures on what kinds of idiom, if any, might be used to represent what the wild now is – or how it might be translated. Gary Snyder's work spans five decades and is still fundamental to considering what language might be capable of in any description of landscape. His multiple attempts at a definition of "wilderness" in his essays, typified by "The Etiquette of Freedom," shows his quest, with his concern in the opening up of multifaceted necessity of wilderness to quotidian life. Alongside a historical definition Snyder offers a darker side, with the possibilities that "wilderness has implied chaos, Eros, the unknown, the realm of taboo, the habitat of both the ecstatic and the demonic."[17] But his earliest poetry gives an answer that is still, perhaps, the most potent.

Having worked as seaman, trail crewmember, and forest lookout in the late 1940s and early 1950s, Snyder embraced Buddhism – and with it a very different form of why language might be used in relation to the natural world. In the poems a mix of fear and ecstasy lets Snyder's own body frame his perceptions of the world – and, conversely, how the materiality of his surroundings shape his consciousness. Both are thus altered. In "Lookout's Journal" (written in 1952–1953 while he worked as a firewatcher) the raw material of Snyder's encounters with nature is reflected in a starkly elliptical form. When he eventually published his "Journal," Snyder took pains that his handwritten "notes" were reflected in the typography of the text:

> Cratershan 15 August
> Almost had it last night: *no identity*. One thinks, "I emerged
> from some general, non-differentiated thing, I return to it." One
> has in reality never left it; there is no return.
>   my language fades Images of erosion.[18]

The poems that came later attempt, in their own way, to be true to this awareness of the eroding limits of language. "Riprap" itself begins:

> Lay down these words
> Before your mind like rocks.
>   placed solid, by hands
> In choice of place, set
> Before the body of the mind
>   in space and time:
> Solidity of bark, leaf, or wall
>   riprap of things:[19]

This embrace of all in blunt materiality – riprap is a cobble of stone laid on rock to make a trail for horses in the mountains – becomes a call for bodily apprehension; one that draws attention to what the words might be capable of, if handled with enough respect and care. But the end of the poem leaves the reader with a sense of profound doubt about the possibility of language as fixing or holding experience: "Crystal and sediment linked hot / all change, in thoughts, / As well as things." A legacy from Imagism is here, but so too is the desire for the perfect object of meditation taken from the wild, something that can – might – only exist as a contemplative force.

Colin Simms has been working and publishing as a poet-naturalist since 1960. He has been mainly based in the northeast of England, but his works range across the high-latitudes of Canada and North America and are populated by the mammals and birds of prey he studies. The poems themselves vary from interlocking sequences to the *bricolaging* of letters with scientific data. But central is the question of what language might work for an encounter with nonhuman species in a wild place. In "Otters in the Kirk Field Burn" alliterative overload is a way of indicating the ground, through the clotted "g's" of waterlogged terrain – "stumble in bramble and off stones in bog and gleg" – but the pace is never enough to catch up with "the wandering dog otter."[20] That distance matters: Simms's work is a poetic form of stalking, which tries to find words for the gap between man and animal. In "Lines" the desire to know a pine marten through a mappable grid position fails, but other – poetical – lines might work. For the meaning of encounter is unpicked *as* the desire to fix the encounter in the last stanzas:

> for this is a survivor and he listens
> "with his heels," his (invisible) sable eyes
> which say what we cannot quite see
> yet are given, if we are able to receive
> radio somehow, the gift of self
>
> of "isness"; which is *his*, not our business
> it is self, or what we see of it
> breath, footprints, scats, or nothing even
> ever misleading We *know* nothing
> which way he went, he went
>
> riddles, still the day sudden
> we'll never find out if it was ...
> or why is all illegible on the edge
> of that edginess, expecting everything –
> except we windfall, given nothing.[21]

This question of "isness," the unalterable "otherness" of the creature engaged with, has become one of significant philosophical import in ecocriticism – including how far poetry might be then able to shape a language of limit, of understanding the gap as *itself* a thing of beauty.[22] Simms has been placed, along with others in the anthology *The Ground Aslant*, as embodying a new form of nature writing that engages with both man in the landscape and with the *strangeness* of what can be found.[23] For example, in "(from some Welsh Fieldwork)" the title shows a tentative partiality, yet the poem begins with precognitive apprehension, as sharp as hairs pricking on the back of a neck: "before I know I'm picking up particular pattern / I'm picking up that pattern of sense and on memory." After this the steps of the creature herself – "footfall against leaf fall" – calibrate the waiting. The poem ends with the stuttering limitations of such an endeavor: "I mutter as she does, sing under my breath and heart I response no matter how foolish, totter toward its art."[24] Yet even completed works tantalize through knowing – often in *mise-*

en-page terms – the gap that language cannot cross. "Loch Maree" shuffles together the names of material substances, rocks, earth, water, alongside Simms's hyphenated coinages for movement. The present participles dart and glide, but then – like the otter ducking below the surface – vanish:

Lochside silverschistsand disturbed-to-black-below
pattern-padded pewter-grad velvet-hollows rain added otter pattern
wind off water levelling sibilant bevelling gritscreen bankscree
whistle reminding you of distant widgeon whee-oo[25]

Erasure of the Human

To imagine a landscape as a wilderness has often been, throughout history, a way to render it into a *tabula rasa* for the imagination, thronged with natural forces and ripe with possibilities – but scythed clear of human presence. This is mendacious when not merely naïve. Even on the smallest scale the presence of an observer changes all – and an observer doesn't even have to attain the wilderness to make his or her effects, as part of rapacious modernity, felt: from the residues of Polychlorinatedbiphenyls in the flesh of Polar Bears to the bleached out plastics endlessly eddying in the Great-Pacific-garbage-gyre. But the desire to erase the human is a constant in some of the most intriguing – and troubling – British and American literature.

Jon Krakauer's *Into the Wild* has become a talismanic text. It is an investigative piece of nonfiction, exploring "the wandering across North America in search of raw, transcendent experience"[26] of a young man – Christopher McCandless. Krakauer tracks McCandless's life, the meanings he and others ascribed to it, and his abject death. McCandless was a young man who abandoned the expectations of 1990s America to reinvent himself as "Alexander Supertramp"[27] and to crisscross the country, doing menial work and testing himself against the elements. He finally changed his name, abandoned all possessions, gave his bank account to charity, burned all cash – and set out for a remote forested corner of Alaska near the Denali National Park. He was untrained for survival, and took only a low-caliber rifle and no long-term supplies. In the melt water and mosquitoes he found life hard and unremitting. His attempt ended in his death from starvation, which he chronicled in his journal – found with his body – which itself formed the basis for Krakauer's book.

Many American writers have narrated the sojourn in the arboreal wilderness as a self-imposed test – a recent example being Thomas Crowe's *Zoro's Field: My life in the Appalachian Woods* of 2005. But *Into the Wild* shows how the *idea* of the wilderness, shaped largely by McCandless's readings of Tolstoy and Jack London, was layered palimpsestically onto a real landscape; one that was, however, not designed for such a test of selfhood, being both physically challenging and also not wild enough – McCandless threw away his map possibly precisely because it would have revealed a road relatively nearby. Krakauer builds his own narrative through parallels between McCandless and himself, and writes of his own younger adventures: "I was on my way, propelled by an imperative that was beyond my ability to control or comprehend."[28] But the imperative the reader can see in *Into the Wild*, with the ghost of McCandless's text behind that of Krakauer's, is that of a romantic fallacy: of masculinity in America as needing a form of testing, and modernity regarded as inadequate for the task. But solitude can still be found as McCandless, in the third person, wrote in an ecstatic note that has its own crescendo of misanthropy:

> Now after two rambling years comes the greatest and final adventure. The climactic battle to kill the false being within and conclude the spiritual pilgrimage. Ten days and nights of freight trains and hitchhiking bring him to the great white north. No longer to be poisoned by civilization he flees, and walks alone upon the land to become <u>lost in the wild</u>.[29]

Yet the unforgiving, non-narratival nature of this wilderness, once lost in it, becomes clear. The abjection of rotting meat – from a moose shot but not smoked, the mounting sense of despair, the wasting of his own body: all are documented by the photographs and diary entries. But as McCandless realized he was dying, amid the abjections of the body and with the bathos of his resting place being an abandoned ex- school bus, his willfully textual reading of the landscape fell away. The last note he left, and signed using his real name, shows fear, not quotations – and a desire for a community to allow human survival:

> SOS. I NEED YOUR HELP. I AM INJURED, NEAR DEATH, AND TOO WEAK TO HIKE OUT OF HERE. I AM ALL ALONE. <u>THIS IS NO JOKE</u>.[30]

J. A. Baker's *The Peregrine* cannot compete in terms of climactic extremity. The terrain it covers, part of Essex, is in one of the most populated British counties, shot-through with human life, industry, and the background banality of modernity. Yet over the course of *The Peregrine* human life, beyond that of the observer, is stilled – and its language finds a way to represent the nonhuman. It purports to be a diary covering a year, but is in fact welded together from years of diaries, its artifice solely dedicated to tracking this ferocious raptor – the peregrine. It begins with a vow:

> Wherever he goes, this winter, I will follow him. I will share the fear, and the exaltation, and the boredom, of the hunting life. I will follow him till my predatory human shape no longer darkens in terror the shaken kaleidoscope of

colour that stains the deep fovea of his brilliant eye. My pagan head shall sink into the winter land, and there be purified.[31]

This purification comes in the casting asunder of human life – no other people feature in his narrative and no places, of any kind, are named. Instead there is just the virtuosic patterning of woods and hedges, similes that shock, and a taxonomy of observation. But what grows throughout the season is the identification of Baker with the bird, until he begins to appropriate its physicalization:

> I found myself crouching over the kill, like a mantling hawk. My eyes turned quickly about, alert for the walking heads of men. Unconsciously I was imitating the movements of a hawk, as in some primitive ritual; the hunter becoming the thing he hunts. I looked into the wood. In a lair of shadow the peregrine was crouching, watching me, gripping the neck of a dead branch. We live, in these days in the open, the same ecstatic fearful life. We shun men.[32]

The "I" moves to a "we," he becomes part of the bird's tribe – or at least wishes to be. But such a translation cannot ever be fully completed, and while humans may mimic birds they are always fated to fail – and thus have to carry a self-knowledge of dark despair: "No pain, no death, is more terrible to a wild creature than its fear of man. … We are the killers. We stink of death. We carry it with us. It sticks to us like frost. We cannot tear it away."[33]

Ruins

Death haunts the growth of "extreme tourism" to new wildernesses – whether the grasses in the ruins of central Detroit or debris blowing through abandoned Pueblos – but it reaches an apogee in the tours now offered to Chernobyl in Ukraine, entering the 30-kilometer exclusion zone that has been abandoned since Reactor 4 exploded in 1986. Yet the radioactive forest and the blockhouse-sarcophagus are only supporting attractions; for central to these tours is the abandoned city of Pripyat. Now overgrown, mainly with birch, willow, and alder, the crumbling Soviet architecture offers a combination of Cold War chic with a distinct pleasure in wilderness and ruins. Films and websites, with their fetishizing of before and after images, are dedicated to its decay – and offer it as a template for the posthuman cities to come. Popular nonfiction offers a corollary, such as Alan Weisman's predictions that revel in the advance of vegetation through New York:

> Ruins of high-rises echo the love songs of frogs breeding in Manhattan's reconstituted streams, now stocked with alewives and mussels dropped by seagulls … Rising water, tides and salt erosion have replaced the engineered

shorelines circling New York's five boroughs with estuaries and small beaches. ... Without natural grazers – unless horses used by hansom cabs and by park policemen managed to go feral and breed – Central Park's grass is gone. A maturing forest is in its place, radiating down former streets and invading empty foundations.[34]

Described here is a vista of destruction, one that no human could ever – by its very rationale for existing – glimpse or appreciate. But it is mapped out in sensuous terms of environmental resurrection; or, to make the spiritual visible, "reincarnation." Only a few traces of a militarized template for understanding the deserted city remains, lurking within the lexical rather than actual jungle, given away only by terms such as "invading." For imagining a city being submerged back into a wilderness has a long history – and one forever connected with violence.

In J. G. Ballard's *Hello America* the characters travel on a quest across the newly desertified "American wilderness,"[35] until they cross the Rockies and find a new tropical rain forest caused by climate change:

> the dawn world of the forest floor, a shadowy realm of suburban stores and houses split apart by huge palms and oaks ... the thousands of leaking swimming pools are slime green tanks crammed with water-lilies, roosting places for flocks of cranes and flamingos ... Los Angeles is a bizarre sight. The great freeways are linear gardens, tapestries of Spanish Moss.[36]

But this is not bucolic: helicopter gunships blaze with their gatlings into the flocks of birds; and in Las Vegas, amid the dense jungle, President Charles Manson plays nuclear roulette with the remaining stockpile of nuclear missiles.

In Richard Jefferies's *After London: or, Wild England* the title itself gives the plot, and the narrative illustrates the lowlands of the Thames valley through the prism of the arts and crafts movement; a new sea has covered London and led to a reversion to subsistence farming. What has happened is retold with violent pleasure by the narrator: "[f]or this marvellous city, of which such legends are related, was after all only of brick, and when the ivy grew over and trees and shrubs sprang up, and, lastly, the waters underneath burst in, this huge metropolis was soon overthrown."[37] Jefferies inspired many, including the poet and walker Edward Thomas, whose *The South Country* included a revenge fantasy for his beloved "Nature":

> I like to think how easily Nature will absorb London as she absorbed the mastodon, setting her spiders to spin the winding-sheet and her worms to fill in the grave, and her grass to cover it pitifully up, adding flowers – as an unknown hand added them to the grave of Nero. I like to see the preliminaries of this toil where Nature tries her hand at mossing the factory roof, rusting the deserted

railway metals, sowing grass over the deserted platforms and flowers of rose-bay on ruinous hearths and walls.[38]

Thomas was not to know what would happen to "rose-bay" – the only species he specifically names. For this plant, with its pink flowers and down-coated leaves, commonly known as Rosebay Willowherb, is thick in all writings about the bombsites that littered post–World War II London. It is the talismanic species in *The World My Wilderness* by Rose Macaulay, an exuberantly strange tale that reinscribes the value of wilderness. Set in postwar London, amid the actual, social and familial ruins, its heroine is Barbary, a seventeen-year-old girl – but one who rejects convention to rather live amid the overgrown and verdancy of bombed buildings. The tumbling and entwining sentences seem mimetic of this resurgent growth:

> Summer slipped on; a few blazing days when London and its deserts burned beneath a golden sun, and the flowering weeds and green bracken hummed with insects, and the deep underground cells were cool like churches, and the long grass wilted, drooped and turned to hay; then a number of cool wet days, when the wilderness was sodden and wet and smelt of decay, and the paths ran like streams, and the ravines were deep in dripping greenery that grew high and rank, running over the ruins as the jungle runs over Mayan temples, hiding them from prying eyes.[39]

When Barbary is forced to holiday with her stepmother in the remoteness of Scotland she finds there, ironically, repressive order that tames nature – and so she escapes back to London where she can find: "a wilderness of little streets ... grown over by green and golden fennel and ragwort, colts-foot, purple loosestrife, rosebay willow herb, bracken, brambles and tall nettles."[40] The text becomes giddy with botanical precision turned into a litany; a floral cloak of amnesia over the jagged pain of death and destruction. It has biographical as well as theoretical poignancy; Macaulay's flat had been burnt to the ground in a firebomb raid during 1941, and her botanizing of the wild flowers was itself a recuperation.[41] Yet verdancy can offer menace as well as balm; such as in John Wyndham's *The Day of The Triffids*, which supposes an apocalyptic calamity being followed by the triumph of the Triffids, a poisonous plant. Survivors make forays to London in the years after the disaster; but the plants that now cover the city, rather than giving concealment to an earlier terror, now *are* the terror:

> The gardens of the Parks and Squares were wildernesses creeping out across the bordering streets. Growing things seemed to press out everywhere, rooting in the crevices between the paving stones, springing from cracks in concrete, finding lodgement even in the seats of abandoned cars. On all sides they were encroaching to repossess themselves of the arid spaces that man had created.[42]

Coda: Wilderness in the Smallest Things

If nature after destruction is a rare example of wilderness winning out against human propensities to map, order, and exploit, it is also a phenomenon that can still be found today – if we recalibrate our sense of scale. While there is a long tradition of *locale* in American nature writing, such as the "land-ethic" of Aldo Leopold's *Sand County Almanac*, it still generally requires goodly acreage to be walked over. But wildernesses can be found in the overlooked cracks in city-life, as the British naturalist Richard Mabey has claimed with such articulate decisiveness across his *oeuvre* from *The Unofficial Countryside* of 1973 to *Weeds* in 2011. For re-enchantment with the local has defined the most interesting turn in the British "new nature writers";[43] typified most acutely in Robert Macfarlane's thinking around – or through – the matter of wilderness and magnitude. Macfarlane's work has to be located within two distinct and ambitious genres: firstly the reinvention of perambulatory pensiveness over the 1990s and 2000s, notably by W. G. Sebald with his thanatos-filled-digressions in *The Rings of Saturn* (1995) and Rebecca Solnit with her activism in *Wanderlust* (2000); but also within the resurgence in a nature writing in Britain, shaped notably by Roger Deakin – a mentor to Macfarlane. Deakin's major works, *Waterlog* (1999) and *Wildwood* (2007), are both built around travel, as testified to by their subtitles: but they are also fixated on the uniqueness of local – tactile – experience, a lesson central to Macfarlane's own loose trilogy. His first volume, *Mountains of the Mind* (2003) was a cultural history of a fascination with elevation and danger, a hymn to a lineage of writers who had been enthralled by mountains – and a record of the author's own engagement with extremity. But in *The Wild Places* Macfarlane undergoes a slow-moving epiphany, a yearlong creeping erosion of his beliefs that wilderness should – or could – only ever be found in remoteness. So he travels through Britain – charting the northern and western fringes in the search for the authentic wild. (Indeed the endpapers of the book present a map of the archipelago of the British Isles as if seen from the North, a cartographic disorientation to foreground the remoter shores). A rage fills the start: a claustrophobia of being caught in an over-farmed and over-inhabited corner of a country, a place where the maps show "a landscape so thickly webbed by roads that asphalt and petrol are its new primary elements."[44] After islands, moors, and woods – and a strenuous attempt to escape the traces of habitation – he travels with Deakin to the Burren limestone plateau in western Ireland. Here, after striding across the windblown surface, he looks into a small fissure called a gryke – and a revelation:

We lay belly-down on the limestone and peered over its edge. And found ourselves looking into a jungle. Tiny groves of ferns, mosses and flowers were
there in the crevasse – hundreds of plants, just in the few yards we could see,
thriving in the shelter of the gryke: cranesbills, plantains, avens, ferns.[45]

His immediate lesson: "the sense of life was immense" – the transcendence
of physical size, grows into a realization that the degree of wildness, and
possibility of finding a wilderness, is thus not dependent on apparent scale.
Indeed places "framed" as wilderness, such as the Highlands of Scotland,
have a long history of tree-burn and forced migration to give such solitude.
The further journeys in this volume – and in *The Old Ways* of 2012, with
its interest in lines ascribed and inscribed by humans in a landscape – are
guided by such revelations. A clear-sighted acceptance that wilderness can
be where we choose to find it, perhaps more precious in the small as well
as large, and might even be in the act of perception itself, closes *The Wild
Places*:

We are fallen in mostly broken pieces, I thought, but the wild can still return
to us … [for] Wildness was here too, a short mile south of the town in which
I lived. It was set about by roads and buildings, much of it was menaced, and
some of it was dying. But at that moment the land seemed to ring with a wild
light.[46]

NOTES

1 Gerard Manley Hopkins, *Poems and Prose* (Harmondsworth, UK: Penguin, 1953), p. 50.
2 William Wordsworth, *The Prelude 1799, 1805, 1850*, eds. J. Wordsworth, M. H. Abrams, and S. Gill (New York: W. W. Norton & Co., 1979), p. 50.
3 H. D. Thoreau, *The Maine Woods* (Princeton, NJ: Princeton University Press, 1983), p. 71.
4 William Cronon, "The Trouble with Wilderness; or, Getting Back to the Wrong Nature" in *Uncommon Ground: Rethinking the Human Place in Nature* (New York: W. W. Norton & Co., 1995), pp. 69–90 (p. 69).
5 Nan Shepherd, *The Living Mountain* (Edinburgh: Canongate, 2011), p. 58.
6 Shepherd, *The Living Mountain*, p. 57.
7 Shepherd, *The Living Mountain*, pp. 10–11.
8 Shepherd, *The Living Mountain*, p. 26.
9 Shepherd, *The Living Mountain*, p. 106.
10 Edward Abbey, *The Monkey Wrench Gang* (London: Penguin, 2004), p. 71.
11 Abbey, *The Monkey Wrench Gang*, p. 71.
12 Abbey, *The Monkey Wrench Gang*, p. 401.
13 Edward Abbey, *Desert Solitaire* (New York: Ballantine, 1971), p. 17.
14 Abbey, *The Monkey Wrench Gang*, p. 61.
15 Abbey, *The Monkey Wrench Gang*, p. 224.
16 Abbey, *The Monkey Wrench Gang*, p. 229.

17 Gary Snyder, *The Practice of the Wild* (Berkeley, CA: Counterpoint, 1990), pp. 3–26, (p. 12).

18 Snyder, "Lookout's Journal," in *Earth House Hold* (New York: New Directions, 1969), p. 18.

19 Snyder, *Riprap and Cold Mountain Poems* (Berkeley, CA: Counterpoint, 2010), p. 32.

20 Colin Simms, *Otters and Martens* (Exeter, UK: Shearsman Books, 2007), p. 50.

21 Simms, *Otters and Martens*, p. 160–161.

22 For the practice of "becoming-animal," see Eric Santner, *On Creaturely Life* (Chicago: University of Chicago Press, 2006).

23 *The Ground Aslant: An Anthology of Radical Landscape Poetry*, ed. Harriet Tarlo (Exeter, UK: Shearsman Books, 2011).

24 Simms, *The Ground Aslant*, p. 110.

25 Simms, *The Ground Aslant*, p. 17.

26 John Krakauer, *Into the Wild* (London: Villard, 1998), p. ix.

27 Itself a literary-moniker, taken from W. H. Davises's *The Autobiography of a Super-Tramp* (1908).

28 Krakauer, *Into the Wild*, p. 136.

29 Krakauer, *Into the Wild*, p. 162.

30 Krakauer, *Into the Wild*, pp. 196–197.

31 J. A. Baker, *The Peregrine, The Hill of Summer & Diaries*, ed. John Fanshawe (London: Collins, 2011), p. 48.

32 Baker, *The Peregrine*, p. 92.

33 Baker, *The Peregrine*, p. 113.

34 Alan Weisman, *The World Without Us* (London: Virgin, 2008), p. 36.

35 J. G. Ballard, *Hello America* (London: Fourth Estate, 2011), p. 53.

36 Ballard, *Hello America*, p. 138.

37 Richard Jefferies, *After London: or, Wild England* (Oxford: Oxford University Press, 1980), p. 36.

38 Edward Thomas, *The South Country* (London: Dent, 1993), pp. 75–76.

39 Rose Macaulay, *The World My Wilderness* (London: Virago, 1997), p. 79.

40 Macaulay, *The World My Wilderness*, p. 53.

41 See Leo Mellor, *Reading the Ruins: Bombsites, Modernism and British Culture* (Cambridge: Cambridge University Press, 2011).

42 John Wyndham, *The Day of the Triffids* (Harmondsworth, UK: Penguin, 2000), p. 197.

43 See, for example, the introduction to the issue of *Granta* "The New Nature Writing" (no. 102, Summer 2008), pp. 1–7.

44 Macfarlane, *The Wild Places* (London: Granta, 2007), p. 10.

45 Macfarlane, *The Wild Places*, p. 168.

46 Macfarlane, *The Wild Places*, p. 321.

PART III

Interdisciplinary Engagements

8

WENDY WHEELER

"Tongues I'll Hang on Every Tree": Biosemiotics and the Book of Nature

these trees shall be my books
And in their barks my thoughts I'll character
          – *As You Like It*, Act 3, scene ii.

Biosemiotics and Natural Constructivism

During the nineteenth century, the idea of a natural oikos, an economy of natural being and relationship, gave rise to the invention, by Ernst Haeckel in 1866,[1] of the term "ecology." Despite its evident emphasis on relationships over things, the dominance of materialism and determinism in the natural sciences, alongside the habitual assumptions of material reductionism as the most appropriate way of understanding ecological development, meant that the idea of relationship was defined in a rather constrained way. Similarly, the Modern Synthesis of Neo-Darwinism, which was developed in the 1930s and 1940s and sought to resolve the discoveries of Mendelian genetics with Darwinian natural selection, gave expression to a mechanistic and reductionist model of evolution. This was later supported by Francis Crick's articulation, in 1958, of the unidirectionality of the Central Dogma's evolutionary thesis: that genetic information flows one way only from DNA to protein. Together these two materialist and deterministic precepts attained the status of nearly unassailable truth. As the philosopher Thomas Nagel has noted, "Physico-chemical reductionism in biology is the orthodox view, and any resistance to it is regarded as not only scientifically but politically incorrect."[2] From the point of view of scientific discovery as an open and ongoing process, the dogmatism to which Nagel refers represents a rather parlous state of affairs.

Now, however, these staples of evolutionary theory are being challenged from a number of sources, and not least by the move – articulated in both physics and biology[3] – from material mechanism to information. The latter (as *more* than a mathematical and semantics-free theory of information and communication,[4] and as something that must offer an account of *meaning* where living organisms are concerned) remains poorly understood, particularly in the case of an informational theory of causation. However, the stage is set, by the work of biosemioticians and other biologists taking the insights of molecular biological research seriously, for a revolution in our understanding of evolution and the importance of ecology. Biosemiotics in particular argues that biological information must be properly understood as biosemiosis – that is the action of signs, and communication and interpretation in *all* living things – all the way from the single cell to complex multicellular organisms. This means that what we understand by "mind" and "knowledge" must necessarily shake off its purely anthropocentric connotations. Claude Shannon's mathematical theory of communication is a theory about the information-carrying capacity of channels. But living organisms are much more than information-carrying mechanistic channels; they are bearers of purposes and readers of meanings. As Jesper Hoffmeyer says, "It is not the genes per se, but their interplay and *interpretation* in the cell that counts."[5] The importance of this biosemiotic insight lies, among many other things, in the way it puts human meaning-making as interpretation and purposiveness back into evolutionary nature where it belongs, and also undoes the unhelpful distinctions between mind and body and nature and culture.[6] All living things are in constant creative semiotic interaction with their environments: each makes the other in a continual process. We can call this natural constructivism.

"Tongues I'll Hang on Every Tree" – Logic in Grass

Pursuing the point about causation, biologist James A. Shapiro, for example, calls for an understanding of the evolutionary mechanisms of information. In an article entitled "DNA as Poetry: Multiple Messages in a Single Sequence,"[7] Shapiro points out that what he calls "coincident messages," that is, multiple messages written within the same DNA coding sequence, cause tremendous problems for a mechanistic account of biological functions. In fact, we understand perfectly well that the same words in human languages can have different meanings according to the contextual interpretation; it appears that DNA code is, similarly, not a mechanical but a semiosic and thus interpretive phenomenon in which cells (and bodies and organisms) have learned to make many context-dependent meanings. This is the understanding that is formally begun by biosemiotics. In joining the biological sciences (bio) and the humanities (semiotics – from semeion, Greek for sign), biosemiotics not only reconnects two ways of thinking that have fallen apart, it also helps us to appreciate again the work of proto-biosemioticians such as Jakob von Uexküll, who understood that every species occupies its own semiotic *umwelt*,[8] and Gregory Bateson, who understood that culture is evolutionarily emergent from nature and reiterates and connects natural patterns and behaviors in cultural ones.[9] This is not to do with laws or determinism but with what Charles Sanders Peirce identified as "nature's tendency to take habits."[10]

Thus, and on the evolutionary principle that nothing comes from nothing, we can look for reiterations of natural patterns in cultural ones. One of these, and perhaps a most characteristic one, will be the play of identity/similarity and difference which creates signification, and which humans call metaphor. Far from being merely a figure of speech, this play of identity and difference, which Bateson called "syllogism in grass," runs through all nature and culture: "Metaphor runs right through Creatura, so, of course, all verbal communication necessarily contains metaphor."[11] As a corollary, we will no longer be surprised to discover semiosis and something like intelligence in cells, and in the entire world of living things, as well as in humans.[12] Neither will we be surprised to discover, as I go on to discuss, that meanings in literature reiterate the mechanisms and patterns of growth in the evolution of multicellular organisms. Culture is natural and evolutionary, and we can see homologous forms and patterning across both natural and cultural artifacts. In common with arguments made by biosemioticians such as Kalevi Kull, Shapiro argues that nature is, in effect, its own reader,[13] and that the innovative readings, which lead to new formulations, are generated by environmental pressures. These activate problem-solving intelligence on the part of cells, and this involves purposeful solutions drawing on, for example, horizontal gene transfer via viral gene swapping, symbiogenesis, genome doubling, and various forms of epigenetic change,[14] all of which Shapiro calls "natural genetic engineering" and biosemioticians call natural constructivism. That different historical and cultural contexts exert pressures for new creative readings of aesthetic objects in humans also seems equally beyond dispute.

These forms of natural metaphor whereby biological function, that is, meaning, is "abducted" or carried over from one site to another emphasize the Batesonian and biosemiotic argument that nothing comes from nothing, and that everything humans do is also done, albeit in more "primitive" form (although not really very "primitive" at all), by earlier stages of evolutionary life. This "carrying over," or bearing of information, which exists as the primary organization of growth and evolution through resonant pattern recognition by an organism's sensorium (sum of its perception), seems to be a marker of life wherever it is found. Norbert Wiener warned against confusing matter, energy, and information: "Information is information, not matter or energy. No materialism which does not admit this can survive at the present day."[15] Nonetheless, it seems that the relation between the three is intimate to say the least.

What is Information?

As quantum physics turned increasingly toward a physics of information, it became possible to write of "the matter myth" and of a new understanding of matter itself as the capability of carrying information. As Paul Davies and John Gribbin wrote in 1991, "what we normally think of as empty space is in fact continually crisscrossed by an incessant traffic of messenger particles such as virtual photons."[16] With this, information became understood as an essential mediating part of our understanding of the physical universe. In the early 2000s, physicist Hans Christian von Baeyer was able to write that "the fundamental building blocks of information," as understood by physicist Anton Zeilinger, are "propositions; [John Archibald] Wheeler calls them answers to questions; and the simplest of those, in turn, is an elementary proposition, a yes-or-no question with an answer that's called a 'bit' of information."[17] This is remarkably redolent of an early proto-biosemiotic claim made by the cybernetician Gregory Bateson when he described the relation between the egg and the spermatozoon just prior to fertilization in the following terms: "we might think of the state of the egg immediately before fertilization as a state of question, a state of *readiness to receive a certain piece of information*, information that is then provided by the entry of the spermatozoon."[18]

By 1985 Susan Oyama had already begun to describe biology in informational terms.[19] In this sense, and edging close to a biosemiotic account as biosemiotician Jesper Hoffmeyer has noted, biological information begins to take on the contextual and semantic aspects, which are absent from physics and mathematical accounts such as Shannon's. Indeed, it is this – the observation that information introduces *differences, which are meaningful* for biological life, and that meanings are functions tied to purposes – that sent the first biologists who recognized this toward theories of meaning and semiosis, and thus turned several of them into the first biosemioticians.[20] This articulated a move, now gathering apace, away from the concept of genetic determinism. As Hoffmeyer writes:

> Oyama … recommended that we give up altogether the idea that the developmental process is directed by some special information that is transmitted by genes. The information that manifests through the life cycle of an individual, Oyama claimed, is rather information that is constructed by and with the developmental process itself. … Oyama's point – which is closely connected

to the one taken in the present book – is that developmental processes depend on "inform-ation" from a range of different sources, and that genes are only one of these sources. The conception of a special genetic programme that unfolds its predetermined logic through embryogenesis is mistaken because this programme – if the programme metaphor should be valid at all – is not self-reliant, but only works at all because it is played out in a context that is derived from elsewhere.[21]

To this we can add not only the growing recognition that "junk DNA" is not junk at all but another kind of information for describing contexts made operative by protein folding, and the role of microbial DNA in the effectively symbiotic life of any organism,[22] but also Susan Lindquist's recent research on prion chaperones and environmental stress in the heritability of acquired characteristics.[23] Thus Lamarck, so long derided (although not, it should be noted, by Charles Darwin), is back.

The biosemiotic view – that all life consists of acts of communication and relatedness, what Charles Sanders Peirce (1839–1914), a major scientific and philosophical influence for biosemiotic understandings, called tychism and agapism – thus assures us that *all* living things communicate and respond in nonmechanistic, nondeterministic ways to their environments. These organic processes cannot be reduced simply to physics and chemistry because an "epistemic cut" exists between any phenomenon and its observer (or measurer).[24] Even a cell has something like awareness, or what Hoffmeyer calls a phenomenological intentionality or "sense of aboutness" – however primitive.[25]

The biologists who first realized this communicative nature of all living things – and this was a development that really happened over two or three generations – eventually realized they needed a theory of semiotics. This was provided in the meeting of biology with both Soviet and North American semioticians. The work of Soviet literary scholar and cultural semiotician Juri Lotman, student of Vladimir Propp at Leningrad State University and founder of the Moscow-Tartu School, was important here; but perhaps most important of all were the unceasing labors of the Hungarian-American semiotician and zoosemiotician, based for many years at the University of Indiana, Thomas A. Sebeok. It was Sebeok who brought together the work of the American scientist, philosopher, and logician Charles Sanders Peirce with the work of the German-Estonian biologist and first ethologist Jakob von Uexküll, and who, through Jakob's son Thure, introduced the Danish and Estonian biologists and semioticians (now known as the Copenhagen-Tartu School) to the American semiotic tradition. This enormous richness of history and development is what gives biosemiotics its scientifically, theoretically, and philosophically deep resources.

Living Metaphor

For the past thirty years at least, a significant part of the humanities has been influenced by an idealist and anthropocentric philosophy, which asserts that our experience of reality is wholly constructed in human language. The idea that this forms the horizon of what we can know about the world, cannot survive evolutionary theory. Thus it cannot survive ecological understandings either. Language (verbal semiosis) is evolutionarily emergent from nonverbal semiosis. The latter, as we know, remains highly significant even for verbally focused human animals.[26] Like all semiosis, language is almost certainly *not* evolved primarily to improve communication (*Homo erectus* managed two million years of successful existence without articulate verbal semiosis); rather, it is evolved to improve the detail with which *Homo sapiens* is capable of modeling the world.[27] In *Models and Metaphor* Max Black pointed out that models are closely related to metaphor[28] – to model the world is to metaphoricize – but this simply means to abstract and abduct patterns of similarity and difference. We shouldn't go around thinking that metaphors are not a real part of the semiotic fabric of the universe and cognition. As is well described by Paul Ricoeur, metaphor – the recognition of difference in similarity – is the *precondition* of human deductive logic and also organizes the world as the "carrying," or carrying over, or bearing across of the creative structures of the world, both natural and cultural. Metaphor comes from the Greek μεταφέρω metafero – to carry; hence metaphor (Greek μεταφορά metafora) means to carry away, via iconic signs, meaning from one place to another; hence Peirce's and Bateson's use of the term "abduction" to identify this logic of discovery. In *La métaphore vive* (*Living Metaphor*, Éditions du Seuil, 1975, translated doggedly in English as *The Rule of Metaphor*), Ricoeur writes:

> metaphor reveals the dynamic at work in the constitution of semantic fields, the dynamic Gadamer calls the fundamental "metaphoric," which merges with the genesis of concepts through similarity. A family resemblance first brings individuals together before the rule of a logical class dominates them. "Metaphor, a figure of speech, presents in an open fashion, by means of a conflict between identity and difference, the process that, in a covert manner, generates semantic grids by fusion of differences into identity."[29]
> I will return to this.

As the work of Jakob von Uexküll has suggested to us,[30] semiosic modeling of the world is what all living organisms must do, thereby co-constructing what von Uexküll calls an *Umwelt*, or semiotic environment. No organism receives the world directly or in an unmediated fashion. What all living things experience are stimuli or signals; let's call them *signs* and let's think about them properly by thinking about what a sign must do in order to function as a sign. In Charles Sanders Peirce's words: "I define a Sign as anything which is so determined by something else, called its Object, and so determines an effect upon a person, which effect I call its Interpretant, that the latter is thereby mediately determined by the former. My insertion of 'upon a person' is a sop to Cerberus, because I despair of making my own broader conception understood."[31] In other words – and this is what biosemiotics urges upon us – let us think properly about the semiotic nature of *all* living organisms and experience. But that modeling of organismic *umwelten* goes hand in hand (or paw in paw) with shaping and being shaped by the world of the particular species *umwelt*. Therefore, while we must eschew the anthropocentric idea of radical socio-linguistic constructivism, we can nonetheless talk about natural constructivism.

Nonverbal semiosis – gesture, expression, movement, sound, olfaction: all the business of the senses and their chemical and neurological supports, in fact – is not the preserve of human animals alone. All these behaviors and functions are semiotic and belong to *all* living things. From the single cell all the way to the complex multicellular organism, and even the super-organisms organic and cultural – both selves and societies – every living thing has a sense of "aboutness" and a living and interpretative "intentional" relation to everything potentially meaningful in its environment. This implies, by the way, that we must try to avoid our anthropocentric bias and rethink what we might mean by such things as "interpretation," "mind," and "knowledge." In some very real sense, all living organisms "know" things and have purposes.[32] You and I know things in that organic embodied way also, but we have more or less lost a language for talking about that kind of knowing made of syllogisms of grass. Or rather we have one in our engagements with art and the sacred and in all the modes, including science, in which we are creative and dream; however, to our very great loss, these apparently no longer count as proper sources of knowledge in the narrowed horizons of contemporary technologized Western cultures.

A Difference Which Makes a Difference

Semiosis – the registering of information as what Gregory Bateson called "a difference which makes a difference"[33] – must be an aspect of biological life right from the start. Life starts with, and is dependent upon, a primordial difference based on the existence of a membrane, or skin, separating self from not-self.[34] The task of life from the start is the negotiation of difference, or the *relation* (which is to say information and communication) between self and not-self, in the task of survival, reproduction, and natural growth. These latter – which are also *work* in the thermodynamic sense – require degrees of creativity, play, and adaptability. The work is made possible by organisms' existence in the midst of cybernetic feedback loops. These have a tendency to generate exploratory strategies – of symbiosis, consortia, parasitism, and so on – which lead to increased multicellular complexity. This has led biosemiotician Jesper Hoffmeyer to describe evolution as the evolution of increasing degrees of semiotic freedom. This evolutionary tendency is bought, however, at the price of the constraining of lower level system components. As Bateson repeatedly suggested, these patterns in nature are repeated in culture, and we have much to learn from them.[35] Among such lessons is the insight that formal limits (natural and social) are not opposed to creativity and adaptation but are, on the contrary, its very condition. As Howard Pattee writes, "Igor Stravinsky (1970) expressed the apparent paradox of constraints in the context of composing: 'The more constraints one imposes, the more one frees oneself from the chains that shackle the spirit ... and the arbitrariness of the constraint serves only to obtain precision of execution.'"[36] We must not, however, make the mistake of equating "natural" with "good." Both the development of technology and of certain kinds of constraining hierarchies are certainly natural, but not all their outcomes are thereby desirable. Learning from what Bateson and biosemiotics understand as the "necessary unity" of mind and nature must not involve uncritical assumptions about "natural goodness." Like all organisms, we must discriminate between life-enhancing and life-destroying organisms socio-technological or otherwise. Learning from natural behaviors, however, can help us think better about the patterns and behaviors that characterize cultural life.

Most biosemioticians would agree with Thomas Sebeok's claim that "Biosemiotics presupposes the axiomatic identity of the semiosphere with the biosphere."[37] Human ways of modeling the world depend, of course, upon human semiotic capacities – language and its discursive forms in myth, religion, art, mathematics, and science – but these, in turn, depend on forms of semiosis, and semiotic patterns and earthly habit formations, which belong in some form to other kinds of life too. We can ponder these forms in order to remind ourselves that *we belong to the earth*; it has made us. This is true, too, of all of earth's life. If we fail to preserve the earth and its biodiversity, we will surely not preserve ourselves in its absence. We are formed by the earth and its ecology – its rocks, rivers, plants, and animals. As Jean-Christophe Bailly passionately argues in *The Animal Side*, echoing Bateson among others, in destroying these relations we destroy ourselves.[38]

What we can learn from biosemiotics concerns the metaphoric and metonymic structure of both natural and cultural evolution. The play of identity and difference by which metaphoric pattern movement is possible should alert us to the two kinds of Aristotelian causation that modern science has excluded. (Aristotle's causes were four: material cause, efficient cause, formal cause, and final cause; modern science tried to expel formal cause and final, or teleological, cause because it thought them contaminated by religious metaphysics.) One important aspect of historical change involves formal causation (not to be confused with formal human logic), and this is clearly influenced by final cause or teleological cause, which relates to function or purpose.

Thus, to take an historical example of abductive formal transformation, the imperatives of developing bourgeois life at what, as a result, became the close of the Middle Ages, meant that a number of regimes of human knowledge came under pressure of change to suit new purposes. One must importantly acknowledge here the alchemy whereby humans are generally not very conscious of what they are doing – and certainly not at the level of cultural behaviors. I am not, in other words, suggesting that such historical semiotic action is *conscious*. Neither am I suggesting that it is or was motivated by Freudian imperatives. So, religion did not in fact go away; it simply altered its form and also its priesthood. Modern science, as it became shaped in the course of the seventeenth century and later, took on many of the forms, which had belonged to Judeo-Christian religion (and some – its earth-nature hostile repudiation of the medieval Book of Nature as a divinely legible "school for souls," for example – which had belonged to gnostic heresies also).[39] The idea of material determinism and immutable physical laws, for example, are a carryover from the monotheistic idea of divine will.[40] Marxism is clearly a formal and materialist reworking of Christian eschatology. The roots of left-wing political thought lie in puritan pietism. Liberalism is a child of Christianity.

Natural Play and Natural Stories

The question of the evolutionary history of cultural forms, and the environmental (i.e., contextual) pressures, which bring about such formal change, is one that will require much further discussion. I want to close this essay with a focus on the ways in which creative play and stories belong both to natural and cultural growth of aesthetic forms. In this way, I intend to indicate the ways in which we can think (as others, indeed, have done before[41]) about the life and liveliness of the aesthetic object in the hands of its readers.

Terrence Deacon has written: "I believe that the experience of being alive and sentient is what it feels like to *be* evolution."[42] A biosemiotic theory of reading suggests our rich connectedness not only to the life of human representations but also to the Book of Nature itself. The experience of reading and thoughtfulness suggests a potential deepening of knowledge in both cases. But it also emphasizes the importance of all the many biosemiotic levels of conscious and nonconscious knowing and interpretation in play in the processes of meaning making. These, in turn, contribute to that greater process whereby meanings can grow (or evolve) over time from the depths of semiosis in the memories of minds and bodies, cells, selves and societies, and the habituations of tribe, place, life forms, and stories, which Australian indigenes call "the dreaming."[43]

Of course, there is no guarantee of growth; conventional responses can inhibit or even diminish development. We can, nonetheless, perhaps see in this the importance of aesthetic semiosis as a crucial part of the possibility of living knowledge in which analysis has a larger synthesis of elements – the insight of a new metaphor – as its final aim. Of course, there are certainly practices where precision and specificity are important: science, technology, and engineering are obvious examples. But too great a focus on consciousness and exactitude may inhibit the play of what Denis Noble calls nature's creative "bodges"[44] through which evolutionary development occurs. Westernized, perhaps especially Protestant, cultures tend to think of play, dream, and *bricolage* as childish, unserious, or unimportant; but all these are sources of abductive logic and thus newness in the world. Darwin's own theoretical ideas concerning the structure of evolutionary processes, for example, did not derive from scientific method but from his correspondence with his cousin Hensleigh Wedgwood, and from Darwin being struck by the idea that biological lineages might develop in the same tree- or bush-like structures as the languages and folktales that his cousin studied.[45] There are many examples of the sources of scientific development lying in such day and night dreams and in forms of serendipity.[46]

The inexactitudes and indeterminacies of aesthetic semiosis and metaphor are the contemplative and creative practices of all human expression, which underpin innovation. A feeling for the play of difference, the pleasure of contrast and similitude in color, shape, tone, and rhythm, all the gradations of repetition, and the slightly altered pattern that makes the painting and the poem a living architecture, is to be alive and sentient, is to *be* evolution. This cumulative feeling for form and its growth is precisely how A. S. Byatt, in contradistinction to the nineteenth-century scientific reductionism described in the first novella ("Morpho Eugenia") in her book, renders Tennyson's poetic gift in the second novella – "The Conjugial Angel" – in *Angels and Insects*:

> He couldn't write out an argument to save his life, he couldn't build up a theory or defend a position. He had been a dumb member of the Apostles, he had decorated the chimneypiece and made sly, quiet jokes, and recited verses

and accepted homage for his great gift, which seemed only partly to belong to himself, whoever he was. But he had thought it out, love and death, those piti-less abstractions, in that cunningly innocent form he had found for Arthur's poems, a form that seemed so straightforward, primitive songlets or chants of grief, but could *feel* its way through an argument, through shifts and shifts of ideas and feelings, stopping and starting, a rhyme closed in a rhyme, and yet moving quietly and inexorably on. In this case, from abstract Personified Love to pure animal sensuality, still sweetly singing on.[47]

The point that Byatt makes – both here and in her other work – is, similar both to Peirce and to Bateson, that scientific ways of knowing (deduction and induction let us say) add to, but do not supersede, other forms of know-ing such as Peirce's logic of abduction. The latter is based on what we call guesswork, intuition, and processes belonging to what Hoffmeyer calls "ani-mal faith."[48] In all cases it is the logic of identity and difference, howsoever consciously poetically or nonconsciously primitively registered as metaphor or a feeling for form, which is inexorably at work here.

Biosemiotician Jesper Hoffmeyer has written:

there is an aspect of *play* in the evolutionary process ... which has been more or less overshadowed ... by the Cyclopsian focus on selection ... "What is characteristic of 'play,'" writes Gregory Bateson "is that this is a name for contexts in which the constituent acts have a different sort of relevance or organization from that which they would have had in non-play." Bateson also suggests the definition of play as "the establishment and exploration of rela-tionship." ... Thus, to the extent that the living world is engaged in an open-ended and nonsettled exploration of relationships between systems ... it can truly be said that nature does, in fact, exhibit play-like behavior. It therefore will be as legitimate to talk about *natural play* as a force in the evolution of life-forms, as it is to talk about *natural selection*. Selection acts to settle things ... thereby putting an end to some element of ongoing play in the system while simultaneously providing for the beginning of whole new kinds of play.[49]

The beginning of new kinds of play, following the stabilization of semiosis by selection lies in the metaphoric capacity of selected signs to grow into what Peirce called "more developed signs." We can notice in poetic language, particularly using Roman Jakobson's schema of the role of combination and selection, or metonymy and metaphor, that a reader and a text grow mean-ings in a remarkably similar form to the way that multicellular life grows. As Terence Turner wrote of Jakobson's literary scheme in 1977, "the uni-verse of relations comprising the narrative as a whole [is transformed] into a set of dynamic principles with the power to generate and control the order manifested by that universe: in a word, to reproduce itself" in narrative time and "memory."[50] It is surely right to say, as Bateson and Hoffmeyer do, that biological as well as aesthetic life is made of stories. Just as a reader plays with resonant patterns in order to discover (and recursively grow) meanings, so evolutionary life – on the basis of a primordial difference initiated by the coming into being of a membrane – plays with patterns of similarity and difference metonymically encoded, recursively in*form*ed and shifting (as the evolutionary systems biologist Denis Noble puts it) "from one metaphor to another."[51]

The relationship between structuralism in semiotics and language and biology has long been identified.[52] As Laura Shintani has noted, Jakobson was fully aware of the correspondences between the genetic code and encoding in language. She writes that, in his review of Francois Jacob's *The Logic of Life: A History of Heredity*, "Jakobson introduces the idea that the linguistic model can be in some respects mapped on to the problem of molecular heredity ... 'Biologists and linguists as well have observed an impressive set of attributes common to life and language since their consecutive emergence ... The makeup of the two codes – the genetic one, discovered and deciphered by molecular biology in our time, and the verbal one, scrutinized by several generations of linguists – has displayed a series of noticeable analogies.'"[53]

"Selection," as Hoffmeyer writes, "acts to settle things." But combination, allowing the possibility of new metaphors emergent from the evolution of hierarchically nested meanings, provides "for the beginning of whole new kinds of play." Such abductions, as Bateson drawing on Peirce observed, are the basis of creative evolution in biology and in human culture. In introducing the idea of *natural play* and stories, alongside *natural selection*, Hoffmeyer (and biosemiotics) reminds us of the "necessary unity" between mind and nature, and of the *living* nature of the patterns that connect them.[54]

NOTES

1 Ernst Haeckel, *Generelle Morphologie der Organismen. Allgemeine Grundzüge der organischen Formen-Wissenschaft, mechanisch begründet durch die von C. Darwin reformirte Descendenz-Theorie* II (Berlin, 1866), p. 286.

2 Thomas Nagel, *Mind and Cosmos: Why the Materialist Neo-Darwinian Conception of Nature Is Almost Certainly False* (Oxford: Oxford University Press, 2012), p. 5.

3 Susan Oyama, *The Ontogeny of Information: Developmental Systems and Evolution*, 2nd edition revised and expanded, with an Introduction by R. Lewontin (Durham, NC: Duke University Press, 2000); H. C. von Baeyer, *Information: The New Language of Science* (London: Phoenix, 2004).

4 Claude Shannon, "A Mathematical Theory of Communication," *Bell System Technical Journal* 27 (July and October 1948), 379–423, 623–656.

5 Jesper Hoffmeyer, *Biosemiotics: An Examination into the Signs of Life and the Life of Signs* (Scranton and London: Scranton University Press, 2008), p. 131.

6 Evelyn Fox Keller, *The Mirage of the Space Between Nature and Nurture* (Durham and London: Duke University Press, 2012).

7 James A. Shapiro, "DNA as Poetry: Multiple Messages in a Single Sequence," posted 01/24/2012 in *Huffington Post* http://www.huffingtonpost.com/james-a-shapiro/dna-as-poetry-multiple-me_b_1229190.html.

8 Jakob von Uexküll, "A Stroll through the Worlds of Animals and Men" in *Instinctive Behavior*, tr. and ed. Claire H. Schiller (New York: International Universities Press, 1957), pp. 5–80. Also published with a new translation as *A Foray into the Worlds of Animals and Humans*, tr. Joseph D. O'Neil, Introduction by Dorian Sagan, Posthumanities 12 (Minneapolis and London: University of Minnesota Press, 2010).

9 Gregory Bateson, *Mind and Nature: A Necessary Unity* (Cresskill, NJ: Hampton, 2002).

10 Charles S. Peirce, "A Guess at the Riddle," in *The Essential Peirce: Selected Philosophical Writings*, vol. 1 (1867–1893), eds. Nathan Houser and Christian Kloesel (Bloomington and Indianapolis: Indiana University Press, 1992), pp. 245–279.

11 Gregory Bateson and Mary Catherine Bateson, *Angels Fear: Towards an Epistemology of the Sacred* (Toronto: Bantam, 1988), p. 28.

12 Hoffmeyer, *Biosemiotics*; James A. Shapiro, *Evolution: A View from the Twenty-First Century* (Upper Saddle River, NJ: FT Science, 2011).

13 Kalevi Kull, "Organism as a Self-reading Text: Anticipation and Semiosis," *International Journal of Computing Anticipatory Systems* 1 (1998), 93–104.

14 John Dupré, "The Polygenomic Organism," in *Nature after the Genome*, eds. Sarah Parry and John Dupré (Malden, MA: Wiley-Blackwell, 2010), pp. 19–31.

15 Norbert Wiener, *Cybernetics: or Control and Communication in the Animal and the Machine* (Cambridge, MA: MIT, 1965), p. 132.

16 Paul Davies & John Gribbin, *The Matter Myth: Dramatic Discoveries That Challenge Our Understanding of Physical Reality* (New York: Simon & Schuster, 1992), p. 239.

17 von Baeyer, *Information*, pp. 227–228.

18 Bateson, *Angels Fear*, p. 118.

19 Oyama, *Ontogeny*.

20 Donald Favareau, "Introduction: An Evolutionary History of Biosemiotics," *Essential Readings in Biosemiotics: Anthology and Commentary* (Dordrecht: Springer, 2010), pp. 1–77. *Springer.com*. Web. 24 Jan 2013. http://www.springer.com/lifesciences/book/978-1-4020-9649-5?detailsPage=free).

21 Hoffmeyer, *Biosemiotics*, p. 103.

22 John Dupré, "Postgenomic Darwinism," in *Darwin*, eds. William Brown and Andrew C. Fabian (Cambridge: Cambridge University Press, 2010), pp. 150–171.

23 Randal Halfmann and Susan Lindquist, "Epigenetics in the Extreme: Prions and the Inheritance of Environmentally Acquired Traits," *Science* 330 (2010), 629–632.

24 Howard H. Pattee, "The Physics and Metaphysics of Biosemiotics," *Journal of Biosemiotics* 1 (2005), 281–301.

25 Jesper Hoffmeyer, "The Natural History of Intentionality," in *The Symbolic Species Evolved*, eds. T. Schilhab, F. Stjernfelt, and T. Deacon (Dordrecht: Springer, 2012), pp. 97–116.

26 Thomas A. Sebeok, "Nonverbal Communication," in *Global Semiotics* (Bloomington & Indianapolis: Indiana University Press, 2001), pp. 105–114.

27 Kalevi Kull, "On Semiosis, Umwelt, and Semiosphere," *Semiotica* 120 (1998), 299–310.

28 Max Black, *Models and Metaphor* (Ithaca, NY: Cornell University Press, 1972).

29 Paul Ricoeur, *The Rule of Metaphor: The Creation of Meaning in Language*, tr. R. Czerny with K. McLaughlin and J. Costello (London: Routledge, 2003), p. 234.

30 Uexküll, "Stroll."

31 Charles S. Peirce, "A Letter to Lady Welby." See letter of 23 December 1908 in "Excerpts from Letters to Lady Welby," in *The Essential Peirce: Selected Philosophical Writings*, vol. 2 (1893–1913), ed. the Peirce Edition Project (Bloomington & Indianapolis: Indiana University Press, 1998), p. 478.

32 Günther Witzany & František Baluška, "Life's Code Script Does Not Code Itself," *Science and Society EMBO Reports* 13 (13 November 2012), 1054–1056, http://www.nature.com/embor/journal/v13/n12/full/embor2012166a.html; Anthony J. Trewavas and František Baluška, "The ubiquity of consciousness, cognition and intelligence in life," *Outlook EMBO Reports* 12 (18 November 2011), 1221–1225, http://www.nature.com/embor/journal/v12/n12/full/embor2011218a.html.

33 Gregory Bateson, "Form, Substance and Difference" [1970], in Bateson, *Steps to an Ecology of Mind*, Foreword by M. C. Bateson (Chicago and London: University of Chicago Press, 2000), pp. 454–471.

34 Hoffmeyer, Chapter 2: "Surfaces within Surfaces," *Biosemiotics*, pp. 17–38.

35 Gregory Bateson, *Mind and Nature: A Necessary Unity* (Cresskill, NJ: Hampton, 2002).

36 Pattee, "Physics and Metaphysics."

37 Thomas A. Sebeok, "Biosemiotics," in *The Routledge Companion to Semiotics and Linguistics*, ed. Paul Cobley (London: Routledge, 2001), p. 164.

38 Jean-Christophe Bailly, *The Animal Side*, tr. C. Porter (New York: Fordham University Press, 2011).

39 Peter Harrison, *The Bible, Protestantism and the Rise of Natural Science* (Cambridge, UK: Cambridge University Press, 1998), p. 17; Peter Harrison, *The Fall of Man and the Foundations of Science* (Cambridge: Cambridge University Press, 2007), p. 15.

40 Paul C. Davies, "From It to Bit," in *Information and the Nature of Reality: From Physics to Metaphysics*, eds. Niels Henrik Gregersen and Paul C. Davies (Cambridge: Cambridge University Press, 2010), pp. 65–91.

41 Wendy Wheeler, "Thought without Concepts in *Angels and Insects*: A. S. Byatt as Crypto-biosemiotician," in *The Semiotics of Animal Representations*, eds. Morten Tønnessen and Kadri Tüür (Amsterdam: Rodopi, 2013), pp. 297–318.

42 Terrence Deacon, "How I Gave up the Ghost and Learned to Love Evolution," *When Worlds Converge: What Science and Religion Tell Us about the Story of the Universe and Our Place in It*, eds. Clifford N. Matthews, Mary Evelyn Tucker, and Philip J. Hefner (Chicago: Open Court, 2002), p. 153.

43 Deborah Bird Rose, *Wild Dog Dreaming: Love and Extinction* (Charlottesville and London: University of Virginia Press), 2011.

44 Noble, *Music*, p. 104.
45 Joan Richardson, *A Natural History of Pragmatism: The Fact of Feeling from Jonathan Edwards to Gertrude Stein* (New York: Cambridge University Press, 2007), pp. 92–93.
46 Margaret Boden, *The Creative Mind: Myths and Mechanisms* (London: Weidenfeld & Nicolson, 1990).
47 A. S. Byatt, *Angels and Insects* (London: Vintage, 1993), p. 263.
48 Hoffmeyer, "Natural History of Intentionality," p. 100.
49 Hoffmeyer, *Biosemiotics*, pp. 196–197.
50 Terence S. Turner, "Narrative Structure and Mythopoesis: A Critique and Reformulation of Structuralist Concepts of Myth, Narrative and Poetics," *Arethusa* 10 (1977), 141–142.
51 Denis Noble, *The Music of Life: Biology beyond the Genome* (Oxford: Oxford University Press, 2006), p. 104.
52 Claus Emmeche and Kalevi Kull, eds., *Towards a Semiotic Biology: Life is the Action of Signs* (London: Imperial College Press, 2011).
53 Laura Shintani, "Roman Jakobson and Biology: 'A System of Systems,'" *Semiotica* 127 (1999), 103–114.
54 Bateson, *Mind and Nature*.

9

JANET FISKIO

Sauntering Across the Border: Thoreau, Nabhan, and Food Politics

Politics

While interdisciplinarity is often understood, following C. P. Snow, as a relation between the "two cultures" of the humanities and the natural sciences, environmental justice reveals that politics is a vital dimension of interdisciplinary thinking for ecocriticism.[1] Interdisciplinary environmental work is frequently conceptualized through the metaphor of the "toolbox," in which all disciplines are expected to contribute harmoniously to solving a common problem that has been previously defined within the framework of Western science.[2] Henry David Thoreau's motif of sauntering offers an alternative model for interdisciplinarity that crosses the lines of literature, science, and politics. In contrast to the toolbox metaphor, sauntering is both playful and provocative, drawing attention to the way that interdisciplinary work involves trespassing material boundaries as well as disciplinary borders. Reflecting on Thoreau's legacy, Rebecca Solnit writes: "'if fields of expertise can be imagined as real fields, fenced off and carefully tilled, then the history of walking is a path that trespasses through dozens of fields.' So are most unfenced lines of inquiry. I learned two kinds of trespassing at the test site, geographical and intellectual."[3] In the context of civil disobedience at the Nevada Test Site, Solnit discovered that the "act of walking through a desert and across a cattle guard into the forbidden zone could articulate political meaning."[4] Similarly, in Thoreau's late natural history essays, sauntering has both theoretical and political meanings. The rewards of sauntering are sweet: wild apples, huckleberries, and intellectual freedom.

Ethnobiologist and food justice activist Gary Paul Nabhan takes up sauntering as a mode of interdisciplinary exploration in the binational terrain of the Sonoran Desert. In this landscape, the materiality of the border disrupts both the human and ecological communities to which he belongs. Nabhan extends Thoreau's interdisciplinary work by theorizing border-crossing, both literal and figurative, as essential to environmental justice and further enriches Thoreau's imagination of sauntering by making community integral to this practice. Community does not, however, signify harmony in Nabhan's work. Instead, his dialogical texts open up space for dissonance and mutual interrogation. Nabhan's work, like Thoreau's, disrupts the boundaries between literature and science, science and politics, academics and activism. Sauntering offers contemporary ecocritics a model for interdisciplinary work that engages critical issues, refusing the rigid separation of disciplines or the cloistering of academic reflection from the work of environmental politics.

In the last decade of his life Thoreau was engaged in a self-consciously interdisciplinary project, tracing a dynamic relationship that did not conform either to Emersonian idealism or to the increasingly positivist and professionalized science of his day.[5] Thoreau himself struggled with the demands of interdisciplinary engagement, seeking to integrate a methodology of close observation with philosophical reflection on the meaning of nature.[6] His scholarly reception shows that critics have had difficulties engaging with the demands of interdisciplinarity. As Nabhan observes in his foreword to *Faith in a Seed*, this scholarly difficulty in appreciating Thoreau's later work reflects the disciplinary entrenchments of both literary and scientific critics.[7] Laura Dassow Walls describes this misreading as the process of "[d]isciplining Thoreau" by simplifying his work into a coherent object of knowledge for literary study, while Solnit warns that "[t]his compartmentalizing of Thoreau is a small portion of a larger partition in American thought, another fence built in the belief that places in the imagination can also be contained."[8]

Thoreau's interdisciplinary engagement spans not only literature and science but also politics, although the question of how to understand the relationship between Thoreau's political and environmental commitments is an ongoing area of discussion.[9] Both Jane Bennett and Shannon Mariotti highlight Thoreau's withdrawals from traditional political forums. While Bennett argues that Thoreau engages in public life "only sporadically and negatively," however, Mariotti argues that scholars have used too narrow a definition of politics; she instead reads Thoreau's practices of withdrawal as a response to the rapid industrialization of Concord.[10] In the political and economic context of modernization, Mariotti argues, Thoreau's walking and huckleberrying are not hermetic retreats, but instead alternate modes of democratic practice that enable resistance to convention, including mainstream political institutions.[11] Similarly, Lance Newman argues that in the later natural history work, especially *Wild Fruits*, Thoreau "connected issues of environmental and social justice into a synthetic critique of the priorities of capitalism."[12] This political thread in Thoreau's work serves as a precursor for contemporary thinkers, such as Nabhan, who disrupt the separation of ecocentric ethics from social justice concerns in a genuine synthesis of environmental justice. During the 1850s, David Robinson observes, "Thoreau worked hard to maintain a cohesive tie between his commitment to the study of nature and his moral obligation as an opponent of slavery."[13] Similarly, Solnit locates Thoreau's walking, huckleberrying, and tax resistance in the context of U.S. slavery and imperialism, observing that "The American landscape in his time was crossed by many invisible lines: those that separated slave and free states; those that demarcated the rapidly shrinking Indian territory and the new reservations; those that laid out the new national borders drawn up at the conclusion of the war on Mexico."[14] Noting that Thoreau recounts leaving jail to lead a huckleberry party in both "Resistance" and *Walden*, Solnit describes his "unresisting walk to jail" as intimately connected to his walks in nature.[15] Consequently, Thoreau's sauntering and savoring of wild foods holds political significance because it is practiced as a form of resistance to the structures of capitalism and private property.[16] This same political resistance is evident in the work of contemporary food justice activists like Nabhan who glean and gather in marginal spaces, and who maintain heirloom species in opposition to industrial agriculture's monocultures.

Appetite and Imagination

In his natural history essays, Thoreau portrays himself as a border figure, an escaped and naturalized member of the community who trespasses both disciplinary and property boundaries.[17] This refusal to adhere to boundaries established by either professional expectations or polite society is thematized through Thoreau's critique of enclosure.[18] His term for this transgression is "sauntering," articulated in the essay "Walking."[19] Sauntering is a form of pilgrimage without a destination, a practice that resists being instrumentalized or domesticated. Thoreau's holy land is found in the Concord woods and, it seems, is often on the property of his neighbors: "The walker in the familiar fields which stretch around my native town sometimes finds himself in another land than is described in their owners' deeds ... These farms which I have myself surveyed, these bounds which I have set up, appear dimly still as through a mist."[20] When sauntering, the boundaries Thoreau has surveyed fade. Sauntering thus serves as a figure for "extravagance," a travel exceeding predictable limits – geographically, politically, and intellectually.[21]

Sauntering offers Thoreau visions that sustain him in the midst of the betrayals of his nation, such as the "shining family" he sees while walking on

Spaulding's Farm.[22] He imagines a blessed man who lives where "no fugitive slave laws are passed."[23] In the context of this reference to the Fugitive Slave Act, Thoreau's declarations of allegiance to the order of Walkers outside of "Church and State and People" and to "the Wild," and his proposal for a "Society for the Diffusion of Useful Ignorance," recall his refusal of allegiance to the state in "Resistance to Civil Government."[24] Taken together, these are declarations of religious, political, and disciplinary apostasy, although in a more playful register than "Resistance." This excursion essay saunters through swamps, bogs down in the territory of political betrayal, and regains its momentum west at the end with the hope that the setting sun will "light up our whole lives with a great awakening."[25] In warning of the "evil days" to come, when "walking over the surface of God's earth shall be construed to mean trespassing on some gentleman's grounds," Thoreau's sauntering figures his advocacy of transgression of both literal boundaries and unjust laws that constrain freedom.[26]

The figure of the saunterer reappears in the later natural history essays, reflecting both the actual process of Thoreau's walking and writing, and the multiple borders they trespass.[27] In "The Succession of Forest Trees," presented at the Middlesex Agricultural Society in 1860, the narrative voice is gently provocative.[28] Thoreau observes the eccentrics who attend the cattle show and notes that many of his neighbors probably include him in that grouping.[29] But this acknowledgement of his misfit status is followed by a reminder of his material trespass: "taking a surveyor's and a naturalist's liberty, I have been in the habit of going across your lots much oftener than is usual, as many of you, perhaps to your sorrow, are aware."[30] Thoreau publicly reminds the property owners of his sauntering across their lands and further asserts his superior knowledge of their domains: "I have several times shown the proprietor the shortest way out of his wood-lot."[31] The owners are strangers to their own borderlands, while Thoreau is the border dweller.

While these opening paragraphs signal the boundaries, both disciplinary and material, that Thoreau insists on crossing, he then states that he will consider "a purely scientific subject."[32] The rhetorical presentation of the subject is infused with the language of scientific demonstration and recounts the practices of repeated observation, objective measurement, and data collection in his efforts to discern the process of succession.[33] As Walls has observed, however, Thoreau's writing in this essay is designed to destabilize accepted modes of scientific thought and writing.[34] His scientific observations both literally and figuratively lead him into the forest and into encounters with squirrels, the overlooked facilitators of forest succession. In this essay Thoreau deviates from the program of objective science, mixing the language of scientific hypothesis and theory testing with awareness of his own emplacement, thus inverting the relationship of observer to object: "One of the principal agents in this planting, the red squirrels, were all the while curiously inspecting me, while I was inspecting their plantation."[35] This deviation from the standard scientific program, like traipsing without permission across his neighbor's fields, is a mode of sauntering, a way of declaring allegiance to his own epistemological project.

Thoreau further develops the motif of sauntering in the essay "Wild Apples," but with a new focus on the lure of these wild fruits. "Wild Apples" links to themes developed in "Walking" with a level of detail and delight that anticipates current rediscoveries of heirloom species as well as the resistance to homogenized production that characterizes the local foods movement.[36] The essay not only catalogs Thoreau's naturalist knowledge of wild apples, including their seed dispersal, flowering and fruiting seasons, and growth habits, but also, as William Rossi observes, "parodies scientific attempts to capture its place-specific varieties in binomial categories."[37] Walls calls the essay a "spiritual autobiography," and Thoreau's identification with the escapees from cultivated fields is clear: "Nevertheless, *our* wild apple is wild only like myself, perchance, who belong not to the aboriginal race here, but have strayed into the woods from the cultivated stock."[38]

Thoreau claims wild apples as the particular domain of the walker, invoking customary rights to glean those apples the farmer leaves on the tree.[39] These seeds "plant themselves" and are dispersed by animal agents but mostly go unnoticed by their owners: "The farmer thinks that he has better in his barrels, but he is mistaken, unless he has a walker's appetite and imagination, neither of which he can have."[40] The escape from domestication, the market, and privatization is essential to the character of wild apples: "The Saunterer's Apple not even the saunterer can eat in the house."[41] The practice of walking is essential to the taste of the apple, conditioning the walker's senses to welcome its flavors with "*papillae* firm and erect on the tongue and palate, not easily flattened and tamed."[42] A walker and gleaner, from sauntering and savoring, has an undomesticated tongue. This is evident as well in the names Thoreau assigns to these apples, an extravagant and playful list with his own Latinate genus and species: "the Apple that grows in an old Cellar-Hole (*Malus cellaris*)"; "the Saunterer's Apple, – you must lose yourself before you can find the way to that."[43] The vernacular names and mock-nomenclature suggest the ways these wild fruits exceed the language of science and agronomy, just as the knowledge of them exceeds scientific positivism.

"Wild Apples" is bookended with laments that articulate the political resistance of sauntering. From the beginning, Thoreau notes that apples possess "a certain volatile and ethereal quality which represents their highest value, and which cannot be vulgarized, or bought and sold."[44] This resistance to commodification cannot preserve the wild apple, however, which is under threat from new cultivated varieties that are fenced in, a further form of domestication of both the fruit and the walker. This critique of privatization is even more explicit in the essay "Huckleberries," where it is linked to the practice of walking through enclosure of public lands.[45] "Huckleberries" sets up a contrast not between wild/domesticated or gleaned/bought, but between free/enslaved.[46] Thoreau compares gathering huckleberries, which generates "a sense of freedom" and "an expansion of all my being," with the cultivation of tobacco, which requires "slavery and a thousand other curses."[47] Thoreau links the privatization of huckleberry fields with the wider political and economic movement of enclosure of the commons, including the tradition of right of way for walkers: "the public retain only a small yard or common in the middle of the village ... and the right of way, by sufferance, by a particular narrow route, which is annually becoming narrower."[48] The saunterer can temporarily escape the domain of private property in the midst of a world whose freedoms are being narrowed by commodification, but Thoreau argues for not only individual but also collective action to protect natural areas as public spaces.[49]

Sauntering Across the Border

The motif of sauntering in Thoreau's late natural history essays figures theoretical and material transgression of borders as a model for interdisciplinary thinking and political engagement. In the course of his career as a scientist and writer, Gary Paul Nabhan has renewed the practice of sauntering in the Sonoran borderlands and extended Thoreau's project through his long-term work with communities to create food justice. Nabhan explicitly acknowledges Thoreau's influence on his academic trajectory in his foreword to *Faith in Seed*:

> At a time in my youth when I wanted to be both a poet and a biologist, those who were close to me – academic advisors, friends, parents – told me that I must choose between these two incompatible pursuits. Faced with this career choice between the arts and the sciences, my response was pure flight behavior: to withdraw from others, to walk for hours on end, and to read Thoreau ... Somehow, in some way, Thoreau altered my life then, for my course as field biologist *and* writer finally emerged out of those months of doubt and difficulty.[50]

Following a path first traced by Thoreau, Nabhan negotiates the borders of disciplines and genres while belonging to multiple communities. In fidelity to the Sonoran borderlands and to indigenous sovereignty, Nabhan crosses geographic, cultural, and political borders between Comcáac and O'odham communities, between Mexico and the United States; between indigenous and Western sciences; between the languages of Cmique Iitom, O'odham, Spanish, English, and scientific Latin.[51] Nabhan's sauntering takes place both on foot and in beat-up pickup trucks, negotiating the disciplinary forces of the border patrol as well as academic discourse. Sauntering here is an act of resistance against the nationalism and economic and industrial colonialism that undermine ecological and cultural survival, taking up Thoreau's call for civil disobedience to unjust laws in the context of environmental concerns. Further, Nabhan enriches the concept of sauntering by making community the locus of his scientific, literary, and political work, enacting the "explicitly communal ethos" of Thoreau's later writings.[52]

Community is essential to Nabhan's dialogical science: a knowledge that is formed through a process of collective epistemology. His texts are multivocal and sometimes cacophonous, rather than holding to the single voice of the naturalist soliloquy.[53] This dialogical form makes an ethical intervention, seeking to communicate a plurality of indigenous knowledges and voices, as well as the collective process that produces this knowledge. For example, the text *Singing the Turtles to Sea* was "Undertaken in Collaboration with the Seri Tribal Governors and the Traditional Council of Elders," including more than a hundred Comcáac contributors.[54] *Turtles* compiles ethnographic narratives, dialogue, history, and scientific theories alongside photographs, carvings, charts, maps, and archival sources. The second part of the text is a status report in a more conventional ethnobiological mode. Nabhan notes, however, that while Comcáac knowledge is presented in the second section "with Western scientific systematics[,] [n]either of these frameworks is assumed to be more or less 'correct' than the other."[55] Nabhan uses a series of voices to mediate these different forms of knowledge. The narrators of Nabhan's ethnographic texts are characters who share autobiographical details with the author. In *Turtles*, this relationship between the author and narrator is particularly complex, since the character of the ethnographer (called "Hant Coáaxoj," or Horned Lizard, by other characters) is only one of the voices the author utilizes; there is also a detached and scientific voice that orchestrates the text and speaks in a more omniscient mode.

The epistemological and ethical difficulties posed by crossing the border of Western science are revealed in the scene that begins the first chapter. The narrator, Hant Coáaxoj, is venturing onto complicated ground – as indicated by the performance of a traditional ceremony near "the village's largest satellite dish" – a terrain of epistemological and ethical uncertainty.[56] During the fiesta he is stalked by the celebrant's "young, slightly inebriated" cousin who "would approach us and very seriously request that we sing an American song or recite our life histories into his tape recorder, so that he could 'save' this event for posterity."[57] This mimicry of the narrator's ethnobiological pursuit frames the dilemma faced by Hant Coáaxoj when he discovers that the Comcáac are eating Green Sea Turtle, an endangered species, as part of the ceremony. Seeking confirmation, the narrator inquires what kind of turtle they are eating, and Ernesto Molina replies "Cooyam," which, the narrator explains, "refer[s] to the younger migratory Green Sea Turtles that arrive from the south in the spring earlier than the rest."[58] This translation displays the wealth of knowledge contained in a single word.

Although at first "incredulous," the narrator recognizes that this ceremony is a form of "communion": "It dawned on me that we were participating in a sacrament … By blessing this young woman's rite of passage with the meat and blood of *moosni cooyam*, they were linking her life to the very creature that swims through their culture's stories, songs, dreams, and diet."[59] The figure of blood runs through this passage and the opening chapter, linking the menarche celebration and the sea turtle's blood through the language of sacrament. Hant Coáaxoj recalls:

> But as I looked up again into the face of the sea turtle shining in the firelight, another wave of emotion washed over me. Because I once shared quarters with a marine biologist who worked tirelessly to protect the nesting beaches of sea turtles, I had for twenty years boycotted any restaurants that featured sea turtle meat, eggs, or soup.
>
> Caught up in the moment, perhaps flattered by the invitation to share sea turtle with Seri friends, had I suffered some ethical lapse?[60]

This vignette poses what seems to be a conflict between the narrator's simultaneous commitments to conservation biology and to the Comcáac community, but the text undermines this false opposition. Relationships are the locus of meaning in this situation, from the young girl's relationship with her community, to the narrator's relationship with marine biologists, Comcáac ecologists, and the turtle who has a face, to the multitude of relationships between humans and reptiles depicted in the text. Nabhan's particular contribution is through the form of this text, which mediates between the Western science of conservation biology and the indigenous science of the Comcáac.

Unresolved questions end the section, as the young cousin who has been weaving through the celebration weaves his way back into the narrative:

> The young Seri anthropologist reappeared with his tape recorder, which no longer held either tape or batteries. Nevertheless, he wanted to talk with me. He held the recorder up in front of my mouth.
>
> "Well," he began, "tell me about your culture. What are your beliefs?"[61]

Because of first-person narrative, we know that this is precisely the question that Hant Coáaxoj is asking himself, as he balances between his commitments to conservation biology and his fidelity to the episteme of the Comcáac community. We also know that he has not found an answer but feels blessed by the challenge.[62] The Comcáac youth turns the tables on the ethnobiological expert, calling for a mutual interrogation, which requires moving beyond the strict form of the scientific article to produce a text that is adequate to expressing the knowledge held by the Comcáac community. The text does not merely document an experience or experiment; it is not a representation of interactions but a participation in an epistemological project, with its concomitant ethical obligations to the nonhuman world and to Nabhan's Comcáac collaborators.

In the introduction that explicates the theoretical orientation of the text, Nabhan articulates the inclusion of the voices of Comcáac collaborators as an ethical mandate:

> Far too often in the past, ethnobiological texts paraphrased, summarized, or homogenized such discussions to the point that the heterogeneity of native speakers' voices could barely be heard … Perhaps we need to foster a brand of ethnobiology that features the expressive individuals who interpret their culture's traditions in idiosyncratic and innovative ways, rather than continuing to stereotype every soul in a community as if they uniformly adhere to the same cultural norms.[63]

The effort to communicate the diversity of Comcáac knowledge and voices is evident in the structure of the chapters and visual appearance of the page. In part 1 of *Turtles*, each chapter begins with quotations from indigenous writers, Western scientists, and philosophers of science. These quotations are followed by a vignette, set off in a distinctive font, that sketches the paradoxes and problems of the chapter. The voice of the vignette's narrator is gregarious, curious, and often the source of humor through mistakes and mishaps. After the opening scenes of each chapter, the self-effacing character of Hant Coáaxoj retreats from the center of attention. Following a break signified by white space, the narrative voice shifts. This new narrative voice (rendered in a more standard font) speaks less often in the first person and uses a more detached perspective and tone, orchestrating Comcáac voices in a discussion of their knowledge of the natural world. This dialogical textual representation is linked to the ethics of practicing collaborative research with indigenous communities. *Turtles* explicitly engages the question of how the benefits of research should accrue to native communities. The second part of the text describes the work of the Comcáac as conservationists and managers and turns to the question of the conservation of Comcáac knowledge. These two elements are tied together in the "'*para-*

ecólogo'" certification program developed by tribal elders and Western scientists, which combines indigenous and Western scientific methods and knowledges to monitor and restore endemic and endangered species.[64] By valuing indigenous knowledge and directing support to the Comcáac community, rather than to universities and outside institutions, this knowledge is sustained through practice.[65] Further, the community retains control over both its knowledge and land.

Nabhan's writings revel in the pleasures that have lured him away from standard scientific investigations. In the essay "Missing the Boat," Nabhan explains how he first wandered from the conventional path of biology and into the rainforest where cultures intertwine with ecological systems. As a college student, Nabhan was scheduled to visit the Galápagos Islands, where he was to be initiated into the realm of evolutionary biology. But, Nabhan writes:

> Instead of spending the summer engaged with the beak of a finch or the cactus-eating habits of the giant tortoises in Darwin's island laboratories, I fell under the spell of a dazzling diversity of tropical South American fruits. I succumbed to the guavas, papayas, bananas, and custard apples cultivated by indigenous farming communities – and to the indigenous folk themselves. Lured by their handiwork, I became as consumed by the "cultural selection" of fruits and seeds as Darwin's disciples are by the "natural selection" of bones and beaks.[66]

Thus begins the story of Nabhan's divergence from the expected trajectory, a theme that runs throughout his work as well as his theories of evolution, pollination, and island biogeography.

Like Thoreau's wild apple gleaner, Nabhan follows his tongue into the borderlands. In *Desert Terroir*, he pursues a trail of aromatic oils from desert herbs.[67] Nabhan identifies a moment he calls "Seek-No-Further" (the vernacular name of a desert apple) when he decided to live his life in the Sonora:

> The Chihuahua catfish had a brief flash of *chile pequin* hellfire seared into it, but then the aromatic oils of the oregano and the crunchiness of the cornmeal took over the dance upon our palates. As I swallowed the last of the catfish, I was overwhelmed by the sense of pleasure rising within me.
> "Seek no further!" I cried out, my *grito* echoing off the limestone walls of Boquillas canyon. "Heaven on earth is here, *mis hijitos*. I shall seek no other!"
> It was the first truly local feast of my entire life.[68]

In this essay, Nabhan's sauntering takes the form of floating through Big Bend on a rafting expedition and encountering local food traditions. The pleasures of this local feast, however, are tempered by Nabhan's awareness of the global forces that impact these households, including the industrial food economy that separates the rafters from this particular place and impoverishes the local community.[69] Nabhan's commitment to local foods began when he met these families who lived along the Rio Grande: "My time among them humbled me, for it suggested that I should never again ignore or waste the harvestable foods within reach of where I stood."[70] In recent years the local economy of this border region has been decimated by the new Homeland Security regime, which prevents rafters from visiting Mexican villages and obstructs "informal trade across the border."[71] Nabhan's concept of food justice on the border takes into account the wide context of environmental and economic justice. Food justice is generally understood as access for all communities to locally grown "fresh, nutritious, affordable, culturally-appropriate" food with attention both to the rights of workers throughout the food system and to ecological impacts of production.[72] Nabhan's work in the Sonora, particularly through his collaborations with indigenous farmers, broadens the concept of food justice to include the restoration and support of native plants and cultural food traditions in a vision of a just and sustainable food system.[73] A comprehensive understanding of food justice requires an analysis of the flows of food, labor, and capital across the border.[74] From the beginning, Nabhan's commitment to local foods has been integrated with a vision of transnational environmental justice, grounded in relationships with those who live on both sides of the border.

Nabhan's sauntering and savoring of local foods inevitably brings him up against the US/Mexico border. While searching for *a'ud nonhakam* (a rare agave), Nabhan is abducted at gunpoint by US border agents who "had [him] up against the hood, frisking the living daylights out of [him]" before releasing him with a warning about drug traffickers.[75] At another point on the Mexican side of the border, he is pulled over – with his children in the pickup – after going into the borderlands to see the night-blooming cereus.[76] These encounters gesture not only to the pervasive regime that fragments the lives of border dwellers, both human and nonhuman, but also to the way that scientific research in the Sonora takes place in a landscape crossed by lines of political power that have material effects. Pursuing ethnobotanical knowledge inevitably requires Nabhan to cross the border, since it artificially imposes a barrier on Sonoran ecological and indigenous communities. For example, the fence undermines Tohono O'odham farming practices, which "unraveled when the intrusion of the border cut their homeland in two."[77] The border fence is not only destructive to "humans and other migratory animals" but also to ancient cactus forests.[78] The three strands of barbed wire do not seem like much of a physical obstacle, but their effect is powerful: "This ecological edge was not identical to the line of the fence but reverberated around it ... I was beginning to sense the fluidity of the borderlands – how phenomena on one side of the fence affected those on the other."[79]

In the context of the border regime, sauntering is an act of pilgrimage – or, invoking Nabhan's identity as an Arab-American, a *hadj* – that requires trespass.[80] Nabhan straddles the borders of multiple communities, including countries, cultures, and disciplines. These pilgrimages are not solitary vision quests, but are always sustained by friendships and chance encounters with angels, and often enacted in community.[81] The final chapter of *Coming Home to Eat* tells the story of a pilgrimage from the Gulf of California to Arizona that he walks with "O'odham, Seri, Yaqui, Hopi, Latino, and Anglo pilgrims."[82] This desert walk both witnesses to the impact of Western colonization on indigenous health and calls for a restoration of native foods and support of food traditions. Nabhan recalls:

> More than any other moment, I remember the instant we crossed the border, that 150-year-old line that has worked to divide our food shed in two, separating river from ocean, deep-sea fisherman from hinterland forager, Mexican from American, Seri from O'odham, me from you ... the very act of simply walking was superseded by the notion that we would be walking across, and that somehow made our journey more political than it had seemed before.[83]

As Nabhan and the other pilgrims reach the border, he notices "a half dozen Mexican hikers, intending to cross the border at the exact same time that we did, when the customs officials and border patrol were most distracted."[84] These travelers are a reminder of the flow of labor that crosses the border, especially for food production; Robert Gottlieb and Anupama Joshi estimate that nearly one million of the workers in the industrial food complex are undocumented.[85] The pilgrims stop at the border to stomp flat store-bought white bread, the symbol of colonization, industrial food production, and broken communities.[86] And we as readers hope that the hikers, simultaneously and silently, have made it safely across.

In a world enframed by neoliberal economic policies, Thoreau's critique of the relentless commodification of every aspect of life is all the more needed. Recent summers have witnessed protestors enacting Thoreau's principles of civil disobedience in defense of the Alberta Tar Sands, North American indigenous nations, Ohio backyards, and coal communities in West Virginia. As the border fence cuts across ancient cactus forests, indigenous communities, and immigrant families, Nabhan's vision of food justice in the Sonora confronts the pervasive presence of the border regime and at the same time invites the reader to a feast. Imagining environmental justice in the twenty-first century requires all the capacities of the humanities and the sciences, academics and activism. Thoreau and Nabhan offer a model for this kind of reimagination of the relationship between literature, science, and politics; between human and nonhuman communities; across borders and contrary to static allegiance to discipline and nation: Saunter. Savor. *Trespass.*

ACKNOWLEDGMENTS

I am grateful for support from the B. Wade and Jane B. White Fellowship for 2012–13 from Oberlin College, which funded my research leave while writing this essay. I would like to thank Lawrence Buell, Rochelle Johnson, T. S. McMillin, Gary Paul Nabhan, and Ted Toadvine for helpful comments on drafts of this essay; Rochelle Johnson and Harlan Wilson for direction through the secondary literature; and Lawrence Buell, Gary Paul Nabhan, and William Rossi for guidance and encouragement on this project.

NOTES

1 C. P. Snow, *The Two Cultures* (New York: Cambridge University Press, 1993).
2 John Foster, "What Price Interdisciplinarity? Crossing the Curriculum in Environmental Higher Education," *Journal of Geography in Higher Education* 23:3 (1999), 359–360.
3 Rebecca Solnit, *Storming the Gates of Paradise: Landscapes for Politics* (Berkeley: University of California Press, 2007), p. 2.
4 Rebecca Solnit, *Wanderlust: A History of Walking* (New York: Viking, 2000), p. 8.
5 I am particularly indebted to Laura Dassow Walls, *Seeing New Worlds: Henry David Thoreau and Nineteenth-Century Natural Science* (Madison: The University of Wisconsin Press, 1995); David M. Robinson, *Natural Life: Thoreau's Worldly Transcendentalism* (Ithaca, NY: Cornell University Press, 2004); and Lance Newman, *Our Common Dwelling: Henry Thoreau, Transcendentalism, and the Class Politics of Nature* (New York: Palgrave, 2005), as well as to Rochelle Johnson and William Rossi for orientation to this discussion.
6 Walls, *Seeing New Worlds*, pp. 4, 150; Newman, *Common Dwelling*, p. 163.
7 Gary Paul Nabhan, "Learning the Language of Fields and Forests," in Henry D. Thoreau, *Faith in a Seed: The Dispersion of Seeds and Other Late Natural History Writings*, Bradley P. Dean (ed.) (Washington, DC: Island Press, 1993), pp. xiii–xiv.
8 Walls, *Seeing New Worlds*, pp. 246–252; Solnit, *Storming*, p. 5.
9 My thanks to Lawrence Buell and Rochelle Johnson for calling my attention to this debate.
10 Jane Bennett, *Thoreau's Nature: Ethics, Politics, and the Wild* (Thousand Oaks, CA: Sage, 1994), p. 42; Shannon Mariotti, *Thoreau's Democratic Withdrawal: Alienation, Participation, and Modernity* (Madison: University of Wisconsin

Press, 2010), p. xvi. For Mariotti's discussion of Thoreau's response to modernization, see especially the chapter "Man as Machine," pp. 85–116.

11 Mariotti, *Thoreau's Democratic Withdrawal*, pp. 6, 98–99; for a more complete discussion, see the chapter "Huckleberrying toward Democracy: Thoreau's Practices of Withdrawal," pp. 117–144.

12 Newman, *Common Dwelling*, p. 162.

13 Robinson, *Natural Life*, p. 6.

14 Solnit, *Storming*, p. 7.

15 Solnit, *Storming*, p. 5; see also *Wanderlust*, p. 8.

16 See Newman, *Common Dwelling*, particularly Chapter 15, for an extended discussion of Thoreau's critique of capitalism, especially as it relates to wild fruits.

17 My thanks to Rochelle Johnson for highlighting this evocative phrase.

18 Newman, *Common Dwelling*, p. 176.

19 Thoreau, *Wild Apples*, p. 59.

20 Thoreau, *Wild Apples*, p. 88.

21 William Rossi, Introduction, in Henry D. Thoreau, *Wild Apples and Other Natural History Essays*, William Rossi (ed.) (Athens: University of Georgia Press, 2002), p. xviii; see also Walls, *Seeing New Worlds*, p. 233.

22 Thoreau, *Wild Apples*, p. 88.

23 Thoreau, *Wild Apples*, p. 91.

24 Thoreau, *Wild Apples*, pp. 60, 75, 85; Henry D. Thoreau, "Resistance to Civil Government," *Reform Papers*, Wendell Glick (ed.) (Princeton, NJ: Princeton University Press, 1973), pp. 79, 84.

25 Thoreau, *Wild Apples*, p. 92.

26 Thoreau, *Wild Apples*, p. 68.

27 William Rossi, "The Journal, Self-culture, and the Genesis of 'Walking,'" *The Thoreau Quarterly: A Journal of Literary and Philosophical Studies* 16 (1984), 140–142.

28 Michael Benjamin Berger, *Thoreau's Late Career and The Dispersion of Seeds: The Saunterer's Synoptic Vision* (Rochester, NY: Camden House, 2000), p. 19, note 13.

29 Thoreau, *Wild Apples*, pp. 93–94.

30 Ibid., p. 94.

31 Ibid., p. 94.

32 Ibid., p. 94.

33 Ibid., pp. 99, 102.

34 Walls, *Seeing New Worlds*, p. 202.

35 Thoreau, *Wild Apples*, p 99. For a discussion of Thoreau's deviation from the positivistic science of his time and the reformulation of the relationship between subject and object in his epistemology, see Alfred I. Tauber, *Henry David Thoreau and the Moral Agency of Knowing* (Berkeley: University of California Press, 2001), pp. 20, 141–142; see also Berger, *Thoreau's Late Career*, and Walls, *Seeing New Worlds*.

36 See, for example, Gary Paul Nabhan (ed.), *Forgotten Fruits Manual and Manifesto: Apples* (Brooklyn, NY: Renewing America's Food Traditions Alliance, 2010).

37 Rossi, "Introduction," p. xxii.

38 Walls, *Seeing New Worlds*, p. 218; Thoreau, *Wild Apples*, p. 149.

39 Thoreau, *Wild Apples*, p. 155.
40 Ibid., pp. 150, 152, 154–155.
41 Ibid., pp. 157.
42 Ibid., p. 158.
43 Ibid., pp. 160–161.
44 Ibid., p. 144.
45 Walls, *Seeing New Worlds*, p. 220; Newman, *Common Dwelling*, p. 176.
46 For a discussion of how the language of slavery in this essay relates to Thoreau's advocacy for John Brown, see Solnit, *Storming*, p. 5, and Newman, *Common Dwelling*, pp. 180–182, 190–191; see also Jack Turner, "Thoreau and John Brown," *A Political Companion to Henry David Thoreau*, Jack Turner (ed.) (Lexington: The University Press of Kentucky, 2009).
47 Thoreau, *Wild Apples*, pp. 192, 193, 187.
48 Ibid., pp. 196, 198.
49 Thoreau, *Wild Apples*, pp. 196–201; Rossi, "Introduction," p. xxiii; see also Newman's reading of the last section of *Wild Fruits*, pp. 180–182.
50 Nabhan, "Learning the Language," p. xi.
51 Gary Paul Nabhan, *Cross-Pollinations: The Marriage of Science and Poetry* (Minneapolis, MN: Milkweed Editions, 2004), p. 10.
52 Rossi, "Introduction," p. xviii.
53 My thanks to Gary Nabhan for this insight.
54 Gary Paul Nabhan, *Singing the Turtles to Sea: The Comcáac (Séri) Art and Science of Reptiles* (Berkeley: University of California Press, 2003).
55 Nabhan, *Turtles*, p. 226.
56 Ibid., p. 15.
57 Ibid., p. 16.
58 Ibid., p. 17.
59 Ibid., pp. 17–19.
60 Ibid., p. 18.
61 Ibid., p. 18.
62 My thanks to Gary Nabhan for this insight.
63 Nabhan, *Turtles*, pp. 4–5.
64 Ibid., p. 222.
65 Ibid., p. 222.
66 Nabhan, *Cultures of Habitat*, pp. 30–31.
67 Nabhan, *Desert Terroir: Exploring the Unique Flavors and Sundry Places of the Borderlands* (Austin: University of Texas Press, 2012).
68 Ibid., pp. 35, 50.
69 Ibid., p. 48.
70 Ibid., p. 35.
71 Ibid., pp. 45–46, 48.
72 This definition is taken from the organization "Just Food": http://www.justfood.org/food-justice.
73 See, for example, Nabhan's work with the organizations Native Seeds/SEARCH (http://www.nativeseeds.org/index.php/about-us/historymission) and Renewing America's Food Traditions (http://www.raftalliance.org).
74 See Nabhan et al., *Hungry for Change: Borderlands Food and Water in the Balance* (Tucson, AZ: The Southwest Center's Kellogg Program in Sustainable Food Systems, 2012) for a discussion of border food justice.

75 Gary Paul Nabhan and Mark Klett, *Desert Legends: Re-Storying the Sonoran Borderlands*, stories by Gary Paul Nabhan, photographs by Mark Klett (New York: Henry Holt, 1994), p. 169.
76 Ibid., pp. 45–46.
77 Ibid., p. 20.
78 Ibid., p. 30.
79 Ibid., p. 33.
80 Ibid., p. 86.
81 My thanks to Gary Nabhan for these insights.
82 Gary Paul Nabhan, *Coming Home to Eat: The Pleasures and Politics of Local Foods* (New York: Norton, 2002), p. 291.
83 Ibid., pp. 295–296.
84 Ibid., p. 297.
85 Robert Gottlieb and Anupama Joshi, *Food Justice* (Cambridge, MA: The MIT Press, 2010), p. 20.
86 Nabhan, *Coming Home*, p. 298.

10

SARAH E. MCFARLAND

Animal Studies, Literary Animals, and Yann Martel's *Life of Pi*

Mosquitoes are nearly universally annoying, globally ubiquitous, and among the deadliest creatures on earth, transmitting dengue fever, malaria, yellow fever, and various encephalitides to humans and other animals. Scientists estimate that mosquitoes have caused half the deaths in human history. Although these diseases tend to be concentrated in poor areas with the attendant problems of inconsistent reporting and inadequate medical access, according to the World Health Organization's estimates, 655,000 people died from malaria, 50–100 million were infected with dengue fever, and 30,000 died from yellow fever in 2010.[1] Current suppression efforts typically involve poisoning landscapes with some of the most destructive and dangerous chemicals ever invented. The promising results of DDT against mosquitoes in an effort to counter malaria and typhus in the mid-1900s, for example, resulted in extensive aerial spraying. This led to the near-elimination of malaria, dengue fever, and typhus, as well as the bald eagle, brown pelican, peregrine falcon, and California condor. Since the publication of Rachel Carson's *Silent Spring* in 1962, the consequences of aggressive chemical pesticides have become notorious and their use legally restricted in many countries. There are still no vaccines or even useful treatments for mosquito-borne diseases like dengue fever, however, so a British biotechnology company has gone one enormous step further in the mosquito control industry: Oxford Insect Technologies created a transgenic mosquito. Oxitec "invented" OX513A, a genetically-modified, human-engineered mosquito species developed and hatched in a laboratory to be released into the world to mate with wild females and produce young that self-destruct. And released it is: in 2009, more than 3 million genetically altered mosquitoes were freed in the Cayman Islands; in 2011, similar open field trials began in Brazil.[2] Like something out of Margaret Atwood's *Oryx and Crake*, scientists are engineering creatures the likes of which have never been seen in nature.

While scientists and others have discussed the controversial and potentially risky decision to release what might be Dr. Frankenstein's monster

into ecosystems and populations – with unimaginable unintended consequences – what people have not asked is what it means to be the mosquito.
To ask that question is to move into the realm of critical animal studies,
where in the words of Donna Haraway, we can "learn how to see faithfully from another's point of view."³ Despite critical animal studies' relatively recent popularity within interdisciplinary ecocriticism, it remains one
of the most philosophically problematic theories in its application because
its concepts can be counterintuitive. In the (largely western) humanistic
tradition, conceptual dichotomies effectively separate isolated, self-certain
subjects from their lived but objectified environments. Generally speaking,
ecocriticism unsettles the nature/culture aspects of this separation and its
innumerable environmental and social consequences; it is "the study of the
relationship between literature and the physical environment" that "takes
as its subject the interconnections between nature and culture, specifically
the cultural artifacts of language and literature."⁴ Within ecocriticism, critical animal studies interrogate the human/animal aspects of the self/other
binary and the arising consequences to subjectivity and species definitions.
For example, in 1934, Jakob von Uexküll published "A Stroll Through the
Worlds of Animals and Men" (orig. in German) in which he ponders the
nature of various nonhuman experiences of the world; how does the world
appear to a tick, for instance, or to a spider? "All animals," he argues, "from
the simplest to the most complex, are fitted into their unique worlds with
equal completeness."⁵ Von Uexküll labels the self-world or phenomenal
world "*umwelt*," the world around an animal as the animal sees it, and suggests that by examining the *umwelt*, we can regard animals as dynamically
perceiving and acting subjects instead of as objects:

> We might assume that an animal is nothing but a collection of perceptual
> and effector tools, connected by an integrating apparatus which, though still
> a mechanism, is yet fit to carry on the life functions. ... The proponents of
> such theories forget that, from the first, they have overlooked the most impor-
> tant thing, the *subject* which uses the tools, perceives and functions with
> their aid.⁶

By putting animals at the center of his speculations, von Uexküll critiques
their exclusion from traditional forms of science, analysis, and representation that consider them only objects to be examined or described.

There is great risk in misrepresenting nonhuman creatures, however,
either as proxies or as objects for human emotional or cognitive projection.
A significant number of texts use animal characters for allegorical purposes,
project anthropomorphically onto their lives, or otherwise erase any nonhuman experience from the textual world. As Mark S. Cladis asserts, "humans
tend to cast everything – even other humans – in their own image."⁷ Many

ecocritics argue that the value of any method of representation in part depends on the human intentions behind it,[8] although others have skeptically argued that anthropomorphism imposes on all thinking about other animals' abilities. But perhaps more interesting is to wonder, how could we possibly know if we are wrong, and in what ways? Thomas Nagel reflects on such impossibilities:

> I want to know what it is like for a bat to be a bat. Yet if I try to imagine this, I am restricted to the resources of my own mind, and those resources are inadequate to the task. I cannot perform it either by imagining additions to my present experience, or by imagining segments gradually subtracted from it, or by imagining some combination of additions, subtractions, and modifications. To the extent that I could look and behave like ... a bat without changing my fundamental structure, my experiences would not be anything like the experiences of those animals.[9]

Nagel moves from here to make an assertion about the subjective nature of experience: that each of us perceives the world from a position where we each, individually, are the center of that experience, and the distance between our understanding of the world and that of another person's or animal's falls on a continuum that ultimately can only be transcended by our respective imaginations. Thus the effort must become one of what I like to call "emphatic empathy" instead of the oppression and harm that does not accord nonhumans agency or subjectivity or, alternatively, romantically portrays them as fur-covered humans.[10]

What would it look like to recognize otherness in the face of nonhuman animals and to acknowledge subjectivity of such a radical sort? In the words of Evelyn Fox Keller, "We need a language that enables us to conceptually and perceptually negotiate our way between sameness and opposition, that permits the recognition of kinship in difference and of difference among kin; a language that encodes respect for difference, particularity, alterity without repudiating the underlying affinity that is the first prerequisite for knowledge."[11] Like Keller, Haraway calls for particularity and specificity and emphasizes the importance of changing perspective into one of situatedness and relation. In arguing against relativism, which she defines as "a way of being nowhere while claiming to be everywhere equally," Haraway says that hers "is an argument for situated and embodied knowledges and against various forms of unlocatable, and so irresponsible, knowledge claims."[12] Her position redefines the relationship between viewer and subject and relabels the object of study by arguing for a new model of seeing: "There are only highly specific visual possibilities, each with a wonderfully detailed, active, partial way of organizing worlds. All of these pictures of the world should not be allegories of infinite mobility and interchangeability, but of elaborate specificity and difference and the loving care people might take to learn how to see faithfully from another's point of view."[13]

These models of situating and speaking knowledge encourage animal studies scholars to recognize that *every* being must be seen as "an actor and agent" in its own life, "not a screen or a ground or a resource, never finally as slave to the master that closes off the dialectic in his unique agency and authorship of 'objective' knowledge."[14] Instead of an anthropocentric relationship that keeps humans centrally significant and nonhumans as metaphors or mirrors for human interests, to give up the position of power is to risk being vulnerable in the face of multiple standpoints. Obviously, to envision the *umwelt* or self-world of nonhuman animals is to speculate in terms of human experience and using human languages; the empathy necessary is somewhat illusory because there is no other way to speculate. Nonetheless, our literary authors can and do, which is what the following pages will examine.

The ultimately wrenching account of love and loss in Yann Martel's *Life of Pi* (2001) can only be fully appreciated after reading the last chapters and then reassessing from the beginning, where nearly every passage takes on new significance as part of the fictional Piscine's greatest wish: for "a long book with a never-ending story. One I could read again and again, with new eyes and a fresh understanding each time."[15] Ostensibly a story about a teenaged boy shipwrecked on a lifeboat with a tiger for 227 days, the novel is really about far more than that: it is about truth and belief, imagination and reality, meaning and authority, religion and science, love and brutality, the parallels between humans and other animals, and the breakdown of these oppositions. The title character recounts his experiences to a fictional authorial voice in a layered narrative that on the one hand defends zoo practices and the study of science but on the other exposes their very flaws, finally privileging imagination over bland fact – the "crude reality" that results in "worthless dreams."[16]

But we should start at the beginning: although this story opens with a fictional "Author's Note" (the first of many indications that the story's undecidability is itself part of the story), there is a beginning we can recognize: "Once upon a time there was a zoo in the Pondicherry Botanical Garden."[17] From his adult perspective, Pi recounts his college studies at the University of Toronto, his childhood in India as the son of a zookeeper, and the events when he was marooned on a lifeboat with a Bengal tiger, a hyena, a wounded zebra, an orangutan, a rat, a cockroach, and some flies, after the ship carrying them to Toronto sank in the middle of the Pacific Ocean. On the lifeboat, the hyena attacks the injured zebra and the orangutan, consuming both, and then is killed and eaten by the tiger. Only Pi and the tiger, misnamed after his captor "Richard Parker," survive to come ashore in Mexico after more than seven months at sea. Later, Pi is asked by investigators why the ship sank, and their incredulity about his tale leads him to tell another that replaces the animals with human survivors (and thus is a story of human brutality, deception, murder, and cannibalism). My straightforward summary does injustice to the intricacies of Martel's narrative, which is actually cunning in its complexity and fails to come to any concrete resolution. The appearance of reality in the novel collapses into the fictional reality and expands back out again until finally the only conclusion we can make is that Martel has successfully unraveled what it means for something to be "real" in the first place.

Because Martel exposes the way the boundaries between humans and animals are established and trespassed in *Life of Pi*, his novel is a potential feast for animal studies scholars, who examine depictions of nonhuman animals and challenge the concepts that frame humanity and animality as discrete categories of difference. Specifically, the relationship between Pi and Richard Parker is multifaceted and slippery, itself deconstructing the various ways that readers try to pin down truth and reality even as it confronts the methods humans (and human readers) employ to define themselves in opposition to and in dominance over the nonhuman world. This is most powerful, perhaps, in the case of Richard Parker's agency, which eventually culminates in the semantic overlap of Pi and Richard Parker in the second story, even as it does not.

Both Pi's tale and his behavior within it foreground the tiger's subjectivity, and we witness the breakdown of power positions and speciesist hierarchies that place humans above other animals. Richard Parker's agency runs throughout the novel. Richard Parker is erroneously named after the man who captured him as a cub; someone filling out paperwork transposed his intended, descriptive name, "Thirsty," with that of his captor. To name something is to accord it subjectivity, to recognize that it has a unique perspective on the world and meaningful relationships. Named animals are individuals; a name belongs to a particular entity, even if it is an accidental designation. The novel, however, reveals his agency in more definitive ways. He is first mentioned in the context of Pi's reminiscences, although at this point readers do not assume he is anything but human, so his subjective experience of the world is perplexing:

> Richard Parker has stayed with me. I've never forgotten him. Dare I say I miss him? I do. I miss him. I still see him in my dreams. They are nightmares mostly, but nightmares tinged with love. Such is the strangeness of the human heart. I still cannot understand how he could abandon me so unceremoniously, without any sort of goodbye, without looking back even once. That pain is like an axe that chops at my heart.[18]

Pi's confusion is redefined once readers realize that he speaks of a tiger, not a man. Importantly, Richard Parker remains a tiger in the novel and does not take on any of the wishful, anthropomorphic characteristics Pi himself describes of zoo visitors, who construct "*Animalus anthropomorphicus*, the animal as seen through human eyes."[19] Instead, the tiger is really and truly a tiger. Even though Pi wishes Richard Parker would recognize him and give a parting sendoff, he knows his desire is part of the human obsession to "put ourselves at the center of everything,"[20] which he resists.

Readers have to struggle against the desire to put the human at the center of our interpretations of this novel, too, so Martel insures that Richard Parker's agency butts up against any predetermined expectations of human superiority readers may have. For example, although Pi lists seven ways in which he might survive the shipwreck and chooses Plan Number Seven, the only one that does not involve some plot to kill the tiger, it is actually Richard Parker who influences the decision in the first place with his own calm acceptance of Pi:

> It was Richard Parker who calmed me down. It is the irony of this story that the one who scared me witless to start with was the very same who brought me peace, purpose, I dare say even wholeness.
>
> He was looking at me intently. After a time I recognized the gaze. I had grown up with it. It was the gaze of a contented animal. ... He was simply taking me in, observing me, in a manner that was sobering but not menacing. He kept twitching his ears and varying the sideways turn of his head. ...
>
> He made a sound, a snort from his nostrils. I pricked up my ears. He did it a second time. I was astonished. *Prusten?*[21]

Prusten, Pi explains, is the quietest tiger call and expresses friendliness and harmless intentions. "Richard Parker did it again, this time with a rolling of the head. He looked exactly as if he were asking me a question."[22] Exchanging a gaze is foundational to many philosophies that underpin critical animal studies. For example, Emmanuel Levinas suggests that by encountering the face of the other, one calls into question one's own subjectness. The very otherness of the other is so complete that it obliterates any ability to categorize it, and what matters is not the particular kind of other so much as what that other can do: the way the sheer otherness of the other momentarily shatters for me – as it would for you – the ability to put things into categories, interpret my being in my world, or understand my very existence in that moment. The face of the other calls upon me in a way that is completely outside any system of meaning I might try to use to understand it and "puts into question the brutal spontaneity of [my] immanent destiny."[23] In fact, my susceptibility to the face of the other is the foundation for my own subjectivity in this Levinasian line of thinking, because "the face opens the primordial discourse whose first word is obligation" and I am obligated to respond,[24] just as Pi does in *Life of Pi*.

The claim of ethical reciprocity in which we make ourselves available to responsiveness invokes John Berger's influential essay "Why Look At Animals?," where he claims that modern industrial societies have extinguished the possibility of shared looks between humans and other animals by imprisoning animals' bodies within the degrading walls of zoo enclosures and otherwise transforming their images into spectacles.[25] In Berger's view, even companion animals like dogs cannot exchange a gaze with their humans because "they have been co-opted into the family" and "in this relationship the autonomy of both parties has been lost."[26] Perhaps as a critique of anthropocentric claims like these, Jacques Derrida describes how his kitten challenges his ability to convey the actuality of his existence via her powerful gaze. His naked body's exposure triggers a malaise brought upon by his inarticulate recognition of the limits of his subjectness – the "who am I at this moment" question he later calls the "abyssal limit of the human."[27] The cat's gaze – her subjectivity – becomes a mirror to reflect Derrida's own humanness, represented by his shame and nakedness. In other words, the cat's gaze represents "the point of view of the absolute other."[28] But Derrida's cat is not just "a" cat; she escapes categorization within the bounds of language. The "bottomless gaze" of the animal demonstrates "the naked truth of every gaze, given that that truth *allows me to see and be seen* through the eyes of the other, in the *seeing* and not just *seen* eyes of the other."[29] His encounter with the gaze of another animal thus disputes several traditional philosophical assumptions, revealing that other animals *can* look, that animality in general does not exist, and that even this cat, who is "family" and familiar (in Berger's terms), can call into question his construction of self (à la Levinas). Thus these philosophers help us elucidate what Pi struggles to communicate about his experience with Richard Parker and his soft vocalization. Both animals make a choice in the passage where Pi hears "prusten": both the human and the tiger decide that they will live or die together, and they choose to live. Thus, while we read Pi's internal decision-making process by which he selects Plan Number Seven, we witness Richard Parker's agency and the effect it produces in Pi after exchanging a disorienting gaze.

Similarly, although Pi coaches Richard Parker to respect his territory on the lifeboat, Richard Parker also trains Pi to read his signals. The tiger can kill and eat the boy at any time but does not, although he swipes at him repeatedly during their mutual efforts as they strive to understand each other's languages. As Pi states, "If I survived my apprenticeship as a high seas animal trainer, it was because Richard Parker did not really want to attack me."[30] Instead of deadly assaults from both sides, they teach each other:

"Eventually I learned to read the signals he was sending me. I found that with his ears, his eyes, his whiskers, his teeth, his tail and his throat, he spoke a simple, forcefully punctuated language that told me what his next move might be. I learned to back down before he lifted his paw in the air. Then I made my point, feet on the gunnel, boat rolling, my single-note language blasting from the whistle, and Richard Parker moaning and gasping at the bottom of the boat."[31] Both imagine the experience and perspective of the other to avoid a dangerous confrontation. In this way, two disparate creatures manage to shepherd each other toward survival.

Also, although some critics have labeled Pi the tiger's "master" (and Pi himself uses this term), the text reveals that he is more rightly called Richard Parker's "steward" *and vice versa*. For example, Pi fills up the tiger's bucket with fresh water and gives him "the lion's share" of whatever food is caught.[32] The traditional human/animal hierarchy is overturned as the boy privileges the tiger's needs over his own human ones. Correspondingly, Richard Parker provides Pi with companionship, motivation, and a purpose. As Pi says, "if he died I would be alone with despair, a foe even more formidable than a tiger. If I still had a will to live, it was thanks to Richard Parker. He kept me from thinking too much about my family and my tragic circumstances. He pushed me to go on living."[33] Neither can survive without the other: Richard Parker offers Pi an escape from despair while Pi is a physical provider for Richard Parker. Thus, firm divisions between domination and submission become complicated by their shared need.

Pi's dependence on Richard Parker helps explain his consternation when the tiger refuses to acknowledge Pi when they finally land on the beach in Mexico. After he leaps onto the beach, the tiger denies Pi the final anthropomorphic moment – the tearful goodbye – reinforcing his animal agency once again in case readers have fallen into romanticizations like Pi suddenly cannot resist doing:

> He didn't look at me. He ran a hundred yards or so along the shore before turning in. His gait was clumsy and uncoordinated. He fell several times. At the edge of the jungle, he stopped. I was certain he would turn my way. He would look at me. He would flatten his ears. He would growl. In some such way, he could conclude our relationship. He did nothing of the sort. He only looked fixedly into the jungle. Then Richard Parker, companion of my torment, awful, fierce thing that kept me alive, moved forward and disappeared forever from my life.[34]

Thus the novel deconstructs the desire to center humans and enables the tiger to maintain his tigerness throughout while acknowledging Pi's very human wish for a conclusive ending to their relationship. Richard Parker's quick escape from the lifeboat, however, is also a comment about freedom being important for all animals, not just humans. The boat restricts the tiger in much the same way as the zoo described in the early sections of the novel, so Richard Parker's departure challenges what appears to be Pi's justification of zoos.

Early chapters of *Life of Pi* include what appears to be a robust defense of zoo practices. The Pondicherry Botanical Garden's zoo is described as a "huge zoo, spread over numberless acres, big enough to require a train to explore it." Part of a garden, there is a "riot of flowers" everywhere, and "suddenly, amidst the tall and slim trees up ahead, you notice two giraffes quietly observing you. The sight is not the last of your surprises. The next moment you are startled by a furious outburst coming from a great troupe of monkeys, only outdone in volume by the shrill cries of strange birds."[35] There are no visible barriers; instead, suddenly giraffes or monkeys or rhinoceros come into view and are described as the ones with the power to gaze. Leisurely visitors sit on benches and enjoy the sights and sounds of the human and nonhuman animals around them.

According to Pi, the zoo's captive animals are relaxed and content (if not even pleased) in their respective spaces because:

> In a zoo, we do for animals what we have done for ourselves with houses: we bring together in a small space what in the wild is spread out. ... An animal will take possession of its zoo space in the same way it would lay claim to a new space in the wild, exploring it and marking it out in the normal ways of its species, with sprays of urine perhaps.[36]

Pi says that the animals' total dependence on humans for their needs is preferable to the perils of the wild, unlike Randy Malamud, who argues that a zoo exhibit "really offers little insight into the natural condition of that species" because of that very dependence and concludes that the only outcome is the substantiation of human superiority.[37] The paradox of zoo animals is clear: the natural within the cultural, they are neither wild nor domesticated. More accurately, zoo inhabitants have the status of exiled refugees, according to Bob Mullan and Garry Marvin: "Denied access to their natural habitat these animals become marginalized from their wild nature and begin to lose access to the mentalities and behaviors which would have been appropriate there. Such animals have a status akin to that of refugees. They are in enforced exile, but a false one at that because realistically there is no 'home' to return to."[38] Pi argues instead that the greatest harm to the zoo animals is the ignorant people who come to look at them, saying "our species' excessive predatoriness has made the entire planet our prey. More specifically, we have in mind the people who feed fishhooks to the otters, razors to the bears, apples with small nails in them to the elephants and hardware variations on the theme. ... The cruelty is often more active and direct," he continues, giving a long list of various harms the visitors have inflicted on the creatures inhabiting the zoo to conclude that the most dangerous animal in the Pondicherry Botanical Garden is the human species.[39]

Nonetheless, Pi's apparent defense of zoos becomes a controversial and arguable issue even among the community of animal studies scholars. For example, Philip Armstrong contends that Pi's defense of zoo practices and the concomitant disregard for the lives of real animals' suffering in real zoos marks this novel as one that "presents humans as innately different from and superior to animals because they possess a greater capacity for rational inventiveness, adaptability to new circumstances, and mobility."[40] Superficially, this appears to be the case. Pi notes that predation, danger, hunger, thirst, parasites, and fear mean that animals are never really free in the wild, regardless of environmentalists' protests to the contrary: "Animals in the wild lead lives of compulsion and necessity," he says, and are "free neither in space nor in time, nor in their personal relations."[41] And he would know, after existing on a lifeboat for seven months of "freedom." He puts it even more straightforwardly, though: "Think about it yourself. Would you rather be put up at the Ritz with free room service and unlimited access to a doctor or be homeless without a soul to care for you?"[42] But the answer to this question is much more complicated even for Pi, despite what appears to be an unquestioning support of zoo practices.

A week after the Tsimtsum sinks, Pi realizes that "with every passing day the lifeboat was resembling a zoo enclosure more and more: Richard Parker had his sheltered area for sleeping and resting, his food stash, his lookout and now his water hole."[43] Obviously, though, neither Pi nor Richard Parker would consider the lifeboat preferable to nearly any other living situation, and it is only because of Pi's efforts to feed and hydrate Richard Parker that the tiger's territory on the lifeboat is any semblance of his enclosure back in the Pondicherry Botanical Gardens. He and Richard Parker share a common fate. In fact, both tiger and boy leave the lifeboat at the first possible opportunity: when the ocean currents bring their boat to a floating algae island with an abundance of edible food and fresh water. Pi ponders the mystery of why Richard Parker returns to the lifeboat each night, incorrectly concluding that he is "attached to his den" there[44] because Pi does not yet know that the island is carnivorous. Until he discovers that harrowing fact, he spends days "eating and drinking and bathing and observing the meerkats and walking and running and resting and growing stronger. My running became smooth and unselfconscious, a source of euphoria. My skin healed.

My pains and aches left me. Put simply, I returned to life."[45] The island, like the Ritz hotel, seems to provide for all of their physical needs.

More importantly for our understanding of the complexities of *Life of Pi*, the island also functions to expose the lie in Pi's claims about animals' acceptance of zoo enclosures and the benefits of the Ritz over a life free and wild. The ambiguity in Pi's justification of zoos is exposed when Pi abandons his island Ritz, asking "How long does it take for a broken spirit to kill a body that has food, water and shelter? ... I preferred to set off and perish in search of my own kind than to live a lonely half-life of physical comfort and spiritual death on this murderous island."[46] He leaves the following night after filling the boat with as much fresh water, dead fish, and meerkat meat that it will hold and awaiting Richard Parker's return, knowing that "to leave him would mean to kill him."[47] Accordingly, Pi himself abandons his Ritz for the uncertainty of the open ocean, indicating that zoos are not so ideal after all.

The zoo as Ritz/island issue is complicated in ways that parallel Martel's complications of any easy interpretation throughout *Life of Pi*: Pi is human and animal; a vegetarian and carnivore; a pacifist and murderer; a Hindu, Muslim, and Christian simultaneously. What Pi means when he defends zoos is equally ambivalent to the questions raised at the end of the novel when, pressured by the Japanese investigators to tell a story that makes sense, Pi tells them a story where the agents are humans instead of animals. Representations of animals have traditionally shown us what we want to see; likewise, the two Japanese investigators "want a story that won't surprise [them]. That will confirm what [they] already know. That won't make [them] see higher or further or differently."[48] In the second account, the hyena is really the ship's French cook, the zebra a wounded Chinese sailor, the orangutan is Pi's mother, and Richard Parker is Pi himself. The second version is a description of human brutality and cannibalism instead of a life-affirming, optimistic tale of a clever boy and a patient tiger. But taken all together, this novel demands an answer to the question of how we define what it means to be human without providing any easy answers. Traditionally, animals are placed perpetually in opposition to humans regardless of the methods used to construct boundaries between species – language ability, culture, intelligence, and so on – yet here we have a story of moral conscience and higher-order thinking when the narrative is about Pi and the tiger, and cruelty and instinctive behavior when the tale is full of humans. People, we like to think, do not behave that way. And yet they do. We are all animals, complex, particular, individual beings.

Throughout *Life of Pi*, Pi acts in ways that acknowledge that Richard Parker can think and feel and live a fully-fleshed life. (This is also true of the other animals he encounters, which we are reminded each time he tells our narrator he prays for the souls of every animal he ate during his voyage because he ended each life and is responsible for its loss.) In these and many other ways too complex to develop further here, the novel demonstrates the kind of mutual respect between individuals that Barbara Smuts defines as genuine personhood: "When a human being relates to an individual non-human being as an anonymous object, rather than as a being with its own subjectivity, it is the human, and not the other animal, who relinquishes personhood."[49] Her definition places the responsibility on the human to recognize the subjectivity of individual others in order to maintain the status of "person." To shift personhood toward behavior instead of locating it in the shape of the human species offers the possibility of mutual respect and reciprocity that crosses not only cultural but species barriers as well, powered by emphatic empathy.

It is only inside the actual encounters with other beings that we can recognize how our own agency and identities are constructed by and simultaneous with those of other animals around us, and it is through those encounters that humans can establish and maintain their personhood. In our stories, like this one by Yann Martel, we can imagine worlds where the challenges to concepts like "humanity" and "animality" are multifaceted, diverse, and various. We cannot be exhaustive in our examples of all key methods of analysis, of course, but determining the ways that complex representations of nonhuman animals can expose the power structures of traditional cultural constructions and depictions, as I have done here, is a good start toward a critical animal studies scholarship. Perhaps it even begins the move toward an empathetic representation of even the tiny, powerful, and unloved mosquito, which of course has its own perspective on the world we share.

NOTES

1 World Health Organization, http://www.who.int/mediacentre/factsheets
2 Oxford Insect Technologies, http://www.oxitec.com/health/our-products/aedes-agypti-ox513a
3 Donna J. Haraway, *Simians, Cyborgs, and Women: The Reinvention of Nature* (New York: Routledge, 1991), p. 190.
4 Cheryll Glotfelty, "Introduction: Literary Studies in an Age of Environmental Crisis," in *The Ecocriticism Reader: Landmarks in Literary Ecology*, Cheryll Glotfelty and Harold Fromm, eds. (Athens: University of Georgia Press, 1996), pp. xviii, xix.
5 Jakob von Uexküll, "A Stroll Through the Worlds of Animals and Men," in *Instinctive Behavior: The Development of a Modern Concept*, Claire H. Schiller, ed. & trans. (New York: International University Press, Inc., 1957), pp. 5–80, 11.

6 von Uexküll, "A Stroll," p. 6.

7 Mark S. Cladis, "On the Importance of Owning Chickens: Lessons in Nature, Community, and Transformation," *Interdisciplinary Studies in Literature and Environment* 7.2 (2000), 199–211, 207.

8 See Karen Warren, Simon Estok, David Abram, and others.

9 Thomas Nagel, "What Is It Like to Be a Bat?" *The Philosophical Review* LXXXIII, 4 (October 1974): 435–50. http://evans-experientialism.freeweb-space.com/nagel.htm

10 For a detailed overview and theorization of nonhuman subjectivity, see Sarah E. McFarland and Ryan Hediger, "Approaching the Agency of Other Animals: An Introduction," in *Animals and Agency: An Interdisciplinary Exploration*, McFarland and Hediger, eds. (Leiden and Boston: Brill Academic Press, 2009), pp. 1–20.

11 Evelyn Fox Keller, "The Gender/Science System: or, Is Sex to Gender as Nature Is to Science?" in *Feminism and Science*, Nancy Tuana, ed. (Bloomington: Indiana University Press, 1989), p. 44.

12 Haraway, *Simians*, p. 191.

13 Haraway, *Simians*, p. 190.

14 Haraway, *Simians*, p. 198.

15 Yann Martel, *Life of Pi: A Novel* (Orlando: Harcourt, 2001), p. 207.

16 Martel, *Pi*, p. xii.

17 Martel, *Pi*, p. xi.

18 Martel, *Pi*, p. 6.

19 Martel, *Pi*, p. 31.

20 Martel, *Pi*, p. 31.

21 Martel, *Pi*, p. 162–163.

22 Martel, *Pi*, p. 164.

23 Emmanuel Levinas, *Totality and Infinity*, A. Lingis, trans. (Pittsburgh, PA: Duquesne University Press, 1969), p. 203.

24 Levinas, *Totality and Infinity*, p. 201. Unfortunately, Levinas explicitly excludes nonhuman animals from the categories of beings who have a face. Matthew Calarco has an excellent counterargument to the logic of Levinas' exclusion in his book *Zoographies* (New York: Columbia University Press, 2008).

25 John Berger, "Why Look At Animals?," *About Looking* (New York: Vintage Books, 1980), pp. 3–28.

26 Berger, "Why Look?," p. 15.

27 Jacques Derrida, "The Animal That Therefore I Am (More to Follow)," in *The Animal That Therefore I Am*, Marie-Louise Mallet, ed., David Wills, trans. (New York: Fordham University Press, 2008), pp. 3, 12.

28 Derrida, "Animal," p. 11.

29 Derrida, "Animal," p. 12.

30 Martel, *Pi*, p. 206.

31 Martel, *Pi*, p. 206.

32 Martel, *Pi*, p. 224.

33 Martel, *Pi*, p. 164.

34 Martel, *Pi*, p. 284–285.

35 Martel, *Pi*, p. 12, 13.

36 Martel, *Pi*, p. 17, 18.

37 Randy Malamud, *Reading Zoos: Representations of Animals and Captivity* (New York: New York University Press, 1998), p. 1, 2.

38 Robert Mullan and Gary Marvin, *Zoo Culture: The Book about Watching People Watch Animals*, second edition (Urbana: University of Illinois Press, 1998), p. 29.

39 Martel, *Pi*, p. 29–31.

40 Philip Armstrong, *What Animals Mean in the Fiction of Modernity* (New York: Routledge, 2008), p. 178.

41 Martel, *Pi*, p. 16.

42 Martel, *Pi*, p. 18.

43 Martel, *Pi*, p. 188–189.

44 Martel, *Pi*, p. 265.

45 Martel, *Pi*, p. 269.

46 Martel, *Pi*, p. 282–283.

47 Martel, *Pi*, p. 283.

48 Martel, *Pi*, p. 302.

49 Barbara Smuts, "Commentary/Response," in *The Lives of Animals* by J. M. Coetzee et al. (Princeton, NJ: Princeton University Press, 1999), p. 118.

PART IV

Major Directions

II

JONI ADAMSON

Environmental Justice, Cosmopolitics, and Climate Change

In the Amazon basin, stories about pink dolphins living in cities under the world's largest river are common. In oral traditions, they show up as lovers, seducers, and are thought of as "humans" who live normal, if somewhat luxurious, lives under the water. In a poem titled "Pink Dolphins," in his chapbook *Amazonia*, Columbian American poet Juan Carlos Galeano writes of dolphins that "dress in pink / to soften the hate in men's eyes."[1] Dolphins in the poem wonder, "How can they hate us if we make love like they do?" Galeano has also published a collection of oral traditions, *Folklore of the Amazon*, in which dolphins transform themselves into humans, and lure the humans with whom they consort to their underwater homes. In one story, a woman named Maria gives birth to twin baby dolphins and her relatives simply take it in stride.[2] Although it is considered bad luck to kill one, local people believe that the celebrated virility of pink dolphins, who "grow pubic hair" at night and "go out stealing women" as Galeano phrases it in the poem, can be transferred to humans through the ritualized use of their organs as amulets. Galeano does not, however, romanticize oral traditions. In his documentary film, *The Trees have Mothers: Amazonian Cosmologies, Folktales, and Mystery*, he takes a hard look at the ways poverty is exacerbated in a region suffering persistent drought, pollution, overfishing, and erosion. The film examines the ways both oral traditions and lack of economic opportunity pull residents into local markets where it is easy to sell dried dolphin penises or vaginas, cut from animals caught accidently in fishing nets.

Drought, caused by warming oceanic and atmospheric temperatures linked to climate change, also threatens dolphins as it dries up tributaries to the Amazon River.[3] In 2012, this caused the numbers of rare pink dolphins to drop by 47 percent.[4] Initially, scientists thought dolphins living in Bolivia, one of the places hardest hit by drought, were a subspecies of *Inia Geoffrensis*, the common Amazonian river dolphin. In 2006, however, Bolivian dolphins, *Inia Bolivensis*, were declared a separate species.[5] Today, with the intense media attention brought to these freshwater mammals by the declaration of its status as a "new" and endangered species, it becomes clearer why the dolphins in Galeano's poem might wonder if humans love them or hate them. The tourist trade is bringing speedboats and motorized canoes full of people curious to see the eight-foot-long, 450-pound, bright-pink animals, causing more frequent dolphin injuries and deaths. In response, the full Bolivian House of Representatives passed legislation declaring *Inia Bolivensis* a "national heritage" animal with "rights" to protection.[6]

This legislation can be seen as a response to the 2009 Copenhagen talks for the United Nations Conference of Parties (COP 15), which were considered largely a failure since the richest nations failed to enter into any binding agreements on climate change. An earlier 2007 United Nations Intergovernmental Panel on Climate Change (IPCC) report had concluded that "worst case scenarios" were already occurring, that sea levels were rising, that oceanic acid levels increasing, that ice sheets moving "beyond the patterns of natural variability within which … society and economy have developed and thrived," and that it would be poor nations that would be most "highly vulnerable" to even modest levels of atmospheric temperature rise.[7] After this report was issued, many of the "most vulnerable nations" decided not to wait for their global north counterparts to act. In 2010, 30,000 delegates from 100 countries gathered in Bolivia for a World People's Conference on the Rights of Mother Earth and Climate Change. They framed a Universal Declaration, which urges all the world's citizens to become more aware of multiple, divergent worlds and to build a politics that would support the "recovery, revalidation, and strengthening of indigenous cosmovisions based on ancient and ancestral indigenous knowledge."[8] Following this conference, in 2011, Bolivia passed the "Law of Mother Earth," giving nature the "right" to maintain and regenerate its life cycles and evolutionary processes; in 2012, they passed the law to protect pink dolphins. This legislation is seen as only the latest in a series of actions demonstrating that global south peoples are taking the lead on climate change.

By 2009, scientists, social scientists, and humanists were also speaking out more forcefully on the lack of action on climate change at the global level. Earlier, atmospheric chemist Paul Crutzen and biologist Eugene Stoermer declared that the Earth had entered a new epoch in its history, which they referred to as the "anthropocene." They argued that a key transformation in the planet's life began some two hundred years ago, when human activity began growing into a "significant and morphological force."[9] In response, anthropologist and ecocritic Debra Bird Rose called for new forms of "writing in the anthropocene" and more attention to "situated connectivities that bind us into multi-species communities."[10] Very quickly after publication of

Rose's manifesto, a group of scholars calling themselves "multispecies ethnographers" began gathering up the sensibilities of Alexander von Humboldt, Charles Darwin, Franz Boas, Claude Lévi-Strauss, Gregory Bateson, Donna Haraway, Eduardo Viveiros de Castro, and Debra Bird Rose, among others, to pull creatures – animals, plants, fungi, and microbes once confined to the category of "that which is killable" – into the realm "of bios," as they launched a mode of research that sets as its goal the "remaking of anthropos as well as its companion and stranger species on the planet Earth."[11]

Storytellers, writers, ecocritics, and their allies have long been musing about what it would mean to "remake anthropos" for a new, more environmentally ethical epoch. Some, like poet and folklorist Juan Carlos Galeano, are reexamining ancient and contemporary indigenous stories about human relationship to animals, with "situated connectivities" to specific geographies, for what they might reveal about linked biophysical and social processes. For example, American National Book Award winning novelist Richard Powers puts an Anishinabe (Ojibwa/Chippewa) folktale about sandhill cranes at the center of his novel, *The Echo Maker*. Sandhill cranes are the oldest living species of bird, notes the novel's narrator, dating back at least 2.5 million years, and are thus only "one stutter step away from pterodactyls."[12] Powers names his novel "echo maker," for the word the Anishinabe use to describe the sound sandhill cranes make in a complex and extended series of coordinated calls heard when a male courts the female he will pair with for life. In the Anishinabe folktale, a girl is standing alone in a meadow. She is suddenly surrounded in a great turning cloud of cranes that "trumpet" to drown out her calls.[13] The "cloud of dust" surrounding the girl gives evidence of the mating dances and various associated behaviors such as bowing, jumping, running, stick or grass tossing, as well as wing flapping.

Powers sets the novel in the very center of North America, the point on the Platte River where cranes have wintered for centuries. This place marks the intersection of two migratory corridors that, for centuries, have put humans and animals at cross-purposes. On one axis, is the "Central Flyway," explains Powers in an interview with Alex Michod, which is used by "hundreds of millions of migratory birds" who rest during migration "along a sixty-mile stretch of the Platte."[14] On the other axis are the great historical American east-to-west routes for Euro-American colonizers who crossed North America on the Oregon Trail, Mormon Trail, Pony Express, transcontinental railroad, Lincoln Highway, and Interstate 80. On one route, cranes fly to the tundras and glacial bays of the iconic North, then back to the Platte. On the other, humans move east and west as they establish the great routes of commerce that have played a role in catalyzing the transition of the Holocene into the Anthropocene. For Powers, "crane girl" becomes what I call in *American Indian Literature, Environmental Justice, and Ecocriticism*, a "seeing instrument" for examining the future of "anthropos" on the planet.[15] As I explain, many writers in the Americas – indigenous and nonindigenous – have employed these kinds of story cycles, both oral and written, as archives of information, or "living books."

   In what follows, then, I examine how contemporary writers are employing iconic riverine and forest geographies, and the animals and oral story cycles associated with them, as an imaginative force for thinking about what anthropologist Julie Cruickshank has called "the origins and [ongoing] transformations of the world and its inhabitants."[16] In order to study the "prehistory" of both multispecies ethnography and environmental justice, I set pink dolphins and sandhill cranes into the context of what Peruvian American anthropologist Marisol de la Cadena and others have described as a "cosmopolitics" that is marking "epochal changes" in the Americas.[17] Following other "multispecies ethnographers," I examine how these stories are offering ecocritics and activists new tools, or "seeing instuments," for making abstract, often intangible global patterns associated with climate change accessible to a wider public.

Dolphin Cities as Seeing Instruments

Juan Carlos Galeano left his native Columbia at the age of eighteen, but returns most summers to hunt, fish, and plant with the mixed Afro-indigenous groups who continue to work for a subsistence living near the Amazon River running through Ecuador, Peru, and Bolivia. Galeano notes that it is still common to hear the cosmological tales he was told as a boy about "spirits of the forest," and these are the stories he has collected in *Folktales of the Amazon* (xvi–xviii). Not surprisingly, dolphins appear frequently in all Galeano's work. The pink dolphin, known for its friendliness and lack of caution around humans (which helps to explain its presence in so many stories) has a highly developed sense of curiosity. In his folktale collection and in his film Galeano documents tales about "Sachamama," the mother of the forest, and "Yakumama," the "Mother of all Water Beings," described as an Anaconda who moves easily through water and presides over the pink dolphins, which are described alternately as "gringos," "policemen," and "rich people" living at the bottom of rivers. The people interviewed in Galeano's film, however, believe that because of the noise of boats and extensive logging, Yakumama, who is neither female nor male but an androgenous representation of "Source of Light/Source of Life," is retreating deeper into the forest and cannot protect her children.[18] Therefore, guided by their oral traditions, humans in the contemporary world must step into Sachamama/

Yakumama's role by passing new laws giving dolphins and other "sentient beings" the "right" to protection.

As Cruikshank explains, from the Global South to the glacial North, indigenous oral "archives" often frame significant geographies such as rainforests and glaciers as "intensely social spaces where human behavior, especially casual hubris or arrogance, can trigger dramatic and unpleasant consequences in the physical world."[19] Today, in a rapidly changing world, formulations of "forest mothers" or glaciers that "listen," Cruikshank writes, are consistently employed "as timeless narratives in a timely way"; they are not assigned to the category of "myth" and applied only to the past as "cultural artifact extraneous to history."[20] Rather, they are employed as authoritative commentary/theory illuminating the consequences of global economic development for local humans, animals, and nonhumans.

Moreover, as anthropologist Michael Uzendoski observes in the "Foreword" to Galeano's folktale collection, contemporary indigenous storytellers and writers are "less concerned with cultural boundaries than they are with natural ones."[21] Stories about human relationships with mother trees, anacondas, and pink dolphins abide by a complex philosophy that has been termed by Brazilian anthropologist Eduardo Viveiros de Castro as "perspectival multinaturalism," a notion that suggests "the world is inhabited by different sorts of subjects or persons, human and non-human, which apprehend reality from distinct points of view."[22] These philosophies speak of humans, animals, and spirits participating in the same world, although with different sensory apparati constituting not just multicultural (human) worlds that imply a unity of nature and a multiplicity of cultures, but multinatural worlds that imply corporeal diversity and its attendant diversity of perspectives.[23] These stories offer those who possess them "a complex navigational system" or "seeing instrument" for understanding human relation to the stars, animals, soils, and planting cycles; they allow humans to "see" spans of history unavailable in a single lifetime and thus offer them access to scales of time necessary to understanding environmental change at planetary levels.[24] Knowledge of small-scale, regional multinatural relationships represented as transformational dolphins (or cranes), or large-scale ecosystemic relationships represented as "Mother of All Water Beings," have been "archived" in their various forms, oral or written, and continue, even today, to offer humans understanding of how "the world came to be through a series of transformations – often violent and predatory" – over the course of geological and biospheric time.[25]

Bodies of oral knowledge from North and South America, Latin America, and the Carribbean began to be systematically collected in the late nineteenth and early twentieth century by the Bureau of American Ethnography, which published reports that can still be found in most U.S. university libraries. Throughout the twentieth and twenty-first centuries these reports have been consulted by numerous anthropologists and ethnographers and also by tribal North American groups suing for land claims in national and state court systems. Renowed indigenous writers such as Louise Erdrich (Anishinabe) and Leslie Marmon Silko (Laguna/Hispana/Anglo) have also used them to research particular aspects of tribal cultural and ecological knowledge that they weave into their contemporary poetry and novels.[26] These reports have a genealogy that extends back to German geologist Alexander von Humboldt's travels in the Amazon at the end of the eighteenth century. In *A Passage to Cosmos*, Laura Dassow Walls describes how Humboldt's wide-ranging research in Europe and South America influenced an intellectual network, which included figures both mainstream and dissident who would deploy "his ideas in often contradictory ways" throughout the nineteenth century and into the twenty-first.[27] One of the "dissidents" was Franz Boas, a German geographer, who studied the Inuit people of what is now the Canadian North in British Columbia, and later shaped the emerging field of anthropology. Calling himself a "cosmographer," Boas considered every phenomenon "worthy of being studied for its own sake" and, at Columbia University, trained a generation of scholars who would shape the field of ethnography, including Edward Sapir, Ruth Benedict, and Zora Neale Hurston. A "cosmographer," he told his students, "studies the history of phenomena, what they are and how they came to be just that way" and "cherishes the very particulars that science uses then throws away."[28] Today, ethnographers continue to collect the oral astronomical, ceremonial, cultural, agroecological, and ethnobotanical knowledges of diverse ethnic groups around the world and treat them as "archives," or sophisticated "cosmographies," rather than simplistic "superstitions." This history helps to explain why Michael Uzendoski describes Galeano's folklore collection as "neo-Boasian." It also points to a "pre-history" for multispecies ethnography and, as I show, the environmental justice movement as well.

The Prehistory of Multispecies Ethnography and Climate Justice

According to Walls, Humboldt's research in the Amazon influenced his most important scientific disciple, Charles Darwin, and, later, a generation of thinkers today recognized as the founders of American environmentalism, including Emerson and Thoreau. After returning to Europe, he published his *magnum opus*, the five volume *Cosmos*, which would influence a generation of thinkers on several continents. Humboldt defined "nature" as "a planetary interactive causal network operating across multiple scale levels, temporal and spatial."[29] Walls traces how his views were inspired by inter-actions with the indigenous peoples he met and later, back in Europe, by his friendships with key figures hailing from the Amazonian basin such as Simón Bolívar. In turn, Bolívar was inspired by Humboldt's views on liberty, the immorality of slavery, and the intelligence and agency of indigenous peoples. Bolívar went on to lead revolutionary movements that shaped the modern nation-states of the Amazonian and Andean regions and, today, his influence can be seen in the emergence of an international "cosmopolitical" movement, led by indigenous and ethnic minority groups based largely in the Global South. The World Conference on the Rights of Mother Earth and the passage of Bolivia's "Law of Mother Earth" can be seen as part of this continuing "evolution/revolution."

Walls's description of the activities of Humboldt and Bolívar also suggests how their friendship laid the groundwork for what would later become the environmental justice movement, and still later, "cosmopolitics." Humboldt was the first to warn about the links between "deforestation, environmental change and depopulation."[30] Arguably, these are the kinds of links associ-ated with climate justice activism today, and they opened a space of pos-sibility for what would become known as "comospolitics" at a much later date. Walls traces Humboldt's references to Indian and slave revolts as she documents Humboldt's views on liberty, the immorality of slavery, and the intelligence and agency of indigenous peoples, and as she discusses how these views acted powerfully on Bolívar's political vision and the revolution-ary movements that shaped the modern nation-states of the Amazonian and Andean regions. As I explain in *American Indian Literature, Environmental Justice, and Ecocriticism*, in an argument that parallels Humboldt's, contem-porary indigenous-authored poetry and fiction pushes the advent of indig-enous social justice and environmental "movements" in the Americas back (at least) to the Pueblo Revolt of 1680 in the Southwest region of North America and to every slave revolt throughout the Americas. More recently, I have updated this argument with a genealogy of indigenous social and envi-ronmental justice political organization in the Global South that predates the 1960s.[31]

Indigenous knowledges should never be romanticized as somehow "authentically" linking particular ethnic groups to "Nature." Contemporary indigenous and ethnic minority writers and activists, however, do employ cosmological oral traditions as what I describe as environmental justice "cultural critique" that continues to have explanatory power in the pre-sent.[32] For example, in *Tracks*, Annishannabe writer Louise Erdrich deploys stories from the oral tradition about transformational animals – bears and wolves – in ways that equip her fictional characters with "theory," which enables them to question the "modern world" through their own multi-natural understandings of human and nonhuman relationship. With its shape-shifting "medicine" healer, Nanapush, who speaks several (human) languages, understands the multinatural (languages) of nonhumans that today scientists are calling "biosemiotics," and serves on the local tribal council, *Tracks* invites readers into an interpretive process that explores "other ways of knowing, other modes of theorizing" and calls readers into active (read: political) participation "in building alternative visions of the world."[33] The novel asserts that indigenous people have continued to inter-act with nonhuman beings existing at multiple scales, both seen and unseen, while participating in the "modern" world.[34]

Characters commonly portrayed as having transformational quali-ties in oral story cycles blur species lines. Erdrich calls upon one such Annishinabe character to draw *Tracks*' "bearwalking" young girl, Fleur. Erdrich employs Fleur's transformational characteristics to address con-temporary social and environmental injustices by suggesting that (cultural, legal, economic, and ecological) "boundaries are permeable."[35] Other characters in the novel suspect that Fleur, a member of the powerful bear clan, may, at times, transform into a bear and "see" from the perspective of a bear. She may thus have access to an "alternative vision" that may assist her in finding "answers to the urgent social and ecological questions fac-ing the community."[36] I argue that if "theory" is a "way of knowing that reveals that what '*is*' is not necessarily the real/true" but "only the existing actuality which is transformable," ... then it becomes entirely "possible to see how traditional folktales, proverbs, trickster stories, and animal tales might be considered 'theory.'"[37] Erdrich encourages readers to think about how they, like Fleur, might alter the power relations at the root of social and ecological imbalances caused by corporate extraction – logging and mining – that began accelerating in the United States on Indian lands after the turn of the twentieth century.

Erdrich is blurring the boundaries between oral and written, past and present, human and animal to create a fictional "multispecies ethnography" that works as cultural critique of the powerful forces at work in the anthro-pocene. She depicts Nanapush encouraging Fleur's daughter Lulu to move between the world of the Anishinabe community and the "modern world" since she will need to know how that world works in order to change it. In a scene in which Lulu is returning home from some very harsh experiences at a boarding school, she rushes into the arms of Nanapush. The novel sug-gests that in the safety of Nanapush's arms, Lulu will learn to make the sig-nificance of Anishinabe culture, historical experiences, and understandings of a multinatural world "visible," while also insisting on her own authority to name the terms of her interaction between multiple social and natural worlds.

What is Anthropos? Writing in the Anthropocene

The brain capacity of pink Amazonian river dolphins is estimated to be 40 percent larger than that of humans. This may be one of the reasons why local people interviewed in Juan Carlo's Galeano's documentary, *The Trees Have Mothers*, sometimes say the pink dolphin is so powerful that it can "take over human minds" and easily "transform" humans into dolphins.[38] In *The Echo Maker*, Richard Powers is also interested in brains and the intelligence of both sandhill cranes and humans, and, to use Debra Bird Rose's words, in the "situated connectivities that bind [humans] into multi-species communities."[39] The novel tells the story of Karin Schluter, who has left her job in another city to come home to Kearney, Nebraska, to help her twenty-seven-year-old brother, Mark, recover from a brain injury. Earlier, Mark's truck careens off a country road after a night spent with friends. He crashes into a ditch on the banks of the Platte River where thousands of magnificent sandhill cranes (*grus canadensis*) settle in their annual migration. After spending a cold, frozen night in his smashed truck, Mark develops Capgras syndrome, a brain condition that causes him to see his loved ones as imposters he suspects of being inhuman. In Mark's case, the inhuman "imposter" is his only surviving family member, Karin.

In an interview with Alec Michod, Powers expresses his fascination with the ways that sandhill cranes, who winter on the Platte River, "are weirdly intelligent, smart in an alien way that [humans are] not quite smart enough to see. And yet, the core parts of their brains are still contained in ours."[40] Over the course of the novel, readers learn that the human brain is a "mind-boggling redesign" but "can't escape its past."[41] Human brains, and bird brains, include a copy of the "reptile's brain," buried in layers of evolution.[42] In other words, the main structures found in every mammal's brain includes a brainstem and cerebellum that is still shaped just like the reptile's. Powers uses Mark's brain injury and crane intelligence to open up the story to all kinds of neurological and ecological traces, telling Michod that cranes "use an entirely different part of their brain as the seat of their intelligence" and their "brain-to-body ratio" makes them "comparable to higher primates."[43] As the novel's narrator states, cranes fly only once with their parents to the North, following landmarks, "water, mountains, woods," and memorizing a "crane map" inside their "crane head." For Powers, this makes both humans and cranes a fitting subject for "writing in the anthropocene." Like other multispecies ethnographers, he strongly suggests that "human-nature is an interspecies relationship."[44]

Over the course of the novel, Powers uses the Anishinabe story about a girl transforming into a crane as a "seeing instrument" to raise questions about human intelligence and apathetic attitudes toward climate change and its often dire consequences for interspecies relationships. Despite the amount of information readily available about the world's changing climate, a 2010 Yale University poll found that only 12 percent of Americans were "very worried" about global warming.[45] In analyzing this trend, environmental educators point out that species extinction is hard for most humans to grasp since they live less than one hundred years, and are often unfamiliar with the history of life on earth – plate tectonics, ancient landscapes and atmospheres, mega-extinctions, and cosmic impacts. Such highly abstract concepts require skilled juxtaposition of scale and an advanced level of cognitive sophistication.

This helps to explain why there are such baffling and disastrous disconnections between the cognitive awareness of climate change and the generally insignificant alterations in lifestyle that humans, specifically in Global North countries, seem prepared to countenance. Powers illustrates this problem with Karin, a character who has spent her entire life living in the same place the cranes shelter in winter. Nevertheless, Karin knows little about cranes. During the prolonged and lonely months of her brother's recovery – in which he comes out of a coma and recognizes everyone except her – Karin reaches out to her community to become a "caring" (as her name and its spelling suggests) volunteer at the sandhill crane reserve. There she learns that the Platte River boasts fifteen dams and provides "irrigation for three states," which lowers the water table, shrinks the wetlands on which the cranes depend, and pushes the half million sandhill cranes remaining on the earth into ever shrinking space. The anxiety of overcrowding, and the disease this breeds among cranes huddling too closely, belies the awe expressed by the tourists who flock to the refuge because they can see "so many birds."[46] In the face of seeming hopelessness for the birds, Karin (who is just as "ordinary" person) begins, in a sense, "becoming crane," when she takes a low-paying job at the crane refuge so that she can work for their survival. Like the girl in the Annishinabe tale who is associated with the annual migration of cranes, each year, Karin will be on the Platte when the cranes arrive, and she will be there when they lift off "for the tundra, peat bogs and muskegs, a remembered origin."[47]

Powers shows that as they fly North, in a cycle that is thousands of years old, the cranes intersect with human migration routes/activities that put them at risk in the anthropocene. At the same time, the birds remind those who know the story of "the capture of the human's daughter" of the connections between humans and cranes and two geographies, one in the North and one at the center of a continent.[48] These geographies are becoming iconic, writes Cruikshank, precisely because global climate change is giving glaciers and "the North" the appearance of being themselves an "endangered species."[49] Thus the crane girl story at the center of Powers' novel becomes an "instrument" for "seeing" multispecies relationships in terms of the biographical, geographical, and political lives of all humans and animals and the places they live. She illustrates how places can "listen" in the sense that they "respond" to hubris or arrogance with sometimes invisible and sometimes dramatic material and ecological consequences. Her story of transformation makes the "invisible" processes necessary to continued biospheric vitality "visible." Karin/crane girl also suggests Powers' notion that "ordinary people" can transform themselves and become "part of something larger."[50]

Cosmos + Politics

In *The Trees Have Mothers*, community members say that Sachamama/Yakumama "listens," is aware of human arrogance, and sometimes transforms him/herself into a desirable shape in order to lead misbehavers away, never to be seen again. However, not all Sachamama stories are about misbehavers. In one version, a boy voluntarily leaves his family to live with pink dolphins. He stays too long, living in luxury, and decides not to return, causing his mother grief. To ease her hardship, he sends her a letter inside a small bag with a few nuggets of gold. When she opens the bag, the gold falls out.[51] This is the version of the story, Galeano observes, that first lured sixteenth-century conquistadors into the forest in search of "El Dorado," with horrible consequences for forest dwellers.[52]

In Galeano's documentary, lost boys and gold become a frame, providing local people with a "seeing instrument" for thinking about the real world disappearance of a twenty-year-old indigenous boy, James Cataschunga. A lifelong city dweller with no experience in the rainforest, James joins his grandfather and cousins to go fishing and is last seen at a forked trailhead leading into the forest. His disappearance near the city of Inquitos, Peru, catalyzes the narration of stories illustrating that for indigenous and ethnic minority peoples living in a rapidly globalizing world, forest mothers have never ceased to exist. Galeano follows Ana, James' mother, as she desperately attempts to locate him over the course of the next eight months. Looking into the camera, holding the boy's plastic identification card and caressing his washed and folded pants and hooded jacket (which are the only remaining material evidence of his existence), Anna speaks of her hope for his return.

Her son worked with her selling grilled fish in an Inquitos food stand that provides the family of six their only means of support. Devastated by his absence, Ana summarizes various explanations for her son's disappearance with reference to dolphins who lead humans to an "enchanted city," where there is no poverty and the people do not "kill themselves with work."[53] Maybe, she speculates hopefully, he has simply gone off to visit a beautiful girlfriend/dolphin and will be back soon.[54]

Like Ana, many of the people interviewed for the film theorize about James' unfortunate disappearance through familiar stories. As they read the situation through the story of the boy sending his mother gold, townspeople remark on the oil companies, mining enterprises, agribusiness, and cocaine producers who, like the conquistadors, do not "ask permission from the mothers of the trees" before they destroy "the whole forest."[55] The story of a boy sending his mother gold becomes a form of cultural critique used to explain the greed of a modern world "thirsty for oil, timber, gold, cocaine, and other Amazonian products like rubber."[56] The people are angry that the big fish they depended on for food "are gone, water is poisonous, and children are dying from contamination, and drought is drying up the Amazon."[57] Here, the connections between dolphins, humans, and gold resurfaces (and helps to explain why a new law to protect the dolphins is necessary). As most residents of the Amazonian basin know, dolphins are threatened not only by drought, but also by mercury contamination of rivers caused by illegal gold mining operations.[58] Stories about human women who give birth to dolphins or human children who go to live with the dolphins become a "seeing instrument" that gives urgency to the knowledge that unseen toxins are moving through human and nonhuman bodies, and the mighty Amazon itself might be turned by climate change into "a ditch."[59] The discussions of James, of his loss, turn into discussions of increasingly complex multicultural, multinational, and multispecies relationships that are being changed by chemical spills, overfishing, water pollution, and poverty.

Galeano's film documents "ordinary" people, in the same sense that Power's character Karin/crane girl is ordinary. Like Karin, they have decided not to wait passively as their communities are polluted and suffer the consequences of climate change. Like the delegates who gathered for the World People's Conference on the Rights of Mother Earth, these people are guided by stories of forest mothers and pink dolphins that suggest, to use the words of the Universal Declaration on the Rights of Mother Earth and Climate Change, that "violations against our soils, air, forests, rivers, lakes, biodiversity, and the cosmos are assaults against us." "Us" is emphasized to mean all living beings – human and nonhuman. Delegates proposed as solution a shift in the world's attention from "living better" to "living well" by which they mean "supporting a society based on social and environmental justice, which sees life as its purpose."[60]

As a growing number of writers, ethnographers, literary critics, and scientists have observed, it is becoming increasingly clear that humans are the primary agents driving climate change. At the same time, as Daniel Fischlin and Martha Nandorfy explain in *The Community of Rights / Rights of Community*, global south environmentalisms are reframing long-held notions about the separation between human/nonhuman as a "community of rights." The idea of "community" suggests a complex allegory for relational identities that would unravel generally accepted notions of "human rights" that pay scant attention to the environmental conditions upon which "humanity" depends for survival. In a globalizing and corporatizing world, some communities are pushing the notion of "rights" and "citizenship" beyond the confines of legalistic and political structures based only on "the human," since these terms often problematically promote notions of identification, symmetry, totality, and unity employed to justify hegemonic and totalitarian actions, by both state and corporations, in the name of community.[61] Coming into a "middle place," as I phrase it in earlier work, these communities are hammering out a "cosmopolitics" that seeks to answer difficult questions about how they might "transform structures and systems that cause climate change and other threats to Mother Earth."[62]

NOTES

1 Juan Carlos Galeano, *Amazonia*, James Kimbrell and Rebecca Morgan, trans. Second edition (Spanish/English) (Inquitos, Peru: Centro de Estudios Teológicos de la Amazonía, 2012), p. 55.

2 Juan Carlos Galeano, *Folktales of the Amazon*, Rebecca Morgan and Kenneth Watson, trans. (Westport, CT and London: Libraries Unlimited, 2009), pp. 19–20.

3 David Adams, "Amazon Could Shrink by 85% Due to Climate Change, Scientists Say," *The Guardian* 11 (March 2009), n.p., http://www.guardian.co.uk/environment/2009/mar/11/amazon-global-warming-trees.

4 Grey, Richard, "Pink River Dolphins at Risk from Drought," *The Telegraph* (7 November 2010), n.p., http://www.telegraph.co.uk/earth/wildlife/8114754/Pink-river-dolphins-at-risk-from-drought.html.

5 The International Union for Conservation of Nature, Redlist of Threatened Species, n.p., http://www.iucnredlist.org/details/10831/0.

6 World Wild Life Fund Global, "The South American River Dolphin (Inia Boliviensis) Declared Bolivia's Natural Heritage" (10 September 2012), n.p., http://worldwildlife.org/stories/the-bolivian-river-dolphin-conservation-ambassador-of-the-amazon.

7 "World Faces 'Irreversible' Climate Change, Researchers Warn," *CNN* (13 March 2009), http://www.cnn.com/2009/WORLD/europe/03/12/irreversible.climate/index.html.

8   Universal Declaration on the Rights of Mother Earth and Climate Change, "Preamble," n.p., http://pwccc.wordpress.com/programa/.

9   Paul J. Crutzen and Eugene F. Stoermer, "The Anthropocene," *Global Change Newsletter* 41 (2000), 17–18.

10 Debra Bird Rose, "Introduction: Writing in the Anthropocene," *Australian Humanities Review* 49 (2009), 87.

11 S. Eben Kirksey and Stefen Helmreich, "The Emergence of Multispecies Ethnography," *Cultural Anthropology* 25 (2010), 545.

12 Richard Powers, *The Echo Maker* (New York: Picador, 2006), p. 3.

13 Powers, *The Echo Maker*, p. 99.

14 Alec Michod, "The Brain Is the Ultimate Storytelling Machine, and Consciousness Is the Ultimate Story: Interview with Richard Powers," *The Believer* (February 2007), n.p., http://www.believermag.com/issues/200702/?read=interview_powers.

15 Joni Adamson, *American Indian Literature, Environmental Justice, and Ecocriticism: The Middle Place* (Tucson, AZ: University of Arizona Press, 2001), p. 145.

16 Julie Cruikshank, *Do Glaciers Listen? Local Knowledge, Colonial Encounters, and Social Imagination* (Seattle: University of Washington Press, 2005), p. 99.

17 Marisol De la Cadena, "Indigenous Cosmopolitics in the Andes: Conceptual Reflections Beyond 'Politics,'" *Cultural Anthropology* 25.2 (2010), 334. See also, Joni Adamson, "Indigenous Literatures, Multinaturalism, and *Avatar*: The Emergence of Indigenous Cosmopolitics," *American Literary History (ALH)*, Special Issue: Sustainability in America 24.1 (2012), 143–167.

18 Valliere Richard Auzenne and Juan Carlos Galeano, Dirs., *The Trees Have a Mother: Amazonian Cosmologies, Folktales, and Mystery* (Tallahassee, FL: Florida State University Film School, 2008). Available at Films on Demand, http://digital.films.com/play/WNHAND. For a definition of "Pachamama/Sachamama/Yakumama," see De la Cadena, "Indigenous Cosmopolitics," 335, 350.

19 Cruikshank, *Do Glaciers Listen?*, p. 11.

20 Cruikshank, *Do Glaciers Listen?*, p. 57.

21 Michael Uzendoski, "Foreword," in Juan Carlos Galeano, *Folktales of the Amazon*, p. xi.

22 Eduardo Batalha Viveiros de Castro, "Cosmological Deixis and Amerindian Perspectivism," *Journal of the Royal Anthropological Institute* 4.3 (1998), 469.

23 Eduardo Batalha Viveiros de Castro, "Exchanging Perspectives: The Transformation of Objects into Subjects in Amerindian Ontologies," *Common Knowledge* 10.3 (Fall 2004), 467.

24 Adamson, *American*, p. 141.

25 Uzendoski, "Foreword," p. x.

26 Adamson, *American*, p. 175–176.

27 Laura Dassow Walls, *The Passage to Cosmos: Alexander von Humboldt and the Shaping of America* (Chicago: The University of Chicago Press, 2009), p. 268.

28 Walls, *The Passage*, p. 212.

29 Walls, *The Passage*, p. 11.

30 Walls, *The Passage*, p. ix.

31 See Joni Adamson, ""¡Todos Somos Indios!": Revolutionary Imagination, Alternative Modernity, and Transnational Organizing in the Work of Silko, Tamez

and Anzaldúa," *The Journal of Transnational American Studies* (May 2012), pp. 1–26.

32 Adamson, *American*, p. 112.

33 Ibid. For more on the semiotic processes at work in nature, or "biosemiotics," see Adamson, "Indigenous Literatures, Multinaturalism and *Avatar*."

34 Cf. Bruno Latour, *We Have Never Been Modern* (Cambridge, MA: Harvard University Press, 1993).

35 Adamson, *American*, p. 106.

36 Adamson, *American*, p. 109.

37 Adamson, *American*, p. 100.

38 Auzenne and Galeano, *The Trees*, n.p.

39 Rose, "Introduction," p. 87.

40 Michod, "The Brain Is the Ultimate Storytelling Machine," n.p.

41 Powers, *The Echo Maker*, p. 17.

42 Ibid., p. 16.

43 Michod, "The Brain Is the Ultimate Storytelling Machine, n.p.

44 Powers, *The Echo Maker*, p. 16; Kirksey and Helmreich, "The Emergence of Multispecies Ethnography," p. 551.

45 Elizabeth Rosenthal, "EPA Makes its Case on Climate Change," *New York Times* (27 April 2010), n.p., http://green.blogs.nytimes.com/2010/04/27/e-p-a-makes-its-case-on-climate-change/?scp=2&sq=poll%20climate%20change&st=cse.

46 Powers, *The Echo Maker*, p. 57.

47 Ibid., p. 97.

48 Ibid., p. 99.

49 Cruikshank, *Do Glaciers Listen?*, p. 6.

50 Alec Michod, "The Brain Is the Ultimate Storytelling Machine," n.p.

51 Galeano, *Folktales*, pp. 19–20.

52 Galeano, *Folktales*, p. 92.

53 Galeano, *Folktales*, p. 91.

54 Auzenne and Galeano, *The Trees*, n.p.

55 Ibid.

56 Galeano, *Folktales*, p. xx.

57 Auzenne and Galeano, *The Trees*, n.p.

58 World Wild Life Fund Global, "The South American River Dolphin," n.p.

59 Galeano, *Folktales*, pp. 28, 35.

60 Universal Declaration, Art. 2, n.p.

61 See Daniel Fischlin and Martha Nandorfy, *The Community of Rights / The Rights of Community* (New Delhi: Oxford University Press/Black Rose Books, 2012).

62 Adamson, *American*, pp. 46–48, 156–159; Universal Declaration, "Preamble," n.p.

12

BONNIE ROOS AND ALEX HUNT

Systems and Secrecy: Postcolonial Ecocriticism and Ghosh's *The Calcutta Chromosome*

When Ronald Ross, former British Colonial officer in India, won the 1902 Nobel Prize for Physiology or Medicine for identifying malaria vectors, his place in Western medicine was assured. Ross identified a parasite, Plasmodium, which infects mosquitoes with malaria, which in turn spread the infection to humans. Ross later broadened appreciation for his accomplishment to a wider audience in publishing his diaries. These writings reinforce a heroic paradigm that disenfranchised those Indian subjects who, in making his research possible, played a role in this discovery. Ross ignored the ideological work – so often assumed absent in scientific discovery – operating within his experiments. Malaria's disproportionate effect on Westerners traveling to tropical and subtropical regions necessarily linked scientific progress to a colonial agenda – facts outside the scope of his diaries. Ross's obliviousness to the colonial politics at work, which we might today attribute to his conditioning by the heroic Western narrative he promulgates, is startling.[1]

In rewriting the history of Ross's discovery in *The Calcutta Chromosome: A Novel of Fevers, Delirium and Discovery* (1995), Amitav Ghosh offers a postcolonial critique by raising the specters of unspoken voices to recover their role in this history.[2] Such perspectives have always been a part of postcolonial conversations: when language is stolen, history is erased or written from the perspective of the colonizer, people are displaced, and education and culture are destroyed, making use of the undocumented and uncorroborated, the "silent" voices, is often among the only means to resist oppression. Indeed, the complications of addressing the silence of the disenfranchised prompted Gayatri Spivak's "Can the Subaltern Speak?," which cautioned critics' efforts to speak "for" the colonized.[3] In ecocriticism, "nature's" silence is also often seen as that which allows for its exploitation, and ecocritics debate the difficulties of trying to "speak a word for nature."[4] Ghosh is keenly aware of these complexities, as his fictional character, famous writer Phulboni, suggests: "I have walked the innermost streets of this most secret of cities, looking always to find her who has so long eluded me: Silence herself ... every word I have ever penned has been written for her. ... If I stand before you now, in this most public of places, it is because I am on the point of desperation and know of no other way to reach her."[5] Phulboni's privilege, and his disclosure of silence's meaning, once, to his beloved, has forever changed his relationship to it, and he can never go back; while he can write on behalf of silence, his entry into fame and discursive narrative traditions means he will be forever separated from it. Ghosh, by contrast, never reveals the workings of silence in his entry into popular detective and science-fiction novel genres. Even so, his narrative structure depends on a paradoxically active notion of silence for its development.[6] Ghosh's writing is particularly instructive not only because he highlights exploitation, but because he rewrites the formal narrative structure to attune his reader to these silences, so that we are empowered to become critical, active readers – detectives – who, as we become better aware of the interdependencies of the various hierarchical strata, are more responsible global citizens; we describe this narrative structure as reflective of postcolonial uneven development.

Ghosh's interest in malaria speaks not only to Ross's moment, but also to our own. According to current malaria statistics from the World Health Organization, each year sees 250 million new cases. While only about 4 per-cent of infected people die, its sheer prevalence, particularly in tropical and subtropical regions, makes it one of the most deadly diseases on the planet. With four different strains, the responses to malaria vary widely, as some strains remain in the host human indefinitely, causing an unpredict-able recurrence. There still is no cure or vaccine. Beyond its sheer deadli-ness, two issues make malaria a concern today. First, antimalarial medicines are quickly becoming ineffective as the disease evolves to counter our best-working defenses.[7] Second, the widespread use of insecticides in the worst-affected areas both encourages chemical-resistant mosquitoes and negatively affects environmental habitats. Ghosh excavates the histories of malaria, but he is also attuned to the possibility of a malaria epidemic today.

To avoiding such dire prognostication and effecting change we must, first, learn from our histories, written and unwritten. And, although the geo-graphical field is different, these ecological and biological issues are nothing less than canon for ecocritics. In her environmental classic *Silent Spring* from 1962, Rachel Carson theorized ecological subjectivity, responding to the massive use of DDT as agricultural pesticide. Carson identified DDT as a particularly dangerous chemical moving through the ecosystem and human bodies. Ironically, DDT was initially used during World War II in the Pacific theater to protect soldiers from mosquitoes carrying malaria. Subsequently applied freely in the United States, the miracle preventative chemical became emblematic of the new recognition of toxicity. Through recognition of pollution from pesticide or nuclear fallout, we recognized our bodily connection to air, earth, and water, the permeability of our bodies within larger ecosystemic flows. Ecology, as Rebecca Solnit put it, should have come as a "vision of harmony," but came as a "nightmare of contamination instead."[8] As a disease that moves through several layers of an ecosystem – microbial, insect, human – malaria certainly reminds us of our bodily connections to the "outside" of our environment. Indeed, malaria, as a "natural" contaminant, forces us to reimagine our bodies as involved in a relation of systems that move through the permeable membranes we pretend distinguish ourselves from the environments we inhabit.[9]

Early research on malaria like Ross's coincided with European colonization of tropical zones of Africa, India, and elsewhere. That malaria became an issue of health for colonists like the English in India lends further layers or interlinking systems of imperial control and "indigenous" resistance. To be an Englishman in India infected with malaria was to be colonized in return on the bodily level. Thus, the quest to decode the mystery of malaria on the part of European powers demonstrates the degree to which the colonial enterprise was an ecological and epidemiological effort as well as an economic and imperial project: to control the malaria bug meant another level of control of colonial spaces. Malaria's medical history also reminds us of the racism inherent in works of so-called scientific progress to halt disease. Ross's efforts to discover the malaria vector demanded that he use test subjects. And despite his offer to pay them, Ross's scientific experiments on natives suggest practices only slightly less sinister than Pfizer's recent experiments in Kano, Nigeria, popularized in John le Carré's novel, *The Constant Gardener*.

Therefore, addressing malaria today demands an awareness of the way in which the environment intersects and affects issues of class and race – global environmental justice. Western ecocriticism has demonstrated a move toward environmental justice issues, analyzing, for example, the geographical proximities between the nuclear military-industrial complex and indigenous lands. But with the emergence of postcolonial ecocriticism, we recognize these exploitative practices are more pronounced when surveyed on a global scale. For example, Ken Saro-Wiwa's cultural defense of the Ogoni peoples of Nigeria involved peaceful protests against Shell Oil's business practices because of its environmental destruction in the Niger Delta. But it was Shell's undocumented collusion with Nigerian government that resulted in Saro-Wiwa's "trial," torture, and hanging in 1995. In such cases, companies like Pfizer or Shell rely on racist assumptions that the global community will ignore events transpiring in Africa, and the profits exceed the cost of unlikely exposure. Critical failure to connect environmental concerns with global economic and human concerns allows for these actions to remain covert, so long as we do not appreciate how narrative structure conspires with hegemonic systems to ensure our ignorance about these interconnections.

Therefore, as part of a postcolonial ecocriticism, all silenced voices, those of women, for instance, are also significant considerations. As often pointed out, women around the world in their relationship to childbearing and rearing have often been endangered by environmental and domestic hazards, and have been the leaders in communities in organizing grassroots resistance in environmental justice cases, as with Wangari Mathai's tree planting efforts. A recent report on immigration highlighted a trend of Manhattan families obtaining Tibetan nannies,[10] reminding us that such flows constitute not only an economics but an ecology of laboring bodies that demonstrate gross economic disparity and tacit colonial relationships, all clothed in parental desire for an exotic, maternal, spiritual influence on their children – an issue addressed by Ghosh with his character Tara. The rights of reproduction and the fact of rape are other important aspects of the language of both postcolonialism and environmentalism. And yet, complexities with respect to gender can never present an all-or-nothing approach. In Bessie Head's *Where Rain Clouds Gather*, for example, heroine Makhaya farms imported crops and endorses land enclosures because they produce more immediate food for the starving village. Gender is often a category over which the sometimes-opposing priorities of postcolonialists and ecocritics become most visible.

In short, we see the emergence of a postcolonial ecocriticism through a study of silences as one iteration of a kind of systems theory, in which strands of the local, racial, national, and global are all important features in an investigation of the interdependencies between ecology, production, reproduction, and modes of production. Following the work of Fritjof Capra, systems and complexity theory enable global analysis that describes social organizations and economics not conceived as the binary opposition to natural and ecological systems of life but rather as part of a common system of flows and affects. Natural systems and human systems are best understood in the terms by which we experience them – as participatory and inter-activating rather than as opposing forces. A systems view of postcolonial ecocriticism must consider not merely the way such forces interact within the form of the novel, of course, but how the novel as discourse participates in a far greater global system of ideas with material effects and implications. In a remarkably lucid exemplar of postcolonial ecocriticism, *Postcolonial Environments: Nature, Culture and the Contemporary Indian*

Novel in English (2010), Upamanyu Pablo Mukherjee characterizes India's postcolonial literatures, its irregular excesses and extremes of literary formal method, as an aesthetic structure reflective of India's postcolonial and environmental "uneven development."[11] Even though Mukherjee locates his research in the geographic particularity of India, he articulates why such efforts at addressing overlapping concerns of environmental and postcolonial issues are so critical:

> Once we have grasped this idea of postcolonial India as a globalized entity within a world system, it is impossible not to see that its condition speaks simultaneously at local and global, specific and general, levels. What is happening in India is also happening, has happened and will happen in the rest of Asia, Africa and Latin America. Since at the heart of both colonialism and neo-colonialism lies the historical fact of unfolding, expanding capital, India (and all other "new" postcolonies) can be seen as part of a singular, but radically uneven, world.[12]

Mukerhjee's work is important to our own for two primary reasons: first, the idea of "uneven development" addresses continuing disparities among "'new' postcolonies" and first world nations in terms of interdisciplinary and activist interest; and second, the assertion that an aesthetic and formal structure are necessary components of this analysis adds new strata of meaning for consideration. But we also found useful Mukherjee's insistence on the applicability of his claims for India to a larger world system. While the particularities of a given location are an imperative consideration, nevertheless, as we move from the local to the global, we find commonalities with other postcolonies everywhere around the globe. Building on his comparative model, we argue that environmental issues the world over are interlinked with one another and with other (economic, political) globalizing systems. Because we cannot address one aspect of these issues without catalyzing others, we cannot so privilege environmental concerns that we ride roughshod over the rights of other marginalized factions; to do so is to ignore the premise that these systems are interconnected. What role ecocriticism plays in the future of literary studies depends on how successfully we practice criticism for social and environmental justice in awareness of a daunting tangle of interrelations. Such high-minded rhetoric may unintentionally echo Charlie Marlow's defense of colonization for the "idea" at the back of it, and may seem to present us with an idea of "justice" that is overly simple. Nevertheless we seek a larger, interconnective theory, demanding self-critical, dialectical recognition of silences and uneven terrains, which we must strive to recognize.

As sci-fi detective novel, *Calcutta Chromosome* uses silences to highlight the various strains of its unevenly developed narrative structure. The dystopian story concerns an Egyptian systems-analyst, Antar, whose computer, Ava, presents Antar with a mystery: a co-worker named Murugan, who disappeared while pursuing his counterhistory of Ronald Ross. In pursuing the explanation for Murugan's disappearance, Antar remembers his history with Murugan, and gradually becomes implicated in the story. In an inconclusive, postmodern ending, Antar appears to find and join Murugan through a melding of his body with Ava's, thus achieving a form of biological and technological reincarnation – a futuristic reimagining of traditional Hindu beliefs.

Ghosh invites a postcolonial, meta-nationalist analysis through his seeming insistence on a global, human identity – Antar is an Egyptian inspired by a Hungarian émigré, now living in New York and remembering an Indian coworker researching an English scientist. There is little "nature" present in settings primarily urban, and, with the exception of the mosquito, virtually no nonhuman animals. Even so, the novel is intriguing, inviting a consideration of its silences, such as the unspoken fact of diminishing global water supply, which, as climate change becomes more evident in the story, means a reduction of India's subtropical zones into more arid ones: water shortages.[13] One of the unspoken interrelationships in the novel is how water shortages mean stress on the environment, but they also mean a reduced habitat for mosquito breeding, and by extension, a reduction in rates of malaria: one world crisis vector diminishing another. Ghosh's novel refuses any apocalyptic pessimism, instead reminding us of how interdependent these various uneven systems are on one another.

In an opening frame involving the discovery of Murugan's burnt identity tag, for example, Ghosh describes Antar's experience of working for the International Water Council, which was accumulating "all the endless detritus of twentieth-century officialdom – paper clips, file covers, diskettes"[14] – data on places that "had a bearing on the depletion of the world's water supplies."[15] But the International Water Council is tied to concerns of colonization and big business, for it had "commandeered … some wretched little Agricultural Extension Office in Ovamboland or Barotseland,"[16] and also taken over Antar's previous employer: "LifeWatch had long since been absorbed, along with many other such independent agencies, into the mammoth public health wing of the newly formed International Water Council."[17] Murugan's LifeWatch ID appears to have come through the "stream" of information via "Lhasa," which is the International Water Council's "command center for Asia," and has the "unique distinction of being the only command center in the world in charge of not one but several major Hydraulic Regions: the Ganges-Brahmaputra, the Mekong, the trans-Yangtze, the Hwang-Ho. The Council's information streams for the eastern half of the continent were all routed through Lhasa."[18] Plentiful business and computer "streams" are juxtaposed against the constrained water supplies in the novel, but lend a seeming "naturalness" to technology as well. It is worth noting that each of these immense river systems has imposed much disputed damming projects that have displaced self-sustaining peoples, removing them from their lands and forcing them into urbanization and poverty. Dams in China and India, as activist writers like Arundhati Roy have made visible, are still contentious, fraught constructions. Ghosh's work, which attributes control of the water systems to the fictional International Water Council, seems to suggest, as Mukherjee's work does, that the rationale for the construction of one dam is much like the rationale for the construction of another; its results – beneficial, harmful, both, but always uneven – we might assume, are shared as well.

Given this initial emphasis on water, the virtual absence of its discussion in the remainder of the novel, except as scene setting, is a telling silence. Antar's position is "programmer and systems analyst,"[19] but he admits he is only a "number-cruncher."[20] The appearance of Murugan's ID card is the first time Antar has been called upon to respond actively to Ava in several weeks, and is only noticed because its damaged obscurity forces Ava to slow down. In an initially simple critique of cyber-technology, we see instead of Antar programing Ava, Ava replacing Antar in virtually every aspect of his work. There is no evidence even of his "number-crunching." Antar, slated for retirement, living in the projects, is already almost invisible and is, by his account and the International Water Council's, a nonessential entity. It is unclear who is controlled and who controlling in these endless loops of power and repeating and diminishing histories. And, of course, as an element in virtually any good science-fiction story, the fears of the computer, or industrialization, enslaving us and making us obsolete is a critical aspect of the story.[21] It is indeed no accident that in appropriating popular genres like science fiction and mystery, Ghosh replicates Ronald Ross's efforts to make "avant-garde" literature and ideas scientifically accessible.

But Ghosh's narrative directs attention to silences, pointing to an uneven narrative structure. We begin to see that the systems Ava analyzes, and Antar halfheartedly oversees on behalf of the International Water Council, are unimportant and even a mystification, given the critical issues of India's, and the world's, imminent water shortages. Ava analyzes everything – but never anything that seems directly to do with water. Indeed, as Antar thinks back to remember his childhood, he recalls watching Investigation Officers in Egypt, and offers an explanation for why they analyze so much information:

> They saw themselves making History with their vast water-control experiments: they wanted to record every minute detail of what they had done, what

they would do. Instead of having a historian sift through their dirt, looking for meanings, they wanted to do it themselves: they wanted to load their dirt with their own meanings.

He sat up with a start and said, in Arabic: "That's what you are Ava, a Dust-Counter, "*Addaad al-Turaab*."²²

Ava hears him and becomes intrigued by the phrase, reproducing it in all "the world's languages in declining order of population" until she gets to "dialects of the upper Amazon":

Antar couldn't bear it any longer. "Stop showing off," he shouted. "You don't have to show me you know everything there is to know. *Iskuti*; shut up."

But it was Ava who silenced him instead, serenely spitting the phrases back at him. Antar listened awestruck as "shut up" took on the foliage of the Upper Amazon.²³

In a novel that seems to have little to say about diminishing sources of water, this scene depicts a crucial realization for Antar, who now finds himself complicit in the project of documenting, but simultaneously ignoring, dwindling water supplies. In this sense, Antar becomes an icon of the post-colonial condition. He is critical of the system as a child, and recognized as the smartest boy in his village, but though his guesses about "dust counting" and erased or modified "history" are correct, they are inspired guesses, dismissed because they are spoken by a child who has never left his village. But Antar's childhood also offers us an illustration of the ideological double bind, and the postcolonial position, and our own. Having traveled out of his village in Egypt, and become a global citizen, he is now in a position to know more about the truth, and maintains his earlier position, but he has compromised himself in order to obtain the truth, and to survive: he practices actions he criticized as a child, and becomes part of the machine that helps to mystify the water issue from the public. Indeed, the current water shortages in Egypt, which link it demonstrably to India's contemporary concerns, may have compelled Antar's departure from his village to New York, though if true, this reason remains unstated – another silent thread of the story. In New York, Antar is enfolded into the system that counts dust, and in the face of this barrage of history, this mountain of documentation and facts produced by Ava, he and his version of history are effectively "silenced." In using Antar to frame the story, Ghosh avoids reductive binaries by positing his protagonist as both disenfranchised and complicit in his silence; Ava is similarly complex in her vocalizing, silencing Antar's voice while she performs a linguistic recovery for the diminishing populations of "the Upper Amazon," whose intricacies become a kind of natural "foliage" in Antar's vision. These histories of silence, for Ghosh, and for theorists of postcolonial ecologies, hold an important place and become a catalyst for action precisely because they are an active, not passive, silence: these histories tell of a ruminating and powerful nature, that will respond unmercifully and regardless of toll when it has been exploited beyond repair; they remind the disenfranchised that histories loop and repeat, and as silence becomes a needed language in which humans must engage, their own histories will privilege them, and disenfranchise others.

The complicity of all the figures is part of what makes the story so interesting. Ghosh deconstructs nature/culture and colonizer/colonized binaries not only by offering "hybrid" or "thirdspace" mediations, but also reminds us that if we are all slaves to our systems, we are also empowered within them. This position is presumptuous in that it may inadequately account for the subaltern, but has the advantage of empowering the victim instead of reinforcing narratives of impotence. Okonkwo, for example, of Chinua Achebe's classic postcolonial text *Things Fall Apart*, conveys the tragedy of Umuofia's colonization not only because he was brutalized by the colonized, but because his own brutality allowed for the cultural perspectives of the colonized to take root.

Water is a quiet subtext and pretext of the novel, which ends with rain pouring into Antar's New York apartment building, specifically into the open window of his friend Tara, while she is off watching children play in the sprinklers. Tara, whom Antar identifies as being Indian, represents Ghosh's nod to women's immigration and labor as nannies. Even though "Tara didn't strike [Antar] as someone who would choose to look after children for a living"[24] and strikes him as obviously undocumented, he agrees to help her find work and dwelling in his building. Her symbolic association with water is important to the novel's conclusion. Although water shortages are a significant underpinning to the story, initially Calcutta, India, where Ronald Ross does his research, does not have a visible water shortage – and we should wonder how colonization has impacted this change. Even later, Murugan's efforts to retrieve a secret history of Ross is interrupted, from the outset, by storms and rain, which bring him to the polluted parts of Calcutta, stagnant areas of the city where mosquitoes are most likely to breed. Such water shortages do not seem to affect New York, which is why, at the end, when Antar finally takes action and interrupts, via computer, the showering Calcutta Director, he fails to note the hypocrisy.[25]

Even though India's river systems depend upon the monsoon season, its arrival, which is always too much water at once, does not mean India has enough water. Indeed, in 2012, the monsoons produced 22 percent less than their usual accumulation.[26] But knowing the monsoons will come provides a degree of comfort, a moment for people to ignore the truth of the diminishing water supply. Similarly, while India and Egypt's slums have been cut off from city water, requiring poor residents to walk for miles to obtain a pot or two for family use, it continues to flow to the middle and upper classes. The fish from these rivers once kept local populations fed, and, through its port location, kept people in work. Farmers who bought Monsanto's hybridized seeds produced more crops but required more water and special chemical pesticides; they are now unable to irrigate their fields and have so damaged the earth with these chemicals they cannot return to less water-dependent crops. The people who "matter" are unaffected enough by the loss of water that the dispossessed are ignored. Thus it is that in Ghosh's story, the Director is not only angry that Antar would venture to contact him without invitation, but is caught – exposed – taking a lengthy shower while he emphasizes the loss of water. He complains that instead of dealing with more pressing issues, he now finds himself inexplicably charged with running a shelter – as if the colonization and globalization he seems aware of have nothing to do with the diminishing water supply.

This recovery of silenced history becomes central to Ghosh's writing. The question of why, given the urgency of this water-shortage backdrop, Antar persists in his electronic efforts to locate the missing Murugan (with whom he has no intimate connection) becomes important. For Antar, to recover Murugan is to recover a different kind of history, and a different kind of knowing. Murugan seeks out Ross in part to reclaim the missing history of malaria, of India, of Hinduism. Here Ghosh points unexpectedly to the little-known and largely undocumented use of malaria as a cure for late-stage syphilis (which causes madness and paralysis) and was advocated by Nobel Prize winner Julius Wagner-Jauregg in 1927; "syphilis" is what catalyzes Murugan's quest, as he admits to Urmila: "'But syphilis is curable now, isn't it?' Urmila said. 'With antibiotics?' 'Sure,' said Murugan. '… except for what it does to your head.'"[27] At this moment, when Ghosh's story appears to veer toward a Pynchonesque, existential ending, Murugan reveals in his search an answer to the same problem metaphorically possessed by Antar: syphilis, *intellectual* anger and impotence, a madness and paralysis of the brain. Finally, Murugan's search is also Antar's search, and, in both cases, the answer seems at least in part to derive from recognizing the power of undocumented, uncorroborated ways of knowing. Silence becomes active and empowered, whether through a refusal to be part of the system of language and naming, as with Simon in Keri Hulme's *the bone people*, or through its reclamation of the exotic, mysterious, unknowable, sublime, as with Mario Vargas Llosa's disappearances in *Death in the Andes*.

However we might describe the human relationship with machine, Ghosh offers a constantly revolving system of hegemonies and disenfranchised computer programmers who have been mastered by the machines they have created, a variation on the "empire" that "writes back." But if the hegemonic system itself is predicated on the Western privileged categories of science and logic, Antar discovers in silence a language Ava cannot possibly understand, which invites him to consider invisible, undocumentable approaches to knowledge. Murugan asks Antar, "Tell me: do you think it's natural to want to turn the page, to be curious about what happened next?" Or, he persists, "Do you think that everything that can be known should be known?" "'Of course,' said Antar. 'I don't see why not.'"[28] In a dialogue – Socratic or Dharmic – that asks the great Western riddle of human existence, Murugan begins with a universalizing of humankind, reducing us all to a curiosity to know in the context of an almost popular detective fiction genre, a "whodunit." Ghosh emphasizes the power of narrative structure as well, framing Murugan's question as a unifier for the story not only of Antar, but also the factual reader, who turns the page precisely because he or she wants to know, an act identified here as "natural." But the question also demands something with respect to history.

As the structure of any detective novel – and any reasonable postcolonial or Marxist theory – suggests, if we can discover what happened, we may be empowered to address what will happen next: to understand our history is to entitle us to a say in our future. This is the premise of any postcolonial effort to recover an unwritten history, to tell the story, to unify a people. But Murugan substantially rephrases his question when Antar declines understanding, and turns it into a Faustian dilemma: do we think everything that can be known, should be known? Here, the questions of suspect medical practices, in the name of a "greater good," are much more unsettling, and Antar's equivocal response, "I don't see why not," becomes dubious, a double negation. Despite our desire to see Antar as a reliable figure in this story, his thoughts are clearly conditioned if he cannot "see why not." Murugan concludes by offering what he thinks he knows about Ross, and the forces that conspired to help him effect his scientific theories about malaria. Antar tells Murugan he cannot see the slightest "proof" or "shred of real evidence." Murugan counters that it is the very lack of evidence that suggests his truth: "secrecy is what this is about: it figures there wouldn't be any evidence or proof."[29] Murugan knows that in the same way Antar is paralyzed within the system of Western hierarchy, logic, and technology, he himself is unable to bring about revelation through his narrative methods, which are similarly part of the system, and do nothing to help him think outside his paralysis and madness. This point is confirmed in Antar's response to Murugan's story, as Antar's questions lead to a dialogue evocative of Arjuna's with Krishna, or Socrates with his interlocutors, that is rhetorically manipulative, logical proofs for what might seem to be illogical underpinnings.

Of course we must be careful about siding too readily with a "secrecy" espoused by the disenfranchised, for it is not only the language of the dispossessed, but the language of the possessed who have something abominable to hide. If slaves were thrown overboard to garner insurance money, the records are absent, not present, made visible by the lack of slaves arriving in port, not a documentation of what happened. Similarly, if companies hope to hide their illegal disposal of toxic contaminants, they are revealed as much by absence as by presence. Such silences are often used to reproduce the victimization of the dispossessed. But listening for critical silences makes us vigilant about deception, and offers us new ways of knowing. For Ghosh's Antar, silence offers the dispossessed opportunities to "force" a mutation in the Calcutta chromosome – an active silence. The Frankenstein story is reversed, and the mutation is here reclaimed by the subaltern as positive, resistive, overturning much of the precedent visible in the story. And so Antar suggests, as other critics have noted, the possibility of silence as active, powerful – laden with romantic tensile potential for both good (a secret goal for immortality through transmigration of souls, in accord with brahmanic principles and through making use of Western science as its tool) and potential injustice (inexplicable disappearances that seem products of vast secret conspiracies connected to the entry of trains into the jungle). But his claim that silence offers us a way to get off the grid, to avoid imbrications into even a linguistic system that claims, names, and marks us as its own should not be underestimated. And Murugan suggests a way for the subaltern to use silence, "secrecy," for its own purposes: "Not making sense is what it's about – conventional sense, that is."[30] He proposes that the subaltern "started with the idea that knowledge is self-contradictory," that "to know something is to change it" and therefore "you only know its history."[31] He concludes: "Maybe they thought that knowledge couldn't begin without acknowledging the impossibility of knowledge ... if it's true that to know something is to change it, then it follows that one way of changing something – of effecting a mutation, let's say – is to attempt to know it, or aspects of it."[32] And so the novel turns in on itself once more: narrative is enslaving and empowering; malaria is both the disease, and through mutation, the potential cure; climate change is harmful and, for certain unique groups, potentially beneficial; computers are the problem and the answer; the postcolony is oppressed, and oppressing; nature is exploited and has ways of recovering and avenging itself; Western science and Hindu reincarnation have sudden affinities in their shared goals of immortality. What Ghosh describes involves an exploration of interstices, and his framing of a novel based on "malaria," with its cycles of historical repetition, with several separate strains that repeat similar symptoms but at different periods and differing severity, is an excellent illustration of uneven development. Ghosh's novel in itself and as representative of postcolonial literature demonstrates the ways in which postcolonial ecocriticism must read for silences – because while ecological issues can be visible in postcolonial texts, they are often quietly in the interstices, inextricably bound within systems of language, justice, economics, and power.

NOTES

1 For more on *Calcutta Chromosome* and Ross's diaries, see Claire Chambers, "Postcolonial Science Fiction: Amitav Ghosh's *The Calcutta Chromosome,*" *Journal of Commonwealth Literature* 38.1 (2003), 57–72.
2 Amitav Ghosh, *Calcutta Chromosome: A Novel of Fevers, Delirium and Discovery* (New York: Avon Books, 1997).
3 For more on Spivak with respect to *Calcutta Chromosome,* see especially Suparno Banerjee, "*The Calcutta Chromosome*: A Novel of Slippage and Subversion," *Science Fiction, Imperialism and the Third World: Essays on Postcolonial Literature and Film* (Jefferson, NC: McFarland & Co., 2010), pp. 50–64 and Tuomas Huttunen, "*The Calcutta Chromosome*: The Ethics of Silence and Knowledge," *Seeking the Self – Encountering the Other: Diasporic Narrative and the Ethics of Representation* (Newcastle upon Tyne, UK: Cambridge Scholars, 2008), pp. 24–38. Postcolonial critics have long noted issues of silence in Ghosh's work, and other postcolonial work; our work builds on theirs.
4 See Scott Russell Sanders, "Speaking a Word for Nature," *Ecocriticism Reader: Landmarks in Literary Ecology,* eds. Cheryl Glotfelty and Harold Fromm (Athens, GA: University of Georgia Press, 1996), pp. 182–195.
5 Ghosh, *Calcutta Chromosome,* pp. 123–124.
6 Both Banerjee and Huttunen also bring up this issue of an active silence. Huttunen, "Ethics of Silence," pp. 27, 37 uses it to argue for a "third" identity that deconstructs binaries and suggests a "universal humanism." Banerjee, "Novel of Slippage," pp. 50–64 further argues that "the very conditions that apparently make the subaltern vulnerable [like silence] hide its source of power."
7 Michaeleen Doucleff, "Signs of Drug-Resistant Malaria Emerge in Vietnam and Myanmar," National Public Radio, 14 November 2012.
8 Rebecca Solnit, *Savage Dreams: A Journey into the Landscape Wars of the American West* (San Francisco: Sierra Club Books, 1994), p. 144.
9 See also Shinn's comparison of malaria in *Calcutta Chromosome* with smallpox as a biological weapon. Christopher A. Shinn, "Homicidal Tendencies: Violence and Global Economy in Asian Pulp Fiction," *Alien Encounters: Popular Culture in Asian America* (Durham, NC: Duke University Press, 2007), p. 118.
10 "With Hats and Umbrellas, Senegalese Fill a City Niche," National Public Radio, 18 September 2012.
11 In later chapters, Mukherjee includes Ghosh's *The Hungry Tide* as an example of this reflected "uneven development." See Upamanyu Pablow Mukherjee,

Postcolonial Environments: Nature, Culture and the Contemporary Indian Novel in English (New York: Palgrave Macmillan, 2010).

12 Mukherjee, *Postcolonial Environments*, p. 7.

13 See also Shinn's identification of the "mythic power of water itself," and the scientific efforts to "control its life-giving properties." Shinn, "Homicidal Tendencies," p. 119.

14 Ghosh, *Calcutta Chromosome*, p. 7.

15 Ghosh, Ibid., p. 7.

16 Ghosh, Ibid., pp. 6–7.

17 Ghosh, Ibid., p. 9.

18 Ghosh, Ibid., p. 12.

19 Ghosh, Ibid., p. 10.

20 Ghosh, Ibid., p. 10.

21 For more on science fiction as Western vs. Eastern genres, see Banerjee, "Novel of Slippage."

22 Ghosh, Ibid., p. 10.

23 Ghosh, Ibid., p. 7.

24 Ghosh, Ibid., p. 18.

25 Ghosh, Ibid., p. 238.

26 *The Economic Times*, July 23, 2012; http://economictimes.indiatimes.com/news/economy/indicators/india-stares-at-drinking-water-crisis/articleshow/15098163.cms?curpg=2

27 Ghosh, *Calcutta Chromosome*, p. 288.

28 Ghosh, Ibid., p. 59.

29 Ghosh, Ibid., p. 104.

30 Ghosh, Ibid., p. 105.

31 Ghosh, Ibid., p. 105.

32 Ghosh, Ibid., p. 105.

13

KAREN THORNBER

Environmental Crises and East Asian Literatures: Uncertain Presents and Futures

East Asia – understood as China, Japan, Korea, and Taiwan – has long been associated with belief systems advocating reverence for nature, as well as numerous indigenous philosophies and religions.[1] Popular perceptions both within and outside East Asia often hold that environmental degradation in the region began in the late nineteenth century, when East Asians, pressured by Western nations, assimilated the latter's technologies and industries. But in fact, East Asian societies have long histories of transforming environments. Rhoads Murphey has gone so far as to argue:

> The Asian record ... makes it clear that, despite the professed values of the literate elite, people have altered or destroyed the Asian environment for longer and on a greater scale than anywhere else in the world, even in the twentieth-century West.[2]

Murphey perhaps overstates the case, since the changes early East Asian peoples made to environments did not have the reach of those instigated by societies in the twentieth-century West.

Nevertheless, the disjuncture between beliefs and behaviors is significant. As the historian Mark Elvin has observed concerning China:

> Through more than three thousand years, the Chinese refashioned China. They cleared the forests and the original vegetation cover, terraced its hill-slopes, and partitioned its valley floors into fields. They diked, dammed, and diverted its rivers and lakes. They hunted or domesticated its animals and birds; or else destroyed their habitats as a by-product of the pursuit of economic improvements. By late-imperial times there was little that could be called "natural" left untouched by this process of exploitation and adaptation ... A paradox thus lay at the heart of Chinese attitudes to the landscape ... On the one hand it was seen ... as a part of the supreme numinous power itself. Wisdom required that one put oneself into its rhythms and be conscious of one's inability to reshape it. On the other hand the landscape was in fact tamed, transformed, and exploited to a degree that had few parallels in the premodern world.[3]

Always in flux, relationships between people and environments became particularly lopsided during the twentieth century, when human populations burgeoned and people developed technologies to transform landscapes more rapidly, more radically, and on a larger scale than ever before.

Late nineteenth- and early twentieth-century industrialization was generally celebrated in East Asia. With few exceptions, the relatively unfettered use of natural resources was central to the narrative of China's, Korea's, and Taiwan's modern economic development, as well as Japan's prosperous growth and overseas empire (1895–1945). Similar discourse surrounded postwar industrialization in the 1950s and early 1960s in Japan, in the 1960s and 1970s in South Korea and Taiwan, and in China in the 1980s. During these decades people generally did not see themselves as significantly damaging environments. Ecosystems were believed so resilient, and their self-restorative powers so great in relation to human demands, that even such activities as disgorging toxic waste were not thought to matter much if at all. As environmental damage became more severe and widespread, this relative nonchalance receded, only to be replaced by a conviction that blighted environments were a necessary cost of rapid, sustained growth. Some triumphalists even argued that belching smokestacks signaled national prosperity. It was not until the late 1960s in Japan, the 1980s in South Korea and Taiwan, and the 1990s in China that a widely shared sense of ecological crisis emerged. This sentiment propelled citizens to organize and demand change, ultimately leading governments and enterprises to adopt policies intended to remediate present environmental damage and to curb it in the future. Subsequent decades witnessed uneven improvement in environmental health and less tolerance for behaviors that blatantly damage ecosystems. Building on this momentum, a green fervor has permeated East Asia, with Taiwan's Green Party (Taiwan Lu Dang, Taioan Lek Tong, 臺灣 綠黨; est. 1996), China's "Green Olympics" (Luse aoyun; 綠色奧運, 2008), South Korea's "Green New Deal" (Noksaek nyudil; 녹색뉴딜2009), Japan's "Green New Deal" (Gurīn nyūdīru; グリーンニューディール, 2009), and countless other "green" endeavors. But despite these steps and a widespread consciousness that current lifestyles are unsustainable, local, national, and regional environmental problems and crises continue. In many cases these problems are simply being exported, not eradicated, creating multiple shadow ecologies.[4]

Given this history, it is not surprising that from their beginnings and especially in the last five decades East Asian literatures have engaged with environmental degradation. This might surprise readers accustomed to the widely publicized conventional Asian literary images of Asian ecological harmony. Indeed, by idealizing people's interactions with their nonhuman surroundings and by giving the impression that East Asian peoples are inherently sensitive to the environment, that they love nature and intermingle peacefully with it, Chinese, Japanese, Korean, and Taiwanese writers have made East Asian literatures famous for celebrating the beauties of nature. Even today, most ecocritical scholarship in the United States, Europe, and East Asia focuses on Anglo-European literatures and increasingly on Western-language postcolonial literatures. But in fact, references to ecodegradation have appeared regularly in East Asian literatures since the 1960s (in Japan and Korea) and 1980s (in China and Taiwan).[5] Some creative works that discuss damage to ecosystems conform to conventional understandings of "nature writing," at least in their place of origin, but many others do not. The tremendous variety of literature in East Asia and throughout the world that addresses ecodegradation – incorporating references that occasionally celebrate, sometimes simply describe, and often condemn harmful changes to environments – testifies to the persistence of damaged environments and to the ecological consciousness, however diaphanous, of literary artists.

This chapter introduces several important works of East Asian writing on environmental degradation: the Chinese writer Wang Ping's short story "Maverick" (2007), the Japanese writer Sakaki Nanao's poems "Itsuka" (Someday, 1995) and "21 seiki ni wa" (In the 21st Century, 1996), and the Korean writer Chŏng Hyŏnjong's (b. 1939) poems "P'um" (Protective Embrace, 1989) and "Tŭlp'an i chŏngmak hada" (The Field Is Forlorn, 1992). Like much creative work on damaged ecosystems, these texts highlight *ecoambiguity* (environmental ambiguity), the complex, contradictory interactions between people and the nonhuman environment. In particular, they underline the uncertainty of environmental conditions – present and future – an especially relevant concern in the wake of Japan's 9.0 intensity Tōhoku earthquake (March 2011).

A number of creative works on damaged environments draw attention to the ambiguity of environmental conditions: narrators and characters lament the current state of affairs, including the absence of particular flora or fauna, but do not indicate whether this absence signals environmental damage, whether it is to be expected, or whether it is in some sense canceled out. Speaking of landscapes as lacking particular nonhuman entities, yet leaving ambiguous the implications of these deficiencies, Chŏng Hyŏnjong's "Protective Embrace" and "The Field Is Forlorn" provide important perspectives on this phenomenon. Unlike Wang Ping's and Sakaki's texts, these poems are not specific to any particular nation, and instead focus on events that transcend particular times and places. As such they can be read as implicating environmental distress writ large.

Chŏng Hyŏnjong's "Protective Embrace" features an individual longing to be held or at least to witness a hug.[6] The poem reads:

> Like trees standing in the rain,
> I wonder where
> I can be held.
> I wonder where the rain is,
> and the location of the tree(s).
> And the protective embrace they make,
> I wonder where it is.[7]

"Protective Embrace" raises a number of questions. Most obvious, and forming the core of the poem, are those concerning the (new) locations of trees, the rain, and their mutual embrace. More subtle and significant in identifying actual ecodegradation are questions about the condition of the observed ecosystem, not to mention its dimensions: the speaker could be referring to a backyard or to an entire planet. He wonders where the rains have gone but gives no indication that the ground is parched. Perhaps the rains are long overdue; perhaps they are only several days late. Perhaps the land is suffering, perhaps not. Even more uncertainty surrounds how much of this landscape's vegetation has been relocated. In the opening line the poem refers to "trees" (*namudŭl*) standing and being held by the rain, yet the next reference to flora is not to "trees" but instead to "tree(s)" (*namu*), the Korean noun *namu* signifying either a single tree or multiple trees. So it is possible that the landscape is devoid of trees. It is equally possible that the poem is commenting on the removal of a single, perhaps favored tree.

The swapping of *namudŭl* with *namu* suggests the latter but leaves open the possibility of the former. Also interesting is that in the first line the poem's speaker compares himself, a single being, to "trees [*namudŭl*] standing in the rain" rather than to a single tree standing in the rain, as the word *namu* would imply. The awkwardness of this phrasing suggests a deliberate move in the poem from plural to singular, one that paradoxically could indicate either intensified or decreased damage to the ecosystem where the poem's speaker stands: perhaps only one tree has survived its removal or perhaps only one tree has been removed. On the other hand, considering the context of the fifth line, "tree" is itself a clumsy translation of *namu* – it is much more likely that the poem's speaker, when mentioning the embrace of rain and flora, would ask about the location of trees, not a single tree. Fogging its references to rain and trees, "Protective Embrace" suggests but does not confirm ecodegradation.

On the other hand, the poem implies that even if the ecosystem as a whole is damaged, its component parts might not be; the poem's speaker wonders where trees have been relocated, not whether they exhibit distress or have disappeared. This is in contrast with Chŏng Hyŏnjong's "The Field Is Forlorn," where animals have been destroyed so plants can flourish:

> In the autumn sunlight, in the autumn air
> in the ripening rice
> dazzling heaven and earth,
> but
> ah, the field is forlorn –
> there are no grasshoppers!
>
> Oh this inauspicious silence –
> Life's golden link has been severed· · · · · · [8]

Chŏng Hyŏnjong's poem is nothing if not intratextually contradictory, a broad frame painting desolation, then destruction (the poem's title and second half) surrounding a portrait of brilliance and fecundity (the poem's first half). Grasshoppers might once have thrived here, but they probably have been eradicated by agrochemicals; the poem does not speak of these substances explicitly, but the combination of a flourishing rice crop and an absence of grasshoppers – a known rice pest easily controlled with chemicals – strongly suggests their use. Removing grasshoppers has made the field forlorn by dissolving a vital part of its ecosystem. But sunlight, air, and rice all dazzle even as grasshoppers disappear; rice production, in fact, depends on their removal. Although the title and second half of "The Field Is Forlorn" attempt to negate the first half, and the first half undercuts the title and second half of the poem, neither position dominates: vital links are broken but heaven and earth still amaze. The contradiction between the casing and the center of Chŏng Hyŏnjong's poem elucidates one of the great paradoxes of farming: the coexistence of production and destruction, indeed the nearly constant reliance of production on eradicating animals and plants, including many designated as "weeds." "The Field Is Forlorn" paradoxically shows ecosystems as damaged, even to the extent of having their most vital parts removed, without losing their vitality.

Chŏng Hyŏnjong's poems and similar texts highlight the difficulties inherent in making sense of current symptoms of possible ecological significance. Other creative works point to the confusion surrounding both human and nonhuman futures in the face of severe, impending environmental damage. Such ambiguous texts, a subset of environmental apocalypse narratives, depict ecological disaster as inevitable and in some cases imminent. On the other hand, unlike many apocalyptic writings that describe in great detail the future that awaits, not to mention those – such as the American author Cormac McCarthy's (b. 1933) best-selling *The Road* (2006) – that actually are set in such a future, the writings examined in this chapter remain notably ambiguous about the conditions that follow disaster. They do so by forecasting outcomes through broad generalizations, conflicting information, or silence. The tension between certainty (of occurrence) and uncertainty (of resulting conditions) is responsible for much of the intra- and extratextual anxiety about environmental futures articulated in creative writing more generally.

Written in English, "Maverick" is the final selection of Wang Ping's anthology *The Last Communist Virgin*.[9] It is one of many recent Chinese creative works that address the high environmental price of the Three Gorges Dam.[10] Wang Ping's story takes place on June 6, 2006; it begins six hours before and concludes six seconds before the demolition of the Three Gorges Dam's cofferdam, the temporary barrier against the Yangzi River used during construction that, when removed, unleashed the full force of the river on the new dam.[11] Although narrated in the early twenty-first century and anticipating an imminent event, the bulk of "Maverick" consists of reiterations of ancient Chinese myths, legends, and folklore; background on Wushan, a county flooded by the Three Gorges Dam; and flashbacks to the principal narrator Wu Pan's childhood experiences in the now flooded town of Wushan. Setting Wang Ping's story apart from most other narratives that address ecodegradation – including many that speak of the devastation caused by or expected from the Three Gorges Dam – is its methodical countdown to devastation that will be anything but methodical; ruin is certain to be followed by even greater chaos, the timing and nature of which are highly uncertain.

Framing "Maverick" is a sequence leading to demolition. The story begins with an epithet on wizards gathering herbs on Soul Mountain from the *Shanhai jing* (Classic of Mountains and Seas), a principal source of Chinese mythology that combines fragments of ethnography and natural history with folklore from shamanistic visions.[12] This is followed by: "This is it, Shan Gui [mountain spirit], June 6, 2006. In six hours, the Coffer Dam will explode. The river will rush in and we'll all go under ... In six hours the river will rise to the red mark – 175 meters, and everything will go – the gorge, the slopes, the mist, and our home under the dawn redwood. The river will become a lake: tame, servile, worthless."[13] Six pages later Shan Gui announces, "In six hours when the Coffer Dam blows up and the water rises, everything along the river will go – the fields, the roads, the villages, the cities, the mountains, and our water fir" (177). With about a page to go before the end of the story, the narrator declares, "The time has come, Shan Gui. In six minutes, the river will rise to the red mark on the trunk" (203). The countdown ticking, on the final page the narrator states: "It [the river] has six seconds to go. In six seconds, the river will no longer be" (204).

The lines that follow this declaration and bring "Maverick" to a close take more than six seconds to read:

> But it will never die.
> At your grave I wait. When the hot wind blows in from the North Pole, the sea will rise like mountains, shattering every chain [dam] on the river's throat and limbs. And you, my mountain spirit, will come home in your original form, free, naked (204).[14]

The cofferdam thus implodes – or is imagined as imploding – as the reader is finishing the story.

Wang Ping's story concludes with a vision of the future at odds with earlier predictions. The forecasts following the announcements at six hours and six minutes remain focused on the relatively immediate effects of a rapidly rising river. Just before announcing that there are six seconds to go, the narrator again speaks of these consequences, noting that archaeologists working feverishly along the gorge are upset over the imminent loss of so many traces of human history, but that it is just as important to think about the damage being inflicted on living human and nonhuman beings:

> Yet who will cry for the tree that survived the ice age and is about to go under? And the green sturgeon that has been spawning in the Gold Sand River for millions of years but is blocked forever behind the dam? Who will cry for the one million people displaced from their homes and land? And you, Shan Gui, who will bring you back from the far north? (203–204)

The reference in this passage to people's abuse of one another resonates with those earlier in the narrative to the suffering the Chinese endured at the hands of their government and its minions, particularly the Red Guards. Elsewhere in the story, the narrator reinforces such sentiments, quoting Shan Gui's mother as urging her to sacrifice herself for the sake of all other sturgeon:

> [Mama said:] You'll hurl yourself against the dam over and over, your flesh splashing over the concrete. You'll be shredded by the turbines, your blood dyeing the reservoir scarlet red. Your violent death may or may not be enough to shock them into finding a new home, but it's the only chance for those stubborn prehistoric creatures. They have seen the rise and fall of dinosaurs, the coming and going of the big ice and floods, the birth of mammals and humans. Will they survive this? We can only hope, before they disappear, before we all disappear ... We want to help them. Those ancient noble souls deserve to have a place on the planet (181–182).

Mama reveals the likely fate of a species that has allegedly endured for millions of years, that has witnessed the rise and fall of countless other species, surviving violent nonhuman phenomena including massive floods and ice ages. This species now has seemingly met its match and is threatened with extinction. The contrast the narrator makes between the sturgeon and most other species is noteworthy in how it highlights not only the unprecedented power of the Three Gorges Dam (i.e., even the sturdiest animals are no match for its turbines), but also the vulnerability of most of the nonhuman, especially to human behaviors.

In contrast, the narrator's final prophecy describes a somewhat different future: in time, it is said, the structures that bury will themselves be buried. This prediction is itself prefigured. Several pages earlier, Shan Gui had claimed that, trapped in a tank of blue chemicals, she has "shut down my body to save my heart. I'm saving my heart for the big wave. When it arrives, a path will open through the steel and glass and concrete. It will take me home" (201). The sturgeon at last will be free; animals at last will triumph. Yet matters ultimately are more complicated. A path might open to take the sturgeon home, one that can penetrate steel, glass, and concrete; the sturgeon might at last recover its "original form," but with just one lone animal remaining it is unlikely that this species has a future. More important, if the seas actually do "rise like mountains" they will shatter "every chain on the river's throat and limbs," or at least make these dams irrelevant. The terrestrial species that can survive such upheaval are few, and the fate of most aquatic species is likely not so different.

What makes the scenario outlined in the final lines of "Maverick" so frightening is that it is not entirely hypothetical. The narrator asserts that what will trigger rising sea levels is "hot wind [blowing] in from the North Pole" – in other words, global warming. The futures the narrator and Shan Gui predict – both immediate and more distant – are analogous. Entire landscapes will be submerged, and soon. Yet it is unclear just what will be flooded, and when, and with what effects on survivors, both people and the natural world, particularly over time. The narrator does not address these ambiguities explicitly. But the contrast between the story's anticipatory structure and its largely retrospective content, together with the disjunction between its precision about the timing of the cofferdam's demolition and its relative silence on the effects of this implosion, not to mention its silence on the timing and effects of the massive flood that is predicted, point to how much is unknown and unknowable about the future conditions of ecosystems. The background information on Wushan makes clear how much already has been lost, as well as how much there is to lose, but beyond the guaranteed flooding of particular spaces, confusion surrounds the prospects for human and nonhuman survivors.

The Japanese writer Sakaki Nanao's "Someday" exhibits even more anxiety and uncertainty about the future.[15] This poem features an individual whose visit to nuclear power plants in and around Tsuruga (Fukui Prefecture, on Japan's western coast) on January 12, 1995 so frightens him that the following day he mistakes a thunderclap and lightning flash for the explosion of a nuclear power plant. Relieved that the boom and flare were false alarms, the speaker nevertheless asserts that it is only a matter of time before an atomic energy facility actually does explode. He then wraps up the poem by noting that these false yet prophetic alarms occurred four days before the Great Hanshin (Kobe) earthquake of January 17, 1995, which killed more than 6,000 people:

> Sun in the dead of winter sinking
> following the shore along the Sea of Japan
> I visited Fukui Prefecture's Mihama nuclear power plant
> then the fast-breeder reactor Monju The next day
> storm-threatened sky dawning
> January 13, noon nuclear power plant Ginza
> On the platform of Tsuruga Station waiting for a train
>
> Clouds turbulent snow off and on the wind gusting
> birds confused · · · Suddenly
> gwoonbari bari bari
> Flash dazzling the eyes
> Deafening roar piercing the ears
>
> Ooh God! Buddha!
> sudden shock
> sudden cold sweat
>
> I'm so thankful that God God
> thunder rumbling
>
> I'm so thankful that
> the nuclear power plant did not explode
>
> But someday · · · [だが いつか・・・]
>
> Four days later [四日のち]
> Kobe's large earthquake [神戸大地震]
> 6,300 dead [死者6,300]1995.1[16]

"Someday" depicts environmental trauma as inevitable. Although understandable considering the troubled histories of the Mihama and Monju nuclear facilities, the speaker's exaggerated reaction to a mere thunderstorm so soon after visiting these sites reinforces the terror nuclear power plants can instill.[17]

Yet the reference to the Kobe earthquake does not shift the source of the traumas the speaker envisions from human behaviors to "natural" phenomena – as does the poem's brief move from nuclear power plants to thunderstorms – so much as it underscores the involvement of both people and the nonhuman in environmental upset. The human death toll of the Kobe earthquake was so high not simply because of the tremendous tectonic energy released but also because the low-lying areas of the city had not been built to withstand extreme shaking.

On the other hand, "Someday" remains notably silent on when the next disaster will occur and what form it will take. The poem concludes with an ambiguous mix of finality and anticipation: finality in that a "someday" has arrived, sooner than expected; anticipation in that there are many more "somedays" to come – including those where nuclear power plants melt down, triggered by earthquakes, as happened in the March 2011 Tōhoku earthquake catastrophe – and that these likely will be more devastating to the planet.[18]

Taking on not the global but the galactic, Sakaki's "In the 21st Century" is place-stamped "Korea Pusan / United Nations Army Cemetery" and time-stamped October 1996, the forty-fifth anniversary of this thirty-five-acre site commemorating Allied servicemen who died in Korea.[19] But as in so many of Sakaki's poems this grounding is overwhelmed by the text itself. Sakaki's poem lists seemingly assured attributes of the twenty-first century. "In the 21st Century" is a visually striking two-page text that consists of eleven numbered sections, six on the first page, divided into two columns (1–3/4–6), and five on the second page, also divided into two columns (7–9/10–11). This relative crowding of information – as though the speaker had lifted material from an official pamphlet, perhaps one obtained at the cemetery – gives the text an aura of authority. The first ten sections begin with the refrain, "In the 21st century" (21 *seiki ni wa*), followed by a catalog of ten items, which are themselves followed first by the subject marker *ga* (が), several spaces, and then the word *nai* (ない; is/are no, will be no). For instance, the first stanza begins:

> (1) In the twenty-first century 21 世紀には
> There will be no true intentions ほんねが　ない
> There will be no pretenses たてまえが　ない
> There will be no string pulling 根まわしが　ない
> There will be no faking やらせが　ない
> There will be no bullying いじめが　ない[20]

Cataloged in the following sections as *not* existing in the twenty-first century are everything from political shenanigans, social problems, and sales taxes to diseases, weapons, environmental pollution, and sites of nuclear disaster such as Chernobyl, Hiroshima, and Nagasaki. The first nine sections also list more desirable phenomena including everything from health drinks and the Internet to Valentine's Day, Nobel Prizes, and peacekeeping organizations, but these are exceptions. In contrast, the tenth section both lists more positive phenomena and specifies that these things will be absent only in specific places. The ten lines following the opening refrain "In the 21st century" begin with a type of person/animal or place (e.g., children, birds, fields), followed by the preposition *ni* (in, at, on), several spaces, characteristics of these places (e.g., smiles, songs, earthworms), the subject marker *ga*, and then the hanging negative *nai*. This section declares that there will be no smiles, songs, earthworms, dragonfly nymphs, mushrooms, fish, sun, cloud shadows, color, or stars in places one would expect them – children's faces, birds, fields, rivers, forests, coral reefs, deserts, the ground, rainbows, and the Milky Way, respectively. So the future of smiles, stars, and so on, is uncertain. Perhaps smiles still will exist, just not on children's faces, and stars will have vanished, but only from the Milky Way.

Dashing these hopes, the eleventh and final section gives two different predictions:

> (11) In the 21st century
> there will be absolutely nothing nothing will be absolutely nothing
> yet somewhere
> —tidings of wind—
> Somewhere in the 21st century
>
> > Urashima Tarō and Otohime
> > are likely to exist
> > Urashima Tarō and Otohime
> > are likely to exist (65).[21]

Certainty becomes ambiguity. Sakaki's poem does not state how or when in the next century these various disappearances will occur, far from idle concerns for a text published in the mid-1990s. More explicitly ambiguous are the longer-term consequences of these disappearances for both people and the nonhuman. If taken literally, the evocation of Urashima and Otohime implies that the bottom of the sea might be spared, remarkable considering the damage done even to the Milky Way. But mention of the two legendary characters also suggests that stories themselves have a chance of surviving. It is unclear whether the stories might exist as tangible or intangible objects (books or oral tales), but their continued presence means not only that people have survived but also that creative production remains part of their lives. After all, "In the 21st Century" repeats the verb *nai* (is/are no, will be no), a word used for the nonexistence of everything but people, leaving the human condition uncertain. The poem appears unwilling to declare its own demise a certainty, much less the demise of the species on which it depends for creation and circulation. Like Wang Ping's "Maverick" and Sakaki's "Someday," "In the 21st Century" asserts that broad environmental destruction is inevitable, but at times the poem is subtly, at times notably, ambiguous about conditions in a postapocalyptic world. Many futures thought to be known are in fact anything but.

Discourse on ecodegradation is nothing if not abundant, and most literature that engages with environmental problems draws directly from personal observations and local predecessors, even as it frequently strives to become more ecologically cosmopolitan and to address concerns with global resonances. But much of this creative writing, even texts that exude self-confidence (e.g., those that assert the future will be one of extremes), interweaves undeniable ambiguities. Creative works that address damage to ecosystems just as often confuse environmental conditions as they depict conditions that are confusing. That is, they feature nonhuman bodies and landscapes whose actualities are difficult to assess, often because of their conflicting attributes (e.g., bodies that appear healthy but display symptoms that suggest they are not; landscapes where some species are obviously thriving and others clearly struggling). They also can confuse the reader by providing fragmented or contradictory information on the conditions of individual bodies and environments about which much more is clearly known (e.g., nonhuman bodies of which only a single facet is described). Such discourse points to the inevitability of uncertainty in both literary and physical environments.

Far from resolving the ecological conundrums it describes, most East Asian and other literature on environmental distress further ambiguates these ambiguities, bringing to light deeper discrepancies. In fact, poetry and prose regularly counter the unstable, inverted pyramids of environmental Ponzi schemes with their own mushrooming miasmas of environmental ambiguity. Creative writing often makes matters even more confusing by remaining silent about its uncertainties: many narrators and characters seem unaware of the discrepancies they depict or exhibit. Indeed, to the extent that they are aware of them, people often suppress the contradictions of their interactions with environments. Analyses of literature can provide sharp lenses for deeper insight into processes of environmental degradation by highlighting creative articulations of these disjunctions. Better appreciating the uncertainties and contingencies of ecodegradation in literature, and in life, should allow for more productive relationships among people and the natural world.

NOTES

1 Research for this chapter was funded in part by the Academy of Korean Studies (AKS-2011-R20).

2 Rhoads Murphey, "Asian Perspectives of and Behavior toward the Natural Environment," in Karen K. Gaul and Jackie Hiltz (eds.), *Landscapes and Communities on the Pacific Rim: Cultural Perspectives from Asia to the Pacific Northwest* (Armonk, NY: M. E. Sharpe, 2000), p. 36.

3 Mark Elvin, *The Retreat of the Elephants: An Environmental History of China* (New Haven, CT: Yale University Press, 2004), pp. 321, 323.

4 The term "shadow ecology" refers to "the aggregate environmental impact on resources outside [a nation's] territory of government practices." Peter Dauvergne, *Shadows in the Forest: Japan and the Politics of Timber in Southeast Asia* (Cambridge, MA: MIT Press, 1997), pp. 2–3.

5 For a summary of the relationship between East Asian literatures and environmental degradation, see Karen Laura Thornber, *Ecoambiguity: Environmental Crises and East Asian Literatures* (Ann Arbor: University of Michigan Press, 2012), pp. 32–98. Arguably the best known East Asian literary texts on environmental degradation are: the Japanese writer Ishimure Michiko's (b. 1927) novel *Kugai jōdo: Waga Minamatabyō* (Sea of Suffering and the Pure Land: Our Minamata Disease, 1969); the Korean writer Cho Sehŭi's (b. 1942) short story "Kigye tosi" (City of Machines, 1977); and the Chinese writer Jiang Rong's (Lü Jiamin, b. 1946) novel *Lang tuteng* (Wolf Totem, 2004). See Karen Thornber, "Acquiescing to Environmental Degradation: Literary Dynamics of Resignation," *Pacific Coast Philology* 47 (2012), 210–231.

6 A diverse and prolific poet, Chŏng Hyŏnjong received a bachelor's degree in philosophy from Yonsei University, and then worked as a journalist and teacher of Korean literature. He began publishing poetry in the mid-1960s and put out the first of many collections in 1972.

7 Chŏng Hyŏnjong, "P'om," in *Chŏng Hyŏnjong si chŏnjip* 1 (Seoul: Munhak kwa Chisŏngsa, 1999), p. 267.

8 Chŏng Hyŏnjong, "Tŭlp'an i chŏngmak hada," in *Chŏng Hyŏnjong si chŏnjip* 2 (Seoul: Munhak kwa Chisŏngsa, 1999), p. 25.

9 Wang Ping was born and raised in China. In 1985 she moved to the United States and in 1999 earned a Ph.D. in comparative literature from New York University. Currently she teaches environmental writing and environmental justice at Macalester College. Wang Ping began publishing fiction in the mid-1990s and poetry in the late 1990s. *The Last Communist Virgin* is her second short-story collection. It won the 2007 Book Award from the Association for Asian American Studies as well as the 2008 Minnesota Book Award. In addition to writing stories such as "Maverick," she has put on several exhibits of her own photographs, including *Beyond the Gate: China in Flux after the Three Gorges Dam* (2007) and *All Roads to Lhasa* (2008).

10 Another key example is the Chinese émigré writer and Nobel Prize winner Gao Xingjian's (b. 1940) *Lingshan* (Soul Mountain, 1989).

11 The cofferdam, located approximately one hundred yards upstream from the Three Gorges Dam, was 1,900 feet long and 460 feet high. Andrew R.

Bridgman, "China Unleashes Yangtze River on Dam," http://www.cbsnews.com/stories/2006/06/06/world/main1686520.shtml.

12 E. N. Anderson, "Flowering Apricot: Environmental Practice, Folk Religion, and Daoism," in N. J. Girardot et al. (eds.), *Daoism and Ecology: Ways within a Cosmic Landscape* (Cambridge, MA: Harvard University Center for the Study of World Religions, 2001), pp. 157–183.

13 Wang Ping, "Maverick," in *The Last Communist Virgin* (Minneapolis: Coffee House Press, 2007), p. 171.

14 Cf. Linda Hogan, *Solar Storms* (New York: Scribner, 1995).

15 Sakaki Nanao was a leader of *Buzoku* (The Tribe), a 1960s and 1970s Japanese countercultural group that included foreigners such as the American poet and environmental activist Gary Snyder (b. 1930). Nanao spent considerable time traveling and hiking in Japan, the United States, and other sites; ecological concerns are at the forefront of much of his work.

16 Sakaki Nanao, "Itsuka," in *Kokoperi* (Minami Izu: Ningen Kazoku Henshūshitsu, 1999), p. 45.

17 Most notable in the context of "Someday" is the December 8, 1995, massive sodium leak and fire at Monju, an incident that forced the suspension of the fast-breeder reactor. Although "Someday" is time-stamped January 1995, the poem was published in a volume released in 1999; Sakaki's reference to Monju might simply have been fortuitous, but he also had ample time to alter references for greater effect. Monju was restarted on May 6, 2010, and reached criticality on May 8, 2010. It has since been temporarily stopped several times.

18 Japan's Niigata-Chūetsu Oki Earthquake (July 16, 2007) was a reminder that the nation most profoundly affected by nuclear fallout not only houses the world's largest nuclear generating station but also operates it on an active earthquake fault. The epicenter of this earthquake was only nineteen kilometers from the Kashiwazaki-Kariwa nuclear power plant. One of the plant's units restarted operation in May 2009 and another in August 2009. Resuming nuclear generation is seen as a key part of reducing Japan's emissions of greenhouse gases. Ajima Shinya, "Restart Raising Questions," *Japan Times* (May 10, 2009), p. 2.

19 Some 2,300 soldiers are buried at the United Nations Memorial Cemetery in Pusan, the only local cemetery supported by the United Nations.

20 Sakaki Nanao, "21 seiki ni wa," in *Kokoperi*, p. 64.

21 Urushima Tarō is the central character of Japan's popular Urashima Tarō legend. One common version of the story has Urashima, after rescuing a turtle being tormented by a group of children, being informed that the turtle is actually Otohime, the daughter of the Emperor of the Sea. He is then taken to the undersea Palace of the Dragon God, where he stays with Otohime and her father. Concerned about his aging mother, he returns to his village, only to discover that many years have passed. Despite warnings against so doing, Urashima opens the box Otohime had given him as a gift at their departure. A cloud of white smoke emerges, and he suddenly is transformed into an old man.

14

KATE RIGBY

Confronting Catastrophe: Ecocriticism in a Warming World

In 1996 Jonathan Bate edited a special issue of *Studies in Romanticism*, to which he contributed an article entitled "Living with the Weather."[1] Here, he characterizes the ecocritical challenge to prevailing literary critical practices as a "Kuhnian paradigm shift ... which could be described in a variety of ways. Perhaps: a New Geographism is replacing the New Historicism. Or, to locate it in a wider context: Cold War Criticism is dying, Global Warming Criticism is about to be born."[2] Preempting recent proposals for a "material ecocriticism" informed by the work of Bruno Latour and Michel Serres, among others,[3] Bate contrasts the critical preoccupations of the Cold War period, focusing exclusively on human language, agency, and social relations, with the ambition of Global Warming Criticism (GWC) to address the inextricability of "nature" and "culture" as disclosed paradigmatically in the weather. In so doing, GWC would break with what Serres terms the "Modern Constitution," which severs the human from the nonhuman, while determining their relationship in terms of mastery and possession.[4] Bate's article, one of the most significant early articulations of the ecocritical project, is noteworthy not only for its prescience, but also for its relative neglect by other ecologically oriented literary critics. Since the mid-1990s, environmental literary and cultural studies have expanded and diversified, acquiring increasing theoretical sophistication in the process. It is only in recent years, however, that many ecocritics have begun to home in on global warming as a key issue in environmental literary and cultural studies. Reflecting on the "relative absence in ecocriticism of its most serious issue," in his *Cambridge Introduction to Literature and Environment* (2011), Timothy Clark rightly predicted that this "must be set to change"[5]: the trickle of publications addressing climate change in a direct and sustained way that I have been able to trace from around 2007 began to swell into a flood beginning in 2010.[6] Over the years since Bate exhorted literary scholars to locate their work in the horizon of an anthropogenically altered climate, however, this horizon has grown considerably more ominous: so much so, in fact, that it

GWC is to live up to its name, it must now face up to the ineluctability of ecocatastrophe.

One of the texts that Bate discusses in "Living with the Weather" is Byron's apocalyptic poem, "Darkness." Conventionally read as a purely cultural weave, referencing and reworking earlier texts and tropes, Byron's vision of a world deprived of the sun's life-giving rays is ecocritically reframed by Bate with reference to meteorological records for the time of its composition during the dreary summer of 1816 on Lake Geneva. These records, Bate explains, bear witness to the global impact of the eruption of Indonesia's Tambora volcano the previous year, occasioning some 80,000 deaths in the immediate vicinity, as well as cooler temperatures, failed harvests, and food shortages in faraway Europe for several years afterward. Not unlike Cormac McCarthy's grim novel *The Road* of 2006, Byron's "dream, which was not all a dream" (l. 1) offers no clues as to the cause of the catastrophe. Rather than raising questions of aetiology – "how has it come to this?" – these works ask us to consider how humans would fare in the face of the total collapse of the biosphere, and in the absence of redemptive divine intervention.

For Bate, the primary ecocritical value of Byron's apocalyptic text lay in its capacity to remind readers in a perilously warming world of human dependence upon those climatic conditions conducive to the flourishing of diverse life on Earth, thereby helping to motivate action toward mitigating anthropogenic climate change. This approach is consistent with the prevailing emphasis across the environmental humanities on the role of social and cultural factors in generating and, potentially, countering ecosocial ills. This has been a broadly utopian project, inspired by the hope that crisis could be prevented from sliding into catastrophe, and bent instead toward ecosocial transformation. Today, however, faced with the necessity of learning to live with – and, optimistically, adapt to – the escalation of extreme weather events and other environmental changes attendant upon those climatic alterations that have now become inevitable,[7] our task can no longer be to ask only how literature might help us to "think fragility,"[8] but also how it might assist us to *confront catastrophe*. In this context, the question of the cultural mediation of what have come to be called "natural disasters" acquires a new pertinence. Because of the overriding concern with socioculturally generated "environmental" problems, the literature of "natural" disaster remains an under-researched field in ecocriticism. Yet the very opposition of "environmental" and "natural" disaster is itself symptomatic of that modernist mindset, which seeks to neatly separate human from nonhuman causes and effects. Moreover, the continuing attribution of today's weatherborne disasters to a violent, amoral, and frequently feminized Nature "over yonder," as Timothy Morton puts it,[9] masks both the human contribution to the warming climate that is ramping up these extremes and the role of sociocultural factors in conditioning the relative vulnerability and resilience of differently situated communities. Troublingly, it also has the potential to fuel ecophobia, shoring up nature-culture dualism at the very time when we most need to dismantle the mental walls of separation and acknowledge both material responsibility, however unevenly shared, for the escalation of extremes, and human ethical accountability to those diverse nonhuman others whose fortunes are increasingly in our famously dexterous, but frequently fumbling hands.[10] Approaching this issue from a material ecocritical perspective, I wish to consider how the imaginary space opened by literary disaster narratives discloses the entanglement – material, but potentially also moral – of human and nonhuman actors and factors in the etiology, unfolding, and aftermath of catastrophes that turn out to straddle the dubious nature-culture divide.

The term "natural disaster" only gained widespread currency in the twentieth century, but the concept began to emerge in the eighteenth in the context of the scientific enlightenment, and it is in the literature of the Romantic period that it first began to be put under pressure. One of the earliest works to do just that is Heinrich von Kleist's short story, "The Earthquake in Chile" of 1806.[11] While the historical referent for this narrative is the massive quake that struck Santiago on May 13, 1647, Kleist's text responds to the philosophical and theological debates that erupted in northern Europe following the Lisbon Earthquake of November 1, 1755. This remains the largest seismic event ever recorded in European history. Subsequently estimated to have measured around 8.5 on the Richter scale, its force was felt on land over an area of more than 15 million square kilometers from North Africa to Scandinavia. From its epicenter deep below the ocean around 200 kilometers west-southwest of Cape St. Vincent, it sent a series of tidal waves coursing across the Atlantic in all directions, cresting up to 15 meters in southern Portugal. Although the waters only topped around 6 meters in Lisbon, the largest concentration of casualties was found here, with around 30,000 people either crushed by falling buildings, many of them in the crowded churches where All Saints' Day celebrations were in process; drowned in the ensuing tsunami; or immolated in the fires that subsequently consumed what remained of the Portuguese capital, then one of Europe's biggest and wealthiest cities.[12] The shockwaves that were felt across much of Europe in consequence of this catastrophe were as much ideational as physical. In a striking instance of the entanglement of natural and social history, the Lisbon Earthquake is frequently cast as a "turning point" or "watershed" dividing Europe's past from its future.[13] Its force was felt all the more powerfully, though, because the grounds of belief were themselves already shifting. While religious conservatives sought to shore up biblical revelation and clerical authority against the rising tide of rationalism by construing the earthquake as God's judgement on the corruptions of this city, other commentators, including John Mitchell, one of the "fathers" of seismology,[14] advocated bracketing divine intentionality in favor of the investigation of purely natural causes. The emergence of a secular scientific approach to those extreme events that theologians had previously classified as "natural evils" held out the promise that greater knowledge of the physical processes involved might allow them to be prevented, or at least predicted, thereby reducing human vulnerability. However, the evacuation of moral significance from the nonhuman world and the veiling of human-nonhuman entanglement implicit in the modern concept of "natural disaster" are in turn proving pretty disastrous.

Kleist's narrative intervention in the Lisbon debate is characteristically equivocal. On the one hand, "The Earthquake in Chile" makes a mockery of theocentric interpretations of Earth's troublesome upheavals by opposing two sets of characters whose competing claims to divine favor effectively cancel each other out. This secularizing tendency is consistent with Voltaire's response to the Lisbon disaster, which famously shattered the enlightened *philosophe's* earlier faith in the providential order of creation: the belief, informed by physicotheology, that this was, as G. W. Leibniz had argued in his *Theodicy* of 1710, "the best of all possible worlds," and that, as Alexander Pope put it in his "Essay on Man," "WHATEVER IS, IS RIGHT."[15] This position was definitively rejected in Voltaire's "Poème sur le désastre de Lisbonne," subtitled "Examen de cet axiome: 'Tout est bien'" ("An examination of the axiom: 'All is well'") of 1756. In his later work, *Candide*, it is in the wake of the Lisbon earthquake, while being flogged at the hands of the Church on the grounds of having "listened with an air of approval" to Pangloss's disquisition on the necessity of "the fall of Man" to this "best of all possible worlds," that the long-suffering protagonist finally rebels. While his tutor is being executed, and he himself is "weltering in blood and trembling with fear and confusion," Candide wonders ruefully, "If this is the best of all possible worlds ... what can the rest be like?"[16] Voltaire's disillusionment with metaphysical optimism is accompanied by a marked disaffection with the earth, which he construes in the ode as given over to evil and destruction: "Il le faut avouer, le mal est sur la terre" ("We must acknowledge that evil is in the world/on the earth").[17] In dismissing physicotheology, Voltaire drives a rationalist wedge between God and Nature, and between Nature and Man: since "la nature est muette" ("Nature is mute"),[18] meaning and morality must be confined to the exclusively human realm. In its revised form, the ode ends with the hopeful affirmation, "Un jour tout sera bien" ("One day all will be well"),[19] but the implication is that this will only come about if and when, nature is thoroughly humanized. While Voltaire's was one of many highly divergent responses to the Lisbon disaster,[20] it is indicative of what would become the prevalent view in eurowestern modernity. Stripped of any lingering traces of the divine, denied both communicative capability and ethical considerability, other-than-human "nature" would henceforth be handed over to scientific knowledge, technological control, and economic exploitation, while the emergent "humanities" were to confine themselves to the exclusively human domain of "culture": the Modern Constitution was framed amidst the rubble of Lisbon.

There is a distinct echo of Voltaire's parody of metaphysical optimism in "The Earthquake in Chile" in the protagonists' self-aggrandizing reflections on "how much misery had to afflict the world in order to bring about their happiness."[21] On the other hand, Kleist's narrative does not unequivocally endorse the French rationalist's moral humanism. For the catastrophe that unfolds in this text is occasioned not so much by the quake itself, as by the sociocultural context in which it occurs and through which it is framed. In this respect, "The Earthquake in Chile" draws closer to Jean-Jacques Rousseau's refutation of Voltaire's view of the Lisbon disaster, as articulated in the open letter that he wrote in response to Voltaire's ode of August 18, 1756.[22] Challenging the Modern Constitution at its very inception, Rousseau stresses the role of sociocultural factors, such as population density, the characteristics of the built environment, and the privileging of material possessions over physical safety, in exacerbating the Lisbon catastrophe, while also defending the underlying rationality and ultimate goodness of the "laws of nature," not all of which, he stressed, were understood. From this perspective – one that was also put forward by Kant in the series of essays that he published in the Königsberg press following the Lisbon earthquake – there is no such thing as a wholly "natural" disaster. Violent events undoubtedly occur in nature, and we should by all means endeavor to understand their material causes, rather than speculating hubristically about divine intentions. The destructivity of their impact could nonetheless be minimized, both Rousseau and Kant argued, by better conforming our collective existence to natural contingencies that might well serve purposes that we cannot comprehend and that were in any case frequently beyond our control. This counter-position is opened up within Kleist's narrative by the representation of the valley outside the city walls as a space within which, in the wake of the quake, an egalitarian, inclusive, and compassionate community emerges, comparable with the actual communities forged by catastrophe discussed by Rebecca Solnit in *A Paradise Built in Hell*.[23]

In Kleist's narrative, this new natural-cultural collective is destroyed, not by the violence of external "nature," but by the interspecific human aggression – specifically, the desire for a scapegoat – which is unleashed by the redeployment of an earlier discourse of oppression.

Kleist first offered "The Earthquake in Chile" for publication in a collection subtitled "moral tales." With this designation, which he subsequently dropped, Kleist aligned his work with the French tradition of "contes moreaux" and perhaps specifically the subgenre of "contes philosophique," of which *Candide* is the most famous exemplar. However, whereas Voltaire uses narrative to mount a philosophical argument by literary means, Kleist's writing is insistently interrogative, using narrative to explore the very process of meaning-making. For what "The Earthquake" makes clear is that the ways in which humans are likely to respond in the face of a catastrophic event are conditioned by the meanings that they attribute to it on the basis of inherited cultural narratives. As cultural theorist Stephen Muecke has shown with respect to the impact of Hurricane Katrina: "the stories told about natural disasters are crucial to the organisation of people's responses in the medium to long term. While the stories of individual events are told in the detail, they are nonetheless already broadly scripted by narrative forms of mythical strength."[24] As a self-reflexive meta-narrative, Kleist's text exemplifies the emergence during the Romantic period of a form of literature that opens an ethical space, within which dominant discourses regarding "nature" and "natural disaster" might be questioned, marginalized perspectives given voice, and new modes of understanding and action enabled.[25]

One of the most remarkable English disaster narratives of this kind is Mary Shelley's dystopian novel, *The Last Man* (1826), which imagines the virtual extinction of the human species as a result of pandemic disease. Not unlike "The Earthquake in Chile," Shelley's text features a narrator whose perspective is subtly subverted by the very tale he tells. According to the "Author's Introduction," the inspiration for this novel was her alleged discovery, in company with a companion, of fragments of prophetic verse in several languages, both ancient and modern, traced on "leaves, bark and other substances," and found deep in the cave of the Cumaean Sybil on the Bay of Naples. In transforming these imaginary archaic verse fragments into the form of a modern prose novel, the author has displaced – although not entirely eclipsed – the voice of the legendary female seer by that of a fictitious male narrator, looking back on the catastrophe of which he is, as far as he knows, the sole survivor at the time of writing, in the year 2,100.

Lionel Verney introduces himself in the opening paragraph in terms that are at once ethnocentric, androcentric, logocentric, and anthropocentric. Proclaiming "man's mind alone" as the "creator of all that was great and good to man," Verney celebrates England as a "sea-surrounded nook," which, "when balanced in the scale of mental power, far outweighed countries of larger extent and more numerous population." Recalling a favorite view of the English landscape "subdued to fertility" by the labors of his "country-men," he likens his native land to a "vast and well-manned ship, which mastered the winds and rode proudly over the waves."[26] Shelley's narrator's profoundly patriarchal perspective instantiates what feminist ecophiloso-pher Val Plumwood terms the "logic of colonisation," grounded in the hier-archical dualism of (masculine) reason and (feminine) nature that underpins the dominant construction of human identity within Western modernity.[27] In this, Verney's voice mimics that assumed in most of the male-authored "last man" narratives that had become popular in the early nineteenth century. As Steven Goldsmith has observed, these texts imagine the end of humanity in such a way as to "reassuringly confirm … the epistemological status quo" by salvaging human consciousness in an immaterial beyond, even as they imagine the obliteration of the human species.[28] Shelley's novel, by contrast, ends up undoing every binary that is implicit in its opening paragraph. In this way, the subaltern wisdom of the Sybil, as appropriated by the implied female author, undercuts the privileged consciousness of her male narrator, allowing a radically different view of human identity, and of natural-cultural catastrophe, to emerge from the narrative.

In his reflections on the Haitian earthquake disaster of January 2010, Junot Diaz recalls that the Greek *apokalypsis* refers not simply to catas-trophe, but to "a disruptive event that provokes revelation." Citing James Berger in *After the End*, Diaz explains that the "apocalyptic event … in order to be truly apocalyptic, must in its disruptive moment clarify and illuminate 'the true nature of what has been brought to end.'"[29] One of the many things that is most revealed by the apocalyptic pandemic in Shelley's novel is that the narrator's earlier view of England's splendid isolation, which was such, he recalls, "that to have forgotten [the rest of the orb] would have cost neither my imagination nor understanding an effort," was utterly illusory. While England is the last nation of the world to succumb to infection, its socioeconomic order, underpinned as it was by the "busy spirit of money-making, peculiar to our country,"[30] had already largely collapsed because of the cessation of international trade. Moreover, while the narrator persists in demonizing the plague as an external agent of humanity's demise, even likening it at one point to the satanic "Arch-Felon" of Milton's *Paradise Lost*, it is made clear that the disease only reaches pandemic proportions on account of the interconnectivities engendered by world trade and colonial conquest. Recalling that the Britain of Shelley's day had been enriched by the only recently outlawed slave trade, it is significant that she identifies the

African continent as the source of this outbreak. Moreover, Verney is shown to become infected through direct bodily contact (the only such instance in the novel) with "a negro half clad, writhing under the agony of disease," who was among the many immigrants, including some from America, given refuge in his grand home (Windsor Castle, no less) and who held him "with a convulsive grasp."[31] Revealing not only England's dependence on the rest of the world, but also the shared corporeal, or, as Stacy Alaimo puts it, "transcorporeal"[32] vulnerability, of erstwhile masters and slaves, colonizers and colonized, Shelley's plague, as Kevin Hutchings has observed, "because of its leveling effect ... becomes, to a certain extent, an emblem of social justice carried out on a global scale."[33] Strangely, Verney is also the only person who recovers from infection, and while his revulsion toward the dying negro has distinctly racist overtones, it is, as Anne K. Mellor suggests, perhaps precisely "from this unwilling but powerful embrace of the racial other ... [that] Verney ... becomes immune to the plague."[34]

The military venture that provides the conduit for the entry of the disease into Europe is prosecuted by Verney's friend and brother-in-law, the Byronic Lord Raymond, who abandons his position as Protector of the English Republic to become a military leader in the Greek War of Independence against the Turks. While Raymond frames his exploits as a struggle of "civilisation" against "barbarism,"[35] the narrator lets slip that the war is also motivated by European commercial interests, and when confronted with the brutality of its prosecution, he is overcome by shame for his species. Having expelled the Islamic invaders from Greece, Raymond, aspiring to subdue all Asia, proceeds to lay siege to Constantinople, the entire population of which eventually succumbs to starvation and disease. Bent on glory and heedless of his own life, following his estrangement from his wife and the death of his lover, Raymond disregards the better judgment of his friends and troops, along with the resistance of his horse and the opposition of his dog, to ride triumphantly into the plague-ridden city. In so doing, he sets off an explosion that kills him outright and releases the contagion that proceeds to ravage the rest of the world. Verney, who intuits more than he admits consciously, prefigures this outcome in the dream that assails him when he succumbs to his bodily needs and falls asleep while searching for Raymond amidst the rubble. Here, his friend appears to him "altered by a thousand distortions, expanded into a gigantic phantom, bearing on its brow the sign of pestilence."[36] When Verney sleeps, it seems, the Sibyl speaks, disclosing the natural-cultural character of the pandemic, which the narrator has such difficulty confronting consciously. That Raymond bears the sign of plague on his forehead suggests metonymically that the human mind is not only dependent on "our animal mechanism," but also that it can become a fatal liability if our "mental creations," as in this case, Raymond's desire to win fame by planting "the Grecian standard on the height of St. Sophia," are disconnected from and privileged over our bodily being and earthly environs, which for Raymond had become no more than "a tomb, the firmament a vault, shrouding mere corruption."[37] This overvaluation of ideation, and the frequently mentioned "self-will" with which it is linked, proves fatal for a number of other characters as well. Raymond's lover, Evadne, dies disguised as a soldier in Raymond's ranks; his wife, Perdita, commits suicide rather than be separated from his graveside; and their daughter, Clara, along with Verney's brother-in-law, Adrian (who are with Verney, sole survivors of the pandemic) drown in a storm while attempting a rash sea-crossing en route to visit her parents' tomb in Greece.

Surviving this disaster also, no thanks to any mental effort or feat of willpower, but rather to the "instinctive love of life" that "animated" his creaturely being, Verney finds enduring consolation neither in wild nature, which is flourishing anew in the absence of human domination, nor amidst the material remains of human and specifically Western civilization in the depopulated city of Rome. Having previously been inspired by his noble friend Adrian, son of the last English monarch, to abandon his "savage" existence as an untutored shepherd and poacher in the Lake District and gain admittance "within that sacred boundary which divides the intellectual and moral nature of man from that which characterizes animals"[38] on Adrian's Windsor estate, Verney ends, as he began: alone with a canine companion. There is a crucial difference, however, in that his new *modus vivendi* is neither savage nor civilized, but integrally natural-cultural, albeit confined to the miniature more-than-human world of the boat, in which he and the dog who had joyously befriended him are left circumnavigating Earth's coastlines in search of other human survivors, with whom to reconstitute a more-than-human collective, regardless of nationality, race, gender, class, or creed.

As well as disclosing the transnational, transpecies, and transcorporeal connectivities that are in play in both the etiology and outcome of the pandemic, the capacious form of this novel allows Shelley to explore diverse human responses to the unfolding catastrophe with a degree of detail and insight that should qualify *The Last Man* as compulsory reading in all of today's burgeoning disaster management courses. These range from opportunistic looting, apocalyptic hedonism, and millenarian hysteria through to pragmatic self-organization on the part of communities and selfless kindness among some individuals. While nationalist and racist prejudices condition initial reactions to the outbreak, including Verney's, and resurface in the face of an influx of foreign refugees, these are ultimately rejected by the narrator and other (if not all) survivors, in favor of the recognition of a common humanity. New structures and styles of leadership emerge, as the wheeler-dealer politics of everyday governance are displaced by the moral guidance provided by the selfless Adrian, who only now assumes the role of protector that his friends had hoped he would take on earlier, working tirelessly to prevent panic and criminality; maintain public hygiene and civil order; and to protect the healthy and aid the sick. As centralized governance breaks down, moreover, Verney is deputed to foster improvisational forms of what would today be termed "adaptive governance" under the leadership of able local figures, who would never have had the chance to enter government under normal conditions, including nonelite youths and women. Gender assumptions are put under pressure in other ways, too: Verney, for example, is forced by grief at the death of his wife to acknowledge an emotional side that he had previously considered exclusively womanly, and to open his heart to other-than-human suffering. Witnessing the colonization of erstwhile human spaces by a plethora of flourishing plants and animals, moreover, he is finally brought to question the anthropocentric "arrogance" of calling ourselves "lords of creation, wielders of the elements, masters of life and death."[39]

Importantly, Shelley's subversion of Verney's logocentric and homocentric assumptions does not culminate in any kind simplistic reversal of the reason-nature dualism. In my reading, it points rather to the necessity of a process of ecological enlightenment, in which the nonhuman is resituated as agentic, communicative, and ethically considerable, while human consciousness is recognized as embodied and interconnected with a more-than-human world that is neither fully knowable nor entirely controllable. Such ecological enlightenment entails also a revaluation of mind as mindfulness: that is to say, the cultivation of the kind of critical self-reflection on one's own "mental creations" that is facilitated by literary narratives such as this one, in its subtle subversion of a patriarchal and anthroparchal symbolic order in denial about its own conditions of possibility and self-destructive tendencies.

Eerily for readers now living in the climatically changing century in which this novel is set, Verney relates how containing the spread of the pandemic and coping with its impacts are rendered more difficult because of the disordered weather conditions that accompany its inexorable progress. These include unusually hot summers, as well as extreme cold snaps, violent storms, and massive sea surges. No explanation is given for the unseasonable and extreme weather, which seems to have settled down again when the narrative concludes. Given that Shelley's late twenty-first century remains minimally industrialized (transport, for example, is still by horse, coach, sailing boat, or hot air balloon!), these conditions are evidently not anthropogenic. They nonetheless hint at connectivities between human and nonhuman worlds that are perhaps not readily visible, but nonetheless materially efficacious and morally significant. Such are those extremes that are today being intensified by the "murderous engine," as Verney calls the plague, of the fossil-fueled industrial revolution that got underway in Shelley's day. [40] If the year 2,100 is not to become the "last year of the world," or at least, the world as we have known and shaped it as is the case for Shelley's lone human survivor, we will need to act quickly in recognition of their revelatory dimension to both limit global warming and prepare for growing levels of climatic and associated social, political, and economic chaos. As the utopian science-fiction writer Kim Stanley Robinson demonstrates in his near-future climate change trilogy,[41] confronting catastrophe does not mean succumbing to despair. On the contrary: it might just open the path to an ecosocial transformation, in which climate change mitigation and adaptation become wedded to a vision of transpecies justice, in keeping with a deepened understanding of "sustainability." Holding to that hope, I would like to conclude with the optimistic words of Robinson's democratically blogging president's last post:

Previous Post:

Eventually I think what will happen is that we will build a culture in which no one is without a job, or shelter, or health care, or education, or the rights to their own life. Taking care of the Earth and its miraculous biological splendor will then become the long-term work of our species. We'll share the world with all the other creatures. It will be an ongoing project that will never end. People worry about living life without purpose or meaning, and rightfully so, but really there is no need for concern: inventing a sustainable culture is the meaning, right there always before us. We haven't even come close to doing it yet, so it will take a long time, indeed it will never come to an end while people still exist.[42]

NOTES

1. Jonathan Bate, "Living with the Weather," *Studies in Romanticism*, vol. 55, no. 3, 1996, pp. 431–448.
2. Ibid., p. 433.
3. E.g., Laura Dassow Walls, "From the Modern to the Ecological: Latour on Walden Pond," in Axel Goodbody and Kate Rigby (eds.), *Ecocritical Theory: New European Approaches* (Charlottesville: University of Virginia Press, 2011); Serenella Iovino and Serpil Oppermann, "Material Ecocriticism: Materiality, Agency, and Models of Narrativity," *Ecozon@* 3 (2012), 75–91.

4 Michel Serres, *The Natural Contract*, trans. Elizabeth MacArthur and William Paulson (Ann Arbor: University of Michigan Press, 1995), pp. 31–32.

5 Timothy Clark, *The Cambridge Introduction to Literature and the Environment* (Cambridge, UK: Cambridge University Press, 2011), p. 11.

6 E.g., Michael Ziser and Julie Sze, "Climate Change, Environmental Aesthetics, and Global Environmental Justice Cultural Studies," *Discourse* 29 (2007), 384–410; Kate Rigby, "Noah's Ark Revisited: (Counter-)Utopianism and (Eco-)Catastrophe," in Andrew Milner, Matthew Ryan and Simon Sellars (eds.), *Demanding the Impossible: Utopia and Dystopia*, special issue of *Arena Journal* 31 (2008), 163–178; Andrew Maxwell, "Postcolonial Criticism, Ecocriticism and Climate Change: A Tale of Melbourne under Water in 2035," *Journal of Postcolonial Writing*, vol. 45, no. 1 (2009), pp. 15–26. There are chapters on climate change in Ursula Heise, *Sense of Place and Sense of Planet: The Environmental Imagination of the Global* (Oxford: Oxford University Press, 2008) and Patrick Murphy, *Ecocritical Explorations in Literary and Cultural Studies: Fences, Boundaries, and Fields* (Plymouth: Lexington Books, 2009). Indicative of the spate of ecocritical engagements with climate change since 2010 are a number of journal special issues, e.g., Astrid Bracke and Marguérite Corporaal (eds.), *Ecocriticism and English Studies*, special issue of *English Studies*, 91:7 (2010) and Andrew Milner, Verity Burgmann, and Simon Sellars (eds.), *Changing the Climate: Utopia, Dystopia and Catastrophe*, special issue of *Arena Journal* 35/6 (2010). A concern with climate change is also noted by Lawrence Buell as an "emerging trend" in "Ecocriticism: Some Emerging Trends," *Qui Parle* 19 (2011), 87–115, overlooking (as does Clark) Bate's early adumbration of Global Warming Criticism.

7 Christopher B. Field et al., *Intergovernmental Panel on Climate Change Special Report on Managing the Risks of Extreme Events and Disasters to Advance Climate Change Adaptation* (Cambridge: Cambridge University Press, 2011); Dim Coumou and Stefan Rahmstorf, "A Decade of Weather Exremes," *Nature Climate Change* 2 (2012), 291–296.

8 Bate, "Living with the Weather," p. 447.

9 Timothy Morton, *The Ecological Thought* (Cambridge, MA: Harvard University Press, 2010), p. 3.

10 On ecophobia, see Simon Estok, "Theorising in a Space of Ambivalent Openness: Ecocriticism and Ecophobia," *ISLE* 15.2 (2009), pp. 203–225. Instances of ecophobic constructions of recent extreme weather events abound, e.g., headline articles in Melbourne's *Age* newspaper referred to the massive cyclone that affected northeastern Australia (hard on the heels of unprecedented flooding) on February 4, 2011, as "YASI'S INVASION" (February 4, p. 4) and its impacts as "NATURE'S RAMPAGE" (February 3, p. 2), totally overshadowing the small p. 5 article in which the growing number of mega-cyclones was linked to increased ocean-surface temperatures. Adam Morton, "Extreme Weather Is Just the Beginning: Garnaut," *The Age* (February 4, 2011), p. 5.

11 Heinrich von Kleist, "The Earthquake in Chile," in *The Marquise of O & other Stories*, trans. David Luke and Nigel Reeves (London: Penguin, 1978), pp. 51–67. For a more detailed ecocritical analysis of this text, see Kate Rigby, "Discoursing on Disaster: The Hermeneutics of Environmental Catastrophe," *Tamkang Review* 39 (2008), 19–40.

12 Jelle Z. de Boer and Donald T. Sanders, *Earthquakes in Human History: The Far-Reaching Effects of Seismic Disruptions* (Princeton, NJ: Princeton University Press, 2005), pp. 90–98.

13 Harald Weinrich, "Literaturgeschichte eines Weltereignisses: Das Erdbeben von Lissabon," *Literatur für Leser. Essays und Aufsätze zur Literaturwissenschaft* (Stuttgart: Kohlhammer, 1971), p. 65; Ana Christina Araujo, "Focus: The Lisbon Earthquake: Part Two. European Public Opinion and the Lisbon Earthquake," *European Review* 14 (2006), 318.

14 Boer and Sanders, *Earthquakes in Human History*, p. 95.

15 Alexander Pope, *An Essay on Man*, ed. Frank Brady (New York: Bobbs-Merrill, 1965), p. 15.

16 Voltaire, *Candide, or Optimism*, trans. John Butt (New York: Penguin, 1947), pp. 34–37.

17 Voltaire, "Poème sur le désastre de Lisbonne," in D. Adams and H. T. Mason (eds.), *Les Oeuvres Completes de Voltaire*, vol. 45a (Oxford: Voltaire Foundation, 2009), p. 341.

18 Ibid., p. 344.

19 Ibid., p. 348.

20 D. Groh et al. (eds.), *Naturkatastrophen: Beiträge zu ihrer Deutung und Darstellung in Text und Bild von der Antike bis ins 20. Jahrhundert* (Tübingen: Gunter Narr, 2003), p. 22.

21 Kleist, "Earthquake," p. 57.

22 Jean-Jacques Rousseau, "Letter to Voltaire," 18 August 1756, trans. R. Spang, in J. A. Leigh (ed.), *Correspondence complète de Jean Jacques Rousseau*, vol. 4 (Geneva: Inst. et Musée Voltaire les Délices, 1967), pp. 37–50.

23 Rebecca Solnit, *A Paradise Built in Hell: The Extraordinary Communities that Arise in Disaster* (New York: Viking, 2009).

24 Stephen Muecke, "Hurricane Katrina and the Rhetoric of Natural Disasters," in Emily Potter et al. (eds.), *Fresh Water. New Perspectives on Water in Australia* (Carlton: Melbourne University Press, 2007), p. 260.

25 See Hubert Zapf, "The State of Ecocriticism and the Function of Literature as Cultural Ecology," in Catrin Gersdorf and Sylvia Mayer (eds.), *Nature in Literary and Cultural Studies: Transatlantic Conversations on Ecocriticism* (Amsterdam: Rodopi, 2006), pp. 49–70.

26 Mary Shelley, *The Last Man*, intro. and notes, P. Bickley (Ware, UK: Wordsworth Editions, 2004), p. 5.

27 Val Plumwood, *Feminism and the Mastery of Nature* (Routledge: London, 1993).

28 Stephen Goldsmith, *Unbuilding Jerusalem: Apocalypse and Romantic Representation* (Ithaca, NY: Cornell University Press, 1993), p. 268. See also Kevin Hutchings, "'A Dark Image in a Phantasmagoria': Pastoral Idealism, Prophecy, and Materiality in Mary Shelley's the Last Man," *Romanticism: The Journal of Romantic Culture and Criticism* 10, no. 2 (2004), pp. 228–229.

29 Junot Diaz, "Apocalypse: What Disasters Reveal," *The Boston Review* 36.3 (May/June 2011), http://www.bostonreview.net/BR36.3/junot_diaz_apocalypse_haiti_earthquake.php.

30 Shelley, *Last Man*, pp. 5, 200.

31 Ibid., p. 268.

32 Stacy Alaimo, "Trans-corporeal Feminisms and the Ethical Space of Nature," in Stacy Alaimo and Karen Hekman (eds.), *Material Feminisms* (Bloomington: Indiana University Press), pp. 237–264.

33 Hutchings, "Dark Image," p. 238.

34 Anne. K. Mellor, "Introduction," in Mary Shelley, *The Last Man*, ed. H. J. Luke (Lincoln: University of Nebraska Press, 1993), p. xxiv.

35 Shelley, *Last Man*, p. 121.

36 Ibid., p. 161.

37 Ibid., pp. 234, 315, 155, 149.

38 Ibid., p. 21.

39 Ibid., p. 184.

40 Ibid., p. 366. James McKusick notes in an early ecocritical discussion of Shelley's novel, that the narrator's identification of the medium of disease transition, in keeping with the medical speculation of her day, is atmospheric. "As the manufacturing cities of England disappeared into a thick haze of photochemical smog, it becomes possible to imagine that human activities might alter the climate and eventually destroy the Earth's ability to sustain human life." James McKusick, *Green Writing: Romanticism and Ecology* (New York: St. Martin's Press, 2000), p. 109.

41 Kim Stanley Robinson, *Forty Signs of Rain* (London: HarperCollins, 2004), *Fifty Degrees Below* (London: HarperCollins, 2005), *Sixty Days and Counting* (London: HarperCollins, 2007). For an excellent ecocritical discussion of this trilogy, see Adeline Johns-Putra, "Ecocriticism, Genre and Climate Change: Reading the Utopian Vision of Kim Stanley Robinson's Science in the Capital Trilogy," *English Studies* 91:7 (2010), pp. 744–760.

42 Robinson, *Sixty Days*, p. 367.

15

STEPHEN RUST

Ecocinema and the Wildlife Film

Species are going extinct en masse. Every 20 minutes we lose an animal species.
If this rate continues, by century's end, 50% of all living species will be gone."
– Wildlife filmmaker Jeff Corwin, *L.A. Times*, November 30, 2009[1]

The 1958 Disney documentary film *White Wilderness*, winner of the 1959 Academy Award for Best Documentary Feature, contains one of the most infamous scenes in motion picture history. In one segment, the camera turns its attention to lemmings and appears to capture one of the most curious behaviors in all of nature – a mass suicide. Cutting between wide angle shots and close-ups, the camera shows a large group of lemmings fleeing from predators, plummeting down terraced slopes, and leaping off a cliff into the icy water below. The film then cuts to an overhead shot as the creatures swim into an expanse of open sea. Punctuated by somber orchestral music, narrator Winston Hibler explains, "All seem to survive the ordeal ... but gradually strength wanes, determination ebbs away, and soon the Arctic Sea is dotted with tiny bobbing bodies."

To be clear, lemmings do engage in mass migrations every four years or so as a result of population explosions, but they do not commit suicide.[2] Yet while scientists have long since dismissed this myth, it continues to be perpetuated by films, television commercials, video games, political rhetoric, and even, so my students tell me, by a few teachers. In the 1982 Canadian Broadcasting documentary *Cruel Camera*, Bob McKeown reported that Disney's production crew had tossed the creatures down the hillside and over the cliff, where they were allowed to drown. In a candid interview, Roy E. Disney admitted to McKeown that although cinematographers often spent weeks in the field filming animals in their natural habitats, many of scenes filmed for Disney's highly acclaimed True-Life Adventures series (1948–1960) were completely staged.

While extreme, this example highlights the integral position that non-human animals have occupied in the development of cinema and the modern cultural imagination. Additionally, the ease with which Disney hid their fakery from viewers underscores an important point for environmental critics. They need to familiarize themselves with the tools and techniques that media producers use to manipulate their audiences' perceptions of the more than human world. As wildlife filmmaker Sir David Attenborough has argued, "The camera is the most convincing of all liars. But in the end, it's the motive of the film-maker that is crucial."[3] Unlike literary texts, cinematic texts do not claim merely to represent the world through complex linguistic arrangements; they claim to represent the world as it actually existed at the time of filming. For ecocritics, therefore, the aesthetic and rhetorical differences between literary and cinematic texts cannot be easily overlooked.

Briefly reviewing the history of the wildlife documentary genre, this chapter traces the rhetorical strategies that have always shaped purportedly realistic film representations of wild animals and their environments. In recent years, the topic of how and why our perceptions of other animals are mediated through the lens of cinema has been the subject of numerous academic studies, including Greg Mitman's *Reel Nature* of 1999, Derek Bousé's *Wildlife Films* of 2000, and Cynthia Chris's 2006 *Watching Wildlife*. As these scholars demonstrate, familiar tropes and patterns such as the hero story, Darwinian survival plots, and sentimental human treatments of nonhuman family life have long been used to shape the narrative structures of films about such diverse animals as lemmings, dolphins, and dung beetles. As the list of threatened and endangered species continues to grow, many filmmakers make use of pastoral and apocalyptic imagery and dramatic musical scores to rouse viewers to take action. This chapter examines the cultural work accomplished by such anthropomorphic projections and competing efforts to represent the independent lives of nonhuman creatures, to protect wild landscapes, and to challenge the practice of large-scale meat production, with attention to such feature-length documentary films as *Microcosmos*, *Being Caribou*, *Grizzly Man*, *March of the Penguins*, *Earth*, *The Cove*, and *Food, Inc.* This chapter contends that as the global ecological crisis deepens, the "cultural logic of ecology" remains equally prevalent in the increasingly globalized world of wildlife film as in literary work responding to threats of climate change, deforestation, and other topics explored throughout this volume.

As contributors to recent anthologies such as *Framing the World* (2010), *Chinese Ecocinema* (2010), and *Ecocinema Theory and Practice* (2012) persuasively demonstrate,[4] ecocinema can inhabit any number of forms; this chapter focuses on portrayals of wild animals in documentaries because from the beginning of filmmaking, nonhuman animals have played an integral and (until recently) underappreciated role in the development of motion picture. For example, one of the first steps toward the development of cinema came in 1878 when Leland Stanford hired photographer Eadweard Muybridge to take a series of split-second images of a thoroughbred horse racing down a track.[5] Using a series of cameras attached to trip wires, Muybridge, who also conducted similar studies of human bodies around this time, successfully demonstrated that when horses run, there is a point in their gait when all four hooves come off the ground, something that the human eye could not accurately detect. Muybridge's images, which circulated widely, were taken on Eastman Kodak celluloid film that contained emulsified gelatin made from cattle.[6]

Motion picture technology was propelled in part, as Mitman notes, by the urge to "reveal living processes and movements unobservable to the human eye."[7] To capture images of bird flight, Etienne-Jules Marey invented a device in 1882 that captured twelve images per second on glass plates, allowing scientists to study wing movement. Inspired by Muybridge, Marey, and others, by 1895, both the Edison company in the United States and the Lumière Brothers in France had developed gear-driven film cameras similar in many respects to those used today. Historically motion pictures have been regarded as part of an inevitable march of technology associated with the Industrial Revolution, yet the name Marey gave his device – the chronophotographic gun – provides at least one indicator of the complex socio-ecological factors at play throughout the development of cinema.

By the time early filmmakers went searching for subjects to entertain audiences at the vaudeville shows and nickelodeons where early cinema found its niche, human industrialization had already begun to take a massive toll on the world's wildlife. The invention of photography in the mid-nineteenth century gave conservationists a powerful tool in their efforts to inform the public of the rapid extermination of species like the passenger pigeon and bison, but such efforts did not immediately extend to cinema. On one hand, as environmental historian Finis Dunaway contends, from "the progressive era through Earth Day, the camera would provide reformers with a way to link politics to visual culture, to turn environmental debates into questions of seeing."[8] On the other hand, many people associated with development of cinematography were (to varying degrees) complicit in the exploitation of nonhuman animals, including Muybridge, who photographed a tiger killing a tethered buffalo for an 1884 study, and Edison, who organized the on-camera death of Topsy the circus elephant for the 1903 short film *Electrocuting an Elephant*.[9]

As cinema developed, both wild and domestic animals quickly became a favorite subject for audiences. *National Geographic Magazine* (established in 1888) often showcased the work of Victorian "camera-hunters" such as George Shiras III and articles arguing for conservation, but early film actualities tended toward images of violent sensationalism – as in *Cockfight* (Edison, 1894) and *The Polar Bear Hunt in the Arctic Seas* (Pathé, 1910) – and animals held in captivity, as in *Lions, London Zoological Garden* (Lumières, 1895) and *Feeding the Russian Bear* (American Mutoscope, 1903). Among the rare exceptions to this trend was *The Sea Lions' Home* (Edison, 1897), the first film to feature wild animals in their natural habitat. Two films portraying the 1909–1910 African expedition led by former U.S. president Teddy Roosevelt to collect animal specimens for display at the American Museum of Natural History highlight the tension between education and entertainment, which has troubled the wildlife film throughout its history. The first of these films, Chicago filmmaker Colonel Selig's *Hunting Big Game in Africa* (1909), was staged at an indoor studio and released when news reached the United States that Roosevelt had shot a lion. Selig's film, a "blood-curdling romance" that features a Roosevelt impersonator shooting a lion purchased from a local zoo, became an immediate hit.[10] According to Bousé, scenes of hunters shooting animals were "wildlife films' chief guarantor of authenticity," until the mid-twentieth century, when scenes of predation became predominant.[11] The second of these films, wildlife photographer Cherry Kearton's *Roosevelt in Africa* (1910), was shot on location and received Roosevelt's personal endorsement. Lacking Selig's dramatic flair, *Roosevelt in Africa* was panned by critics and viewers but well received by museums, which is where the vast majority of wildlife films would be viewed until the theatrical release of Disney's True-Life Adventures after World War II.

Between the world wars, the popularity of fiction films and the establishment of commercial studio industries in the United States, France, Germany, Japan, and elsewhere relegated most wildlife films to museums, schools, and other educational venues. Although nonhuman animals featured prominently in many classical-era films, particularly during the silent era when the German Shepherd Rin Tin Tin became an international icon, most filmic animals (like landscapes) served as symbolic backdrops to the psychological motivations of human characters. Thus, as Chris notes, despite growing pressure on filmmakers to "avoid fakery and temper the sensationalism of their work with scientific accuracy and conservationist messages," the financial success of wildlife films continued to "depend on the degree to which they embraced sensationalism."[12] The pioneer of underwater filmmaking, Jean Painlevè, for example, whose films include *L'Hippocampe* ("The Sea

Horse," 1934) and *Amours de la pieuvre* ("The Love Life of the Octopus," 1965), believed that filmmakers could be capable of balancing storytelling and science. The most widely seen wildlife documentaries of the period, however, such as Martin and Osa Johnson's films *Simba* (1927) and *Congorilla* (1929), commonly display animal cruelty and a disturbing tendency to conflate nonwhite humans with monkeys.[13] As the success of fiction films like *King Kong* and the cartoons of Disney and Warner Brothers illustrate, audiences during the classical era clearly favored anthropomorphized caricatures of animals over the real thing, which is deeply ironic considering that the rate at which wild animals became threatened with extinction increased dramatically during this period.

Throughout the twentieth century, many wildlife species experienced sharp declines attributable to such factors as exploding human populations, deforestation, pesticides, and lax environmental regulations. By the time stricter laws protecting air, water, and threatened species were enacted in the United States and elsewhere in the 1970s, humanity had already instigated what scientists are now calling the Sixth Extinction. As biologist and filmmaker Jeff Corwin explains, "The fifth extinction took place 65 million years ago when a meteor smashed into the Earth, killing off the dinosaurs and many other species and opening the door for the rise of mammals. Currently, the sixth extinction is on track to dwarf the fifth."[14] In 2007 CNN television special *Planet in Peril*, Corwin contends that habitat destruction remains the single greatest threat to biodiversity preservation because most species (particularly insects and amphibians) have evolved to live in specific habitats – an issue first explored in 1954, in Disney's *The Vanishing Prairie*.

The Vanishing Prairie marks an important turning point in the wildlife film genre by calling attention to the endangered status of several high-profile species, including bison, whooping cranes, and black-tailed ferrets. Apart from a single mention of civilization's encroachment on the grasslands, however, the film avoids any mention of suburbanization and other anthropogenic threats to these species. Prairie dogs, for example, are described as "vanishing" as a result of the persistent efforts of predators rather than farmers and ranchers, and it is even suggested that whooping cranes may be complicit in their own demise because they lay only one egg each year. Similar to *Bambi* (1942), the film's cartoonish musical track and voice-over narration anthropomorphize the animals' behaviors by punctuating their behaviors with melodramatic effects, yet there is no mention of hunting. Adhering to the Disney motto, "Nature writes the screenplays," human beings – both "man" (i.e., white Americans) and "the red man" (i.e., indigenous peoples) – are absent from the mise-en-scène, which is ostensibly set in the period following the last ice age. Rather than tackling complex ecological concerns head-on, Disney films maintained the traditional wilderness narrative of earlier generations by demarcating nature as a space separated from human culture. To their credit, the True-Life Adventures do encourage viewers to appreciate the natural world on its own terms, a stance also taken by Jacque Cousteau in films like *The Silent World* (1956). By 1960, when the last True-Life Adventure *Jungle Cat* was released, Disney had established the basic (albeit often conflicting) tropes of the wildlife filmmaking still in use today, such as an appreciation of nonhuman animals for their own sake, a focus on charismatic species and family groups, and expert staging. Despite the critical and financial success Disney achieved, however, wildlife films once again disappeared from the big screen during the next several decades as the genre shifted to television.

Between the 1960s and 1990s, narrative films centered on human beings living in close proximity with wild animals – dangerous or otherwise – came to dominate the theatrical market for wildlife entertainment. Such films include *Flipper* (1963), *Born Free* (1966), *Jaws* (1975), *Never Cry Wolf* (1983), *Gorillas in the Mist* (1988), and *Free Willy* (1993). *The Hellstrom Chronicle* (1971), Ed Spiegel and Walon Green's documentary on the struggle between humans and insects, may be the one exception to this rule, although it is as much science fiction as science. As demand shifted, syndicated wildlife programs – including *Zoo Quest* (1954–1963), *Wild Kingdom* (1963–1988, 2002–), *National Geographic Specials* (1964–), *The Undersea World of Jacques Cousteau* (1968–1973), *Nature* (1982–), and *The Crocodile Hunter* (1997–2006) – became a ubiquitous feature of the ever-expanding television universe, owing in large part to their relatively low production costs. In 1996, Animal Planet became the first television channel devoted entirely to shows featuring wild and domesticated animals, followed by National Geographic Wild in 2006.

While a thorough review of television wildlife documentaries is beyond the scope of this essay, several features of this genre are useful for situating the resurgence of theatrical wildlife documentaries in recent years. First, like the feature-length documentaries discussed later in the chapter, they tend to take one of two forms, focusing either on intrepid researcher adventures like Marlin Perkins, Jane Goodall, and Steve Irwin, or on members of charismatic mascot species like whales and tigers. Second, while far more concerned with species preservation than earlier films in the genre, they share many aspects of both the safari films of the 1910s–1930s and the Disney films of the 1940s–1950s. Both forms typically focus on members of tight-knit family groups and the life cycle of mascot species. Dian Fossey, for example, was featured in several *National Geographic Specials* that highlighted her relationship with a single group of mountain gorillas in Rwanda before her murder in 1985. Third, helicopters, zoom lenses, infrared cameras, and other technologies have offered filmmakers new ways of accessing animal behavior, but when edited into short segments, these techniques problematically instill what Bousè describes as a sense of "false intimacy" in viewers.[15] As Chris notes, such technologies have also allowed wildlife programs to become more explicit in their displays of sexual reproduction and predation, often using such moments to draw analogies between human and wildlife behavior akin to social Darwinism.[16] Fourth, staged scenes exploiting captured or trained animals remain a prominent feature of wildlife television, particularly on cable. The practice is so widespread, in fact, that the Canadian Broadcasting Corporation (CBC) produced an updated version of *Cruel Camera* in 2008 to highlight the issue. Finally, although television wildlife programs often focus on threatened or endangered species, these shows rarely engage in complex social and political arguments, making them palatable to mainstream audiences and highly adaptable to a global media market.

This list may suggest that wildlife television is somehow antithetical to the aims of ecocritical thought and action, but this is not entirely the case. As the neoliberal mindset of hyperindividualism began to take root in Western culture during the 1980s and 1990s, television wildlife shows (like fiction films) offered many viewers a sense that they were not alone in their concern for the environment. Ursula Heise, for example, has argued that such mediated moments of interspecies communication are capable of fostering a nascent sense of ecocosmopolitanism, which she describes as our best hope for a sustainable future.[17] The problem with commercial television programs, however, is that their messages are inseparable from the constant flow of targeted consumer advertising with which they are embroiled. As a capitalist enterprise, television revolves around advertising, not content, because advertising brings in the majority of revenue. Steve Irwin, for example, before he was killed by a stingray in 2006, sought to shift the genre beyond "the days of sittin' back on the long lens on the tripod and lookin' at wildlife way over there." Irwin wanted to inspire action, not just talk. Yet what are viewers to make of such claims when they are immediately interrupted by commercials for automobiles, fast food, and other products associated with environmental injustice?

Released in 1996, *Microcosmos*, created by Claude Nuridsany and Marie Pérennou, became the first wildlife film to break out of the independent film festival circuit and reach mainstream theatrical audiences, signaling the dawn of a new era in the genre. Its use of robotic cameras, digital editing, and a multilayered soundtrack composed of real and studio-generated insect sounds accompanied by a lush musical score and a single line of narration set a new standard for technological achievement and demonstrated the viability of theatrical wildlife films in the global market. Pixar animators also studied the film while making their multimillion-dollar blockbuster *A Bug's Life* (1998).[18] Humans are absent from the film's mise-en-scène, and anthropomorphism is minimized by the absence of narration. As the film's original title, *Le peuple de l'herbe* ("The People of the Grass"), and musical score suggest, however, the liminal space between human and nonhuman continues to haunt the cultural imagination, a topic that has been discussed at length by such thinkers as Jacques Derrida, Donna Haraway, Franz de Waal, and Cary Wolfe.[19] In an interview with film scholar Scott MacDonald, Nuridsany and Pérennou decry excessive anthropomorphism for turning animals into "zoomorphic puppets" but contend that "refusing any type of anthopomorphism is to assume that humans and animals have no commonality, and that human beings are absolutely unique (if not divine)."[20] The success of *Microcosmos* also set the stage for another wordless French production, Jacques Perrin's *Winged Migration* (2001), to earn more than $30 million at the global box office.

Upon their release, *Microcosmos* and *Winged Migration* appeared to signal that the theatrical wildlife film not only had become viable again but that it had broken free of the tendency to focus almost exclusively on mascot species. However, as the political rhetoric surrounding environmental issues has heated up in the early twenty-first century, filmmakers have generally returned to the familiar trope of the charismatic species, particularly those appealing to mainstream audiences.

The related approaches taken by *March of the Penguins* (2005), *An Arctic Tale* (2007), and *Earth* (2009) to the depiction of wildlife threatened by climate change highlight the difficult choices faced by filmmakers in their efforts to balance education and entertainment. Although most greenhouse gases are released in the populated countries of the Northern Hemisphere, in 2001, the connection between penguins and climate change became apparent after two icebergs created by melting sea ice slammed into the Ross Ice Shelf in Antarctica, decimating two emperor penguin colonies.[21] Although the event was a key inspiration behind *March of the Penguins*, it is not mentioned in the film. In an interview with *National Geographic*, director Luc Jacquet defended his decision: "It's obvious that global warming has an impact on the reproduction of the penguins. But much of public opinion appears insensitive to the dangers of global warming. We have to find other ways to communicate to people about it, not just lecture them."[22] By focusing on love and family over science, they offered viewers a blank slate on which they could project their own assumptions about the environment. Marketed to both arthouse and multiplex filmgoers and endorsed by critics from both sides of the political aisle, *March of the Penguins* won the Oscar for Best Documentary Feature in 2006 and grossed an astonishing $117 million worldwide, a record for wildlife films that stands to this date.

Two years later, *National Geographic* released *Arctic Tale*. Scripted by Kristen Gore and narrated by Queen Latifah, the film was nominated for a coveted Panda award at Bristol's Wildscreen Film Festival (the Oscars of the wildlife film industry), but performed below expectations in limited theatrical release, earning less than $2 million worldwide. In spite of a well-planned marketing strategy, including a joint advertising venture with the coffee chain Starbucks, the film's "preachy" references to global warming and melodramatic depictions of polar bears and walruses did not sit well with many viewers and critics.[23]

Inspired by the success of *March of the Penguins*, Disney announced its intention to reenter the theatrical market for wildlife films in 2008 through the creation of Disneynature, an independent production unit based in Paris. The first Disneynature film, *Earth*, is a re-edited version of director Alistair Fothergill's BBC series *Planet Earth* (2006). Disney meticulously crafted the film's release pattern and marketing strategy, screening it internationally between 2007 and 2008 before premiering it in the United States on Earth Day in 2009. The soundtrack and narration were altered to reflect viewers' cultural differences. As Claire Molloy argues, Disneynature films are conceived first and foremost as capitalist commodities designed to maximize the company's profits.[24] As such, they offer a glimpse into the cultural logic of ecology by revealing the close-knit ties between economics and cultural perceptions of environment. Disney's success at promoting itself as a "green brand" is a clear indicator that consumers have become increasingly concerned with environmental issues and are seeking to align themselves with like-minded companies. In the film, which earned more than $100 million worldwide, Disney's appeals to eco-conscious viewers are apparent in the Disneynature logo (an iceberg in the shape of Cinderella's castle) and several overt references to anthropogenic environmental change.

As these traditional wildlife films have become popular, a small group of films based on the adventurer model have also gained recognition, including *Being Caribou* and *Grizzly Man*. Released in 2004, as the political battle over oil drilling in the Alaska National Wildlife Refuge was heating up in the United States and Canada, *Being Caribou* follows the efforts of Karsten Heuer and Leanne Allison to track the annual caribou migration. The film became the darling of the festival circuit (earning more than twenty awards) but it was not picked up for theatrical distribution, further highlighting the difficulty for films produced outside the corporate model to reach wider audiences. As Salma Monani contends, the film's "strong focus on the adventure story of two [white] Euro-Americans makes it easy for viewers to overlook native representations or to simplify them," suggesting that many wildlife films have yet to fully overcome the ethnocentric problems associated with the safari film era.[25]

Grizzly Man also follows the story of an activist seeking to escape the confines of human civilization and retreat (to borrow novelist John Krakauer's phrase) into the wild. Unlike other wildlife adventure narratives, however, the film is highly critical of its protagonist, the late Timothy Treadwell, who was killed and eaten in 2003, along with his girlfriend Amie Huguenard, by one of the bears he had been living with in a remote area of Alaska's Katmai National Park. Although it did not receive an Oscar nomination, the film earned $4 million at the box office. It has also received considerable scholarly attention, in part because a wide range of possible meanings are made possible by the intercutting that occurs between Treadwell's home video footage, director Werner Herzog's voice-over narration, and interviews with Treadwell's friends and fellow conservationists. Treadwell is given significant screen time to make his case that living with the grizzlies helped him to overcome the social indoctrination that teaches most of us to perceive nature as entirely separated from human culture. His gruesome death, however, which is not shown on camera, becomes an opportunity for Herzog and his interviewees to describe Treadwell as a naïve dreamer who failed to recognize that there are boundaries between human and nonhuman animals that should not be crossed. From an ecocritical perspective, what is particularly troubling about the film is that the grizzlies' struggle for survival in a world where their primary food source, salmon, are threatened by overfishing, dams, and climate change becomes entirely overshadowed in Herzog's vision by Treadwell's tragic hubris.

By way of conclusion, I now turn to two highly-acclaimed films produced by Participant Media: Robert Kenner's *Food, Inc.* and Louis Psihoyos's *The Cove*. Founded in 2004 by former Ebay president Jeff Skoll, Participant is not a corporate giant just yet, but its interests do include books, television, digital videos, and theatrical films (including *Syriana*, *North Country*, and *An Inconvenient Truth*). According to media mogul Richard Branson, "All of the organizations Jeff Skoll has founded share a common vision of living in a sustainable world of peace and prosperity."[26] Nominated for an Oscar in 2009, *Food, Inc.* tackles the issue of industrial agriculture in the United States, while *The Cove*, which won the Oscar for Best Documentary Feature in 2010, documents the annual capture and slaughter of dolphins near the Japanese town of Taiji. These films' entangled discourse surrounding the humanity's consumption of other animals for meat and entertainment presents a compelling challenge for those interested in environmental media scholarship.

Food, Inc. opens with an establishing shot of a traditional red farmhouse. As the camera tracks into a close-up, however, the image fades from live action to illustration, taking the viewer from the farm to the supermarket as farmhouse dissolves into the logo on a package of butter. This is the first of many shots intended to press the film's case that corporate food production has transformed the United States from the pastoral past to the suburban present. Like *King Corn, Super Size Me,* and other recent food documentaries, Kenner's film argues that Americans have become more obese and unhealthy by consuming cheaply produced animal products purchased at fast-food drive-in windows while a handful of corporations like Monsanto and Tyson have replaced traditional farming methods with industrial agribusiness. Elsewhere, the film employs slick graphics, horror-style handheld shots from inside slaughterhouses, and a racially problematic combination of interviews with white food writers, organic farmers, and an overweight working-class Hispanic family. *Food, Inc.* borrows the same tactics as corporate advertisers to manipulate viewers, thus challenging ecocritics to accept Attenborough's claim that it is the intentions of the filmmaker that matter the most. A study of more than twenty thousand viewers conducted by the University of Southern California's Annenberg School for Communication found that viewers were "significantly more likely to encourage their friends, family & colleagues to: learn more about food safety, shop at their local farmers market, eat healthy food, [and] consistently buy organic or sustainable food."[27] This point is driven home by a scene in which the camera is situated outside a warehouse that the filmmakers are not allowed to enter. When the film then cuts to a similar building to show close-ups of birds wading in their own manure the point is made that food corporations care more about profits than farmers, consumers, and animals.

The Cove highlights the fact that while globalization is offering us new avenues for cross-cultural communication, it is also making our differences more visible, particularly in relation to meat consumption. Thus, while on one level *The Cove* is a wildlife film, on another it can be read as a food film. The plot centers on Richard O'Barry, who was the lead dolphin trainer for the television series *Flipper* (1964–1967) but became a preservationist after one of the dolphins that played Flipper "committed suicide" in O'Barry's estimation by refusing to breathe. This melodramatic tale reinforces the viewer's desire to see O'Barry succeed in his efforts to protect the more than 20,000 dolphins that are slaughtered for food each year in Taiji, as well as the smaller number that are captured and sold to aquariums and encounter therapy centers. There are few moments in the history of cinema so chilling as the shots of O'Barry and his crew listening to these highly intelligent creatures become increasingly agitated as they are driven into a hidden cove and trapped by nets to await the slaughter. Dolphins are highly sonic creatures and the sounds they produce make it difficult for any viewer to come away from the film without feeling that the dolphins are aware of their predicament. None of the footage in the film, if the filmmakers are to be believed, has been staged. However, the film's effort to implicate the Japanese government for its continued refusal to abide by international treaties against whaling occasionally slips into a xenophobic indictment of Japanese culture, prompting *The Guardian*'s film critic David Cox to ask, "Westerners … kill and eat cows. Easterners eat dolphins. What's the difference?"[28] One difference is that dolphin meat contains extremely high levels of mercury, making them unfit for human consumption. Another is that humans have engineered modern cows to the point where they can no longer survive in the wild. And while Cox fails to recognize these differences, his question raises concerns that will keep such debates alive and well into the future, or at least until the last dolphins are gone. At this writing, the slaughter in Taiji continues unabated.

Can we really blame folks like Richard O'Barry, Steve Irwin, or even Timothy Treadwell for devoting their lives to protecting some of the last living examples of a time long before the invention of cinema, when humanity did not consider itself the pinnacle of creation, even if their efforts appear at times to be so misguided? We did not ask to be born into such perilous times; nor is it easy to look around us each day and see so many carrying on with business as usual, particularly now that we can all sense what is coming. For even as the specter of nuclear apocalypse has abated somewhat in the post-Cold War era, we are facing the very real possibility that life as we know it could be radically altered by the needless destruction of our planet's rich biodiversity. Although the wildlife documentary genre has been troubled throughout its brief history by commercialism, sensationalism, and even downright fakery, as the films discussed in this chapter illuminate, the horrors that we humans have collectively enacted on our fellow creatures typify the hubris of anthropocentrism that is situated at the heart of the Earth's unfolding tragedy.

NOTES

My thanks to Janet Fiskio and Carter Soles for their insights and suggestions.

1 Jeff Corwin, "The Sixth Extinction," *Los Angeles Times* (November 30, 2009), http://articles.latimes.com/2009/nov/30/opinion/la-oe-corwin30-2009nov30.
2 Nils Stenseth, "Population Cycles in Voles and Lemmings," *Oikos* 87 (1999), 427–461.

3 David Attenborough, "How Unnatural Is TV Natural History," *The Listener* (May 7, 1987), 12.

4 Paula Willoquet (ed.), *Framing the World: Explorations in Ecocriticism and Film* (Charlottesville: University of Virginia Press, 2010); Jiayan Mi (ed.), *Chinese Ecocinema in the Age of Environmental Challenge* (Hong Kong: Hong Kong University Press, 2009); and Stephen Rust, Salma Monani, and Sean Cubitt (eds.), *Ecocinema and Practice* (New York: Routledge, 2012).

5 Kristin Thompson and David Bordwell, *Film History: An Introduction* (Boston: McGraw-Hill, 2010), 4–6.

6 Nicole Shukin, *Animal Capital: Rendering Life in Biopolitical Times* (Minneapolis: University of Minnesota Press, 2009), 87–130.

7 Greg Mitman, *Reel Nature: America's Romance with Wildlife on Film* (Cambridge, MA: Harvard University Press, 1999), 8.

8 Finis Dunaway, *Natural Visions: The Power of Images in American Environmental Reform* (Chicago: University of Chicago Press, 2005), xvii.

9 Derek Bousè, *Wildlife Films* (Philadelphia: University of Pennsylvania Press, 2000), 42.

10 Mitman, *Reel Nature*, 10.

11 Bousé, *Wildlife Films*, 43.

12 Cynthia Chris, *Watching Wildlife* (Minneapolis: University of Minnesota Press, 2006), 20.

13 Ibid., 18–20.

14 Corwin, "The Sixth Extinction."

15 Bousé, *Wildlife Films*, 28.

16 Chris, *Watching Wildlife*, 106.

17 Ursula Heise, *Sense of Place and Sense of Planet: The Environmental Imagination of the Global* (New York: Oxford University Press, 2008), 56.

18 David Price, *The Pixar Touch* (New York: Random House, 2008), 160.

19 See, for example, Jacques Derrida, *The Animal That Therefore I Am* (New York: Fordham University Press, 2008); Donna Haraway, *When Species Meet* (Minneapolis: Minnesota University Press, 2007); Franz De Waal, *The Ape and the Sushi Master* (New York: Basic, 2001); and Cary Wolfe, *Animal Rites: American Culture, the Discourse of Species, and Posthumanist Theory* (Chicago: University of Chicago Press, 2003).

20 Scott MacDonald, *Adventures of Perception: Cinema as Exploration* (Berkeley: University of California Press, 2009), 195.

21 Gerald Kooyman, et al., "Effects of Giant Icebergs on Two Emperor Penguin Colonies in the Ross Sea, Antarctica," *Antarctic Science* 19 (2007): 31–38.

22 Stefan Lovgren, "Interview: March of the Penguins director Luc Jacquet," *National Geographic News* (June 24, 2005), http://news.nationalgeographic.com/news/2005/06/0624_050624_marchpenguin.html.

23 Daniel Engber, "March of the Lesbian Walruses," *Slate* (July 26, 2007), http://www.slate.com/articles/health_and_science/green_room/2007/07/march_of_the_lesbian_walruses.html.

24 Claire Molloy, "'Nature Writes the Screenplays': Wildlife Films and Commercial Eco-Entertainment," *Ecocinema Theory and Practice*, 169–188.

25 Salma Monani, "Wilderness Discourse in Adventure-Nature Films: the Potentials and Limitations of Being Caribou," *ISLE* 19 (2012), 117.

26 Richard Branson, "Can Movies Save the World?" *Canadian Business* (March 19, 2012), 14.

27 Johanna Blakely, "Research Study Finds That a Film Can Have a Measurable Impact on Audience Behavior," *University of Southern California Annenberg School of Communication* (February 22, 2012), http://www.learcenter.org/pdf/FoodInc.pdf.

28 David Cox, "The Cove's Message Is Gruesome, but Facile," *The Guardian* (October 26, 2009), http://www.guardian.co.uk/film/filmblog/2009/oct/26/the-cove-documentary.

CHRONOLOGY OF PUBLICATIONS AND EVENTS

Foundations

Pastoral

3rd Century B.C.E	Theocritus, *Idylls*
c. 3 B.C.E	Virgil, *Eclogues* and *Georgics*
1579	Edmund Spenser, *The Shepheardes Calendar*
1590	Philip Sidney, *Arcadia*
1594	William Shakespeare, *A Midsummer Night's Dream*
c. 1600	*As You Like It*

The Sublime

1699	Joseph Addison, *Remarks on Several Parts of Italy*
1709	Third Earl of Shaftesbury, *The Moralists, A Political Rhapsody*
1756	Edmund Burke, *A Philosophical Enquiry into Our Ideas of the Sublime and the Beautiful*
1790	Immanuel Kant, "On the Sublime" in *The Critique of Judgment*

Romantic Poetry of Nature

1800	William Wordsworth, *Preface to Lyrical Ballads*
1816	Percy Bysshe Shelley, "Mont Blanc"
1819	John Keats, "To Autumn"

Nature Writing and Natural History

1836   Ralph Waldo Emerson, *Nature*

1854   Henry David Thoreau, *Walden, or, Life in the Woods*

1859   Charles Darwin, *The Origin of Species*

1911   John Muir, *My First Summer in the Sierra*

Proto-Environmental Non-Fiction and Ecocriticism

1949   Aldo Leopold, *A Sand County Almanac*

1962   Rachel Carson, *Silent Spring*

1964   Leo Marx, *The Machine in the Garden*

1973   Raymond Williams, *The Country and the City*

The Development of Environmental Literary Criticism or Ecocriticism

1974   Joseph Meeker, *The Comedy of Survival: Studies in Literary Ecology*

1975   Annette Kolodny, *The Lay of the Land: Metaphor as Experience and History in American Life and Letters*

1978   William Rueckert, "Literature and Ecology: An Experiment in Ecocriticism"

1990   Glen Love, "Revaluing Nature: Toward an Ecological Criticism"

       Gary Snyder, *The Practice of the Wild*

1991   Jonathan Bate, *Romantic Ecology: Wordsworth and the Environmental Tradition*

1992   Formation of the Association for the Study of Literature and the Environment (ASLE) at the Western Literary Association Conference, Reno, Nevada

1993   Greta Gaard, ed., *Ecofeminism: Women, Animals, Nature*

1994	Formation of the Association for the Study of Literature and Environment in Japan (ASLE-Japan)
1995	Terry Gifford, *Green Voices: Understanding Contemporary Nature Poetry*
	Kate Soper, *What Is Nature?*
	William Cronon, "The Trouble with Wilderness, or, Getting Back to the Wrong Nature"
1996	Cheryll Glotfelty and Harold Fromm, eds., *The Ecocriticism Reader*
1997	Colin Riordan, ed., *Green Thought in German Culture: Historical and Contemporary Perspectives*
1998	Formation of the Association for the Study of Literature and Environment, UK (now ASLE UK and Ireland)
	Richard Kerridge and Neil Sammells, eds., *Writing the Environment: Ecocriticism and Literature*
	Scott Slovic, *Seeking Awareness in American Nature Writing*
	Patrick Murphy, Terry Gifford, and Katsunori Yamazato, eds., *Literature of Nature: An International Sourcebook*
2000	Lawrence Coupe, ed., *The Green Studies Reader: From Romanticism to Ecocriticism*
2001	Founding of the Association for the Study of Literature and Environment in Korea (ASLE-Korea)
	Joni Adamson, *American Indian Literature, Environmental Justice, and Ecocriticism*
	Joni Adamson, Mei Mei Evans, and Rachel Stein, eds., *The Environmental Justice Reader: Politics, Poetry, Pedagogy*
2002	John Parham, ed., *The Environmental Tradition in English Literature*

2003 Founding of the Association for the Study of Literature and Environment, Australia and New Zealand (ASLE-ANZ)

Glen Love, *Practical Ecocriticism: Literature, Biology, and the Environment*

Cary Wolfe, ed., *Zoontologies: The Question of the Animal*

Ken Hiltner, *Milton and Ecology*

Michael P. Branch and Scott Slovic, eds., *The ISLE Reader: Ecocriticism, 1993–2003*

2004 Founding of the Association for the Study of Literature and Environment in India (ASLE-India) and the Organization for Studies in Literature and Environment in India and other Asian countries (OSLE-India)

Greg Garrard, *Ecocriticism*

Kate Rigby, *Topgraphies of the Sacred: The Poetics of Place in European Romanticism*

Founding of the European Association for the Study of Literature, Culture, and Environment (EASLCE)

2005 Founding of the Association for the Study of Literature, Environment, and Culture-Australia and New Zealand (ASLEC-ANZ)

Founding of the Association for Literature, Environment, and Culture in Canada (ALECC)

Elizabeth DeLoughrey, Renée K. Gosson, and George B. Handley, eds., *Caribbean Literature and the Environment: Between Nature and Culture*

2006 Robert N. Watson, *Back to Nature: The Green and the Real in the Late Renaissance*

Catrin Gersdorf and Sylvia Mayer, eds., *Nature in Literary and Cultural Studies: Transatlantic Conversations on Ecocriticism*

2007	Founding of the Association for the Study of Literature and Environment in Malaysia (ASLE-Malaysia)
	Axel Goodbody, *Nature, Technology, and Cultural Change in Twentieth-Century German Literature*
	Timothy Morton, *Ecology Without Nature*
2008	Founding of the Association for the Study of Literature and Environment in Taiwan (ASLE-Taiwan)
	Jacques Derrida, *The Animal That Therefore I Am* (English trans.)
	Dan Wylie, ed., *Toxic Belonging? Identity and Ecology in Southern Africa*
	Laird Christensen, Mark C. Long, and Freg Waage, eds., *Teaching North American Environmental Literature*
	Ursula Heise, *Sense of Place and Sense of Planet: The Environmental Imagination of the Global*
	Philip Armstrong, *What Animals Mean in the Fiction of Modernity*
	S. Murali, ed., *Nature and Human Nature: Literature, Ecology, Meaning*
2009	Alfred Siewers, *Strange Beauty: Ecocritical Approaches to Early Medieval Landscape*
	Graham Huggan and Helen Tiffin, *Postcolonial Ecocriticism: Literature, Animals, Environment*
2010	Bonnie Roos and Alex Hunt, *Postcolonial Green: Environmental Politics and World Narratives*
	Adrian Taylor Kane, ed., *The Natural World in Latin American Literatures: Ecocritical Essays on Twentieth-Century Writings*
	Catriona Mortimer-Sandilands and Bruce Erickson, eds., *Queer Ecologies: Sex, Nature, Politics and World Narratives*

2011   Rob Nixon, *Slow Violence and the Environmentalism of the Poor*

Leo Mellor, *Reading the Ruins: Modernism, Bombsites, and British Culture*

2012   Greg Garrard, ed., *Teaching Ecocriticism and Green Cultural Studies*

Stephen Rust, Salma Monani, and Sean Cubitt, *Ecocinema Theory and Practice*

FURTHER READING

General Sources

The Association for the Study of Literature and Environment, www.asle.org/, ASLE's website lists international affiliate members, upcoming conferences, online materials introducing ecocriticism, and resources including syllabi and an online ecocritical library and bibliography at: http://www.asle.org/site/resources/ecocritical-library/

Journals

AJE: Australasian Journal of Ecocriticism and Cultural Ecology (The official publication of the Association for the Study of Literature, Environment and Culture-Australia and New Zealand, ASLEC – ANZ), http://www.nla.gov.au/openpublish/index.php/aslec-anz

The Goose (electronic journal of the Association for Literature, Environment and Culture in Canada, ALECC), http://www.alecc.ca/goose.php

Green Letters: Studies in Ecocriticism (journal of the UK and Ireland affiliate of ASLE, published commercially by Taylor and Francis)

The Indian Journal of Ecocriticism

The Journal of Ecocriticism, J o E (open-access, peer-reviewed electronic review of ecocriticism and ecoliterature), http://ojs.unbc.ca/index.php/joe

Resilience: A Journal of the Environmental Humanities (University of Nebraska Press)

Related non-literary journals: *Environmental Ethics, Environmental History, Environmental Humanities, Environmental Philosophy, Environmental Politics, Environmental Values.*

Foundations

Bate, Jonathan, *Romantic Ecology: Wordsworth and the Environmental Tradition* (London and New York: Routledge, 1991).

The Song of the Earth (Cambridge, MA: Harvard University Press, 2000).

Buell, Lawrence, *The Environmental Imagination: Thoreau, Nature Writing, and the Formation of American Culture* (Cambridge, MA: Harvard University Press, 1995).

Writing for an Endangered World: Literature, Culture, and Environment in the U.S. and Beyond (Cambridge, MA: Harvard University Press, 2001).

The Future of Environmental Criticism: Environmental Crisis and Literary Imagination (Malden, MA: Blackwell, 2005).

Coupe, Laurence (ed.), *The Green Studies Reader: From Romanticism to Ecocriticism* (London: Routledge, 2000).

Fisher, Philip, *Hard Facts: Setting and Form in the American Novel* (New York: Oxford University Press, 1985).

Gaard, Greta (ed.), *Ecofeminism: Woman, Animals, Nature* (Philadelphia: Temple University Press, 1993).

Glotfelty, Cheryl and Harold Fromm (eds.), *The Ecocriticism Reader: Landmarks in Literary Ecology* (Athens: University of Georgia Press, 1996).

Kerridge, Richard and Neil Sammels (eds.), *Writing the Environment: Ecocriticism and Literature* (London: Zed Books, 1998).

Kolodny, Annette, *The Lay of the Land: Metaphor as Experience and History in American Life and Letters* (Chapel Hill: University of North Carolina Press, 1975).

Marx, Leo, *The Machine in the Garden: Technology and the Pastoral Ideal in America* (New York: Oxford University Press, 1964).

Meeker, Joseph, *The Comedy of Survival: Studies in Literary Ecology* (New York: Scribner, 1974).

Nash, Roderick, *Wilderness and the American Mind* (New Haven: Yale University Press, 1967.

Nicolson, Marjorie, *Mountain Gloom and Mountain Glory*, orig. pub. 1959 (Seattle: University of Washington Press, 1997).

Parham, John (ed.), *The Environmental Tradition in English Literature* (Aldershot: Ashgate, 2002).

Snyder, Gary, *The Practice of the Wild* (New York: North Point Press, 1990).

Williams, Raymond, *The Country and the City* (London and New York: Oxford University Press, 1973).

Theories

Abram, David, "Philosophy on the Way to Ecology," *The Spell of the Sensuous: Perception and Language in a More-Than-Human World* (New York: Pantheon Books, 1996), pp. 31–72.

Biro, Andrew (ed.), *Critical Ecologies: The Frankfurt School and Contemporary Environmental Crises* (Toronto: University of Toronto Press, 2011).

Brown, Charles S. and Ted Toadvine (eds.), *Eco-Phenomenology: Back to the Earth Itself* (Albany: State University of New York Press, 2003).

Goodbody, Axel and Kate Rigby (eds.), *Ecocritical Theory: New European Approaches* (Charlottesville: University of Virginia Press, 2011).

Heise, Ursula, *Sense of Place and Sense of Planet: The Environmental Imagination of the Global* (New York: Oxford, 2008).

Luke, Timothy, *Ecocritique: Contesting the Politics of Nature, Economy, and Culture* (Minneapolis: University of Minnesota Press, 1997).

Mazel, David, *American Literary Environmentalism* (Athens: University of Georgia Press, 2000).

Morton, Timothy, *The Ecological Thought* (Cambridge, MA: Harvard University Press, 2010).
   Ecology without Nature: Rethinking Environmental Aesthetics (Cambridge, MA: Harvard University Press, 2007).
Plumwood, Val, *Environmental Culture: The Ecological Crisis of Reason* (London: Routledge, 2002).
   Feminism and the Mastery of Nature (London: Routledge, 1993).
Sandilands, Cate, *The Good-Natured Feminist: Ecofeminism and the Quest for Democracy* (Minneapolis: University of Minnesota Press, 1999).
Soper, Kate, *What Is Nature? Culture, Politics, and the Nonhuman* (Oxford: Blackwell, 1995).

Interdisciplinary Engagements

Basso, Keith, *Wisdom Sits in Places: Language and Landscape among the Western Apache* (Albuquerque: University of New Mexico Press, 1996).
Beer, Gillian, *Darwin's Plots: Evolutionary Narrative in Darwin, George Eliot, and Nineteenth-Century Fiction* (London: Routledge & Kegan Paul, 1983).
Buell, Frederick, *From Apocalypse to Way of Life: Environmental Crises in the American Century* (New York: Routledge, 2003).
Campbell, SueEllen, Alex Hunt, Richard Kerridge, and Ellen Wohl, *The Face of the Earth: Natural Landscapes, Science, and Culture* (Berkeley: University of California Press, 2011).
Hoffmeyer, Jesper, *Signs of Meaning in the Universe* (Bloomington: University of Indiana Press, 1996).
Love, Glen, *Practical Ecocriticism: Literature, Biology, and the Environment* (Charlottesville: University of Virginia Press, 2003).
Phillips, Dana, *The Truth of Ecology: Nature, Culture, and Literature in America* (New York: Oxford, 2003).
Walls, Laura Dassow, *The Passage to Cosmos: Alexander von Humboldt and the Shaping of America* (Chicago: University of Chicago Press, 2009).
   Seeing New Worlds: Henry David Thoreau and Nineteenth-Century Natural Science (Madison: University of Wisconsin Press, 1995).
Wheeler, Wendy, *The Whole Creature: Complexity, Biosemiotics, and the Evolution of Culture* (London: Lawrence and Wishart, 2006).

Applied Environmental Approaches

Adamson, Joni, *American Indian Literature, Environmental Justice, and Ecocriticism* (Tuscon: Arizona University Press, 2001).
Carruth, Allison, *Global Appetites: American Power and the Literature of Food* (New York: Cambridge University Press, 2013).
Gifford, Terry, *Green Voices: Understanding Contemporary Nature Poetry* (Manchester: Manchester University Press, 1995).
Goodbody, Axel, *Nature, Technology, and Cultural Change in Twentieth-Century German Literature* (Houndmills: Palgrave Macmillan, 2007).
Harrison, Robert Pogue, *Forests: The Shadow of Civilization* (Chicago: University of Chicago Press, 1992).

Hiltner, Ken, *Milton and Ecology* (Cambridge and New York: Cambridge University Press, 2003).

What Else Is Pastoral? Renaissance Literature and the Environment (Ithaca: Cornell University Press, 2011).

Huhndorf, Shari, *Going Native: Indians in the American Cultural Imagination* (Ithaca: Cornell University Press, 2001).

Hutchings, Kevin, *Imagining Nature: Blake's Environmental Poetics* (Montreal: McGill-Queens University Press, 2002).

Romantic Ecologies and Colonial Cultures in the British Atlantic World 1750–1850 (Montreal: McGill-Queens University Press, 2009).

Knickerbocker, Scott, *Ecopoetics: The Language of Nature, the Nature of Language* (Amherst: University of Massachusetts Press, 2012).

Mellor, Leo, *Reading the Ruins: Modernism, Bombsites, and British Culture* (Cambridge, UK: Cambridge University Press, 2011).

Parham, John, *Green Man Hopkins: Poetry and the Victorian Imagination* (Amsterdam and New York: Rodopi, 2010).

Rigby, Kate, *Topographies of the Sacred: The Poetics of Place in European Romanticism* (Charlottesville: University of Virginia Press, 2004).

Siewers, Alfred, *Strange Beauty: Ecocritical Approaches to Early Medieval Landscape* (London: Palgrave McMillan, 2009).

Slovic, Scott, *Seeking Awareness in American Nature Writing* (Salt Lake City: University of Utah Press, 1998).

Stein, Rachel, *Shifting the Ground: American Women Writers' Revisions of Nature, Gender, and Race* (Charlottesville: University of Virginia Press, 1997).

Wardi, Anissa J., *Water and African-American Memory: An Ecocritical Perspective* (Gainesville: University of Florida Press, 2011).

Watson, Robert N., *Back to Nature: The Green and the Real in the Late Renaissance* (Philadelphia: University of Pennsylvania Press, 2006).

Westling, Louise, *The Green Breast of the New World: Landscape, Gender, and American Fiction* (Athens: University of Georgia Press, 1996).

New Directions

Environmental Justice

Adamson, Joni, Mei Mei Evans, and Rachel Stein (eds.), *The Environmental Justice Reader: Politics, Poetics, and Pedagogy* (Tuscon: Arizona University Press, 2002).

Stein, Rachel, *New Perspectives on Environmental Justice: Gender, Sexuality, and Activism* (Rutgers, NJ: Rutgers University Press, 2004).

Westerman, Jennifer and Christina Robertson (eds.), *Working on the Earth: The Intersection of Working-Class Studies and Environmental Justice* (New York: Lexington Books, 2011).

New Nature Writing

Lopez, Barry, *Arctic Dreams: Imagination and Desire in a Northern Landscape* (New York: Scribner, 1986).

McFarlane, Robert, *The Wild Places* (London: Penguin, 2008).

Nabhan, Gary Paul, *The Desert Smells Like Rain: A Naturalist in Papago Indian Country* (San Francisco: North Point Press, 1982).
Ortiz, Simon, "Our Homeland, a National Sacrifice Area," *Woven Stone* (Tuscon, University of Arizona Press, 1992), pp. 337–363.
Robinson, Tim, *Connemarra: The Last Pool of Darkness* (London: Penguin, 2009).
Solnit, Rebecca, *Savage Dreams: A Journey into the Landscape Wars of the American West* (Berkeley: University of California Press, 2000).

Pedagogy

Christensen, Laird, Mark C. Long, and Fred Waage (eds.), *Teaching North American Environmental Literature* (New York: The Modern Language Association, 2008).
Garrard, Greg (ed.), *Teaching Ecocriticism and Green Cultural Studies* (London: Palgrave Macmillan, 2012).

Postcolonial

DeLoughrey, Elizabeth M. and George B. Handley, *Postcolonial Ecologies: Literatures of the Environment* (New York: Oxford, 2011).
Huggan, Graham and Helen Tiffin, *Postcolonial Ecocriticism: Literature, Animals, Environment* (London: Routledge, 2009).
Roos, Bonnie and Alex Hunt, *Postcolonial Green: Environmental Politics and World Narratives* (Charlottesville: University of Virginia Press, 2010).

Animal Studies

Armstrong, Philip, *What Animals Mean in the Fiction of Modernity* (New York: Routledge, 2008).
Daston, Lorraine and Gregg Mitman (eds.), *Thinking with Animals: New Perspectives on Anthropomorphism* (New York: Columbia University Press, 2005).
Derrida, Jacques, *The Animal That Therefore I Am* (New York: Fordham, 2008).
Henninger-Voss (ed.), *Animals in Human Histories: The Mirror of Nature and Culture* (Rochester: University of Rochester Press, 2002).
Malamud, Randy, *Reading Zoos: Representations of Animals and Captivity* (New York: New York University Press, 1998).
McFarland, Sarah and Ryan Hediger (eds.), *Animals and Agency: An Interdisciplinary Exploration* (Boston: Brill, 2009).
McHugh, Susan, *Animal Stories: Narrating across Species Lines* (Minneapolis: University of Minnesota Press, 2011).
Midgley, Mary, *Animals and Why They Matter* (Athens: University of Georgia Press, 1998).
Rothfels, Nigel (ed.), *Representing Animals* (Bloomington: Indiana University Press, 2002).
Westling, Louise, *The Logos of the Living World: Merleau-Ponty, Animals, and Language* (New York: Fordham University Press, 2013).

Wolfe, Cary, *Animal Rites: American Culture, the Discourse of Species, and Posthumanist Theory* (Chicago: University of Chicago Press, 2003).

Wolfe, Cary (ed.), *Zoontologies: The Question of the Animal* (Minneapolis: University of Minnesota Press, 2003).

Climate Change

Bhaskar, Roy, Cheryl Frank, Karl Georg Høyer, Peter Naess, and Jenneth Parker (eds.), *Interdisciplinarity and Climate Change* (London and New York: Routledge, 2010).

Diamond, Jared, *Collapse: How Societies Choose to Fail or Succeed* (New York: Viking, 2005).

Kolbert, Elizabeth, *Field Notes from a Catastrophe: Man, Nature, and Climate Change* (New York: Bloomsbury USA, 2006).

Lovelock, James, *The Revenge of Gaia: Earth's Climate Crisis and the Fate of Humanity* (New York: Basic Books, 2007).

Maxwell, Anne, "Postcolonial Criticism, Ecocriticism, and Climate Change: A Tale of Melbourne under Water in 2035," *Journal of Postcolonial Writing* 45 (2009), 15–26.

Media Studies

Brereton, Pat, *Hollywood Utopia: Ecology in Contemporary American Cinema* (Bristol, UK: Intellect Ltd., 2004).

Cubitt, Sean, *EcoMedia* (Amsterdam: Rodopi, 2005).

Ingram, David, *Green Screen: Environmentalism and Hollywood Cinema* (Exeter: University of Exeter Press, 2000).

Lu, Sheldon and Jiayan Mi (eds.), *Chinese Ecocinema: In the Age of Environmental Challenge* (Seattle: University of Washington Press, 2010).

MacDonald, Scott, *The Garden in the Machine: A Field Guide to Independent Films about Place* (Berkeley: University of California Press, 2001).

Mitman, George, *Reel Nature: America's Romance with Wildlife on Film* (Cambridge, MA: Harvard University Press, 1999).

Murray, Robin L. and Joseph K Heumann, *Ecology and Popular Film: Cinema on the Edge* (Albany: State University of New York Press, 2009).

That's All Folks: Ecocritical Readings of American Animated Features (Lincoln: University of Nebraska Press, 2011).

Rust, Stephen, Salma Monani, and Sean Cubitt (eds.) *Ecocinema Theory and Practice* (New York: Routledge, 2012).

Willoquet-Maricondi, Paula (ed.), *Framing the World: Explorations in Ecocriticism and Film* (Charlottesville: University of Virginia Press, 2010).

Material Ecocriticism

Alaimo, Tracy, *Bodily Natures: Science, Environment, and the Material Self* (Bloomington: Indiana University Press, 2010).

Opermann, Serpil and Serenella Iovino (eds.), *Material Ecocriticism* (Bloomington: Indiana University Press, 2013).

General Anthologies

Armbruster, Karla, and Kathleen R. Wallace (eds.), *Beyond Nature Writing: Expanding the Boundaries of Ecocriticism* (Charlottesville: University of Virginia Press, 2001).

Becket, Fiona and Terry Gifford (eds.), *Culture, Creativity, and Environment: New Environmentalist Criticism* (Amsterdam and New York: Rodopi, 2007).

Bennett, Michael and David W. Teague (eds.), *The Nature of Cities: Ecocriticism and Urban Environments* (Tuscon: University of Arizona Press, 1999).

Cranston, C. A. and Robert Zeller (eds.), *The Littoral Zone: Australian Contexts and Their Writers* (Amsterdam and New York: Rodopi, 2007).

Cusick, Christine (ed.), *Out of the Earth: Ecocritical Readings of Irish Texts* (Cork: Cork University Press, 2010).

DeLoughrey, Elizabeth, George Handley, and Renee K. Gosson (eds.), *Caribbean Literature and the Environment: Between Nature and Culture* (Charlottesville: University of Virginia Press, 2005).

Dixon, Terrell (ed.), *City Wilds* (Athens: University of Georgia Press, 2002).

Fuchs, Eleanor and Una Chaudhuri (eds.), *Land/scape/theater* (Ann Arbor: University of Michigan Press, 2002).

Gaard, Greta and Patrick D. Murphy (eds.), *Ecofeminist Literary Criticism: Theory, Interpretation, Pedagogy* (Champaign: University of Illinois Press, 1998).

Gersdorf, Catrin and Sylvia Mayer (eds.), *Nature in Literary and Cultural Studies: Transatlantic Conversations on Ecocriticism* (Amsterdam and New York: Rodopi, 2006).

Kane, Adrian Taylor (ed.), *The Natural World in Latin American Literatures: Ecocritical Essays on Twentieth-Century Writings* (Jefferson, NC: McFarland Publishing, 2010).

LeMenager, Stephanie, Teresa Shewry, and Ken Hiltner (eds.), *Environmental Criticism for the Twenty-First Century* (New York: Routledge, 2012).

Lu, Shuyuan (ed.), *Nature and Culture: A Sourcebook of Ecocriticism* (Shanghai: XueLin Press, 2006).

Lu, Shuyuan (ed.), *Nearing the Primeval Forest: Ecodiscourses of Forty Humanities Scholars* (Shanghai: Shanghai Literary and Artistic Publishing House, 2008).

Lynch, Tom, Cheryll Glotfelty, and Karla Armbruster (eds.), *The Bioregional Imagination: Literature, Ecology, and Place* (Athens: University of Georgia Press, 2012).

Mazel, David (ed.), *A Century of Early Ecocriticism* (Athens: University of Georgia Press, 2001).

Mortimer-Sandilands, Catriona and Bruce Erickson (eds.), *Queer Ecologies: Sex, Nature, Politics, Desire* (Bloomington: Indiana University Press, 2010).

Murali, S. (ed.), *Nature and Human Nature: Literature, Ecology, Meaning* (New Delhi: Prestige Books, 2008).

Murphy, Patrick, Terry Gifford, and Katsunori Yamazato (eds.), *Literature of Nature: An International Sourcebook* (Chicago: Fitzroy, Dearborn, 1998).

Oppermann, Serpil, Ufuk Özdağ, Nevin Özkan, and Scott Slovic (eds.), *The Future of Ecocriticism: New Horizons* (Cambridge: Cambridge Scholars Press, 2011).

Selvamony, Nirmal, Nirmaldasan, and Rayson K. Alex (eds.), *Essays in Ecocriticism* (Chennai and New Delhi: OSLE-India and Sarup & Sons, 2007).

Volkmann, Laurenz, Nancy Grimm, Ines Detmers, and Katrin Thomson (eds.), *Local Natures, Global Responsibilities: Ecocritical Perspectives on the New English Literatures* (Amsterdam: Rodopi, 2010).

Wylie, Dan (ed.), *Toxic Belonging? Identity and Ecology in Southern Africa* (Cambridge: Cambridge Scholars Publishing, 2008).

INDEX

Cambridge Companions to...

Lightning Source UK Ltd.
Milton Keynes UK
UKOW02f2342141016

285286UK00001B/293/P